Spiritual Socialists

SPIRITUAL SOCIALISTS

Religion and the American Left

Vaneesa Cook

PENN

UNIVERSITY OF PENNSYLVANIA PRESS

PHILADELPHIA

Copyright © 2019 University of Pennsylvania Press

All rights reserved. Except for brief quotations used for purposes of review or scholarly citation, none of this book may be reproduced in any form by any means without written permission from the publisher.

Published by
University of Pennsylvania Press
Philadelphia, Pennsylvania 19104-4112
www.upenn.edu/pennpress

Printed in the United States of America
on acid-free paper

10 9 8 7 6 5 4 3 2 1

Library of Congress Cataloging-in-Publication Data
ISBN 978-0-8122-5165-4

*To Jennifer, Jeremi, and Chuck
for being an invaluable and everlasting part of my becoming*

CONTENTS

Introduction. Cultivating the Kingdom of God   1

Chapter 1. Reconstructing Socialism in the Wake of World War I   20

Chapter 2. The Kingdom of God in the City and the Country   56

Chapter 3. Spiritual Power and the Kingdom Abroad   96

Chapter 4. The Religious Left and the Red Scare   132

Chapter 5. Socialism of the Heart   170

Conclusion. Spiritual Socialists in the Twenty-First Century   209

Notes   221

Index   253

Acknowledgments   261

INTRODUCTION

Cultivating the Kingdom of God

In the 1940s and 1950s, the American Left was in disarray. Chastened by the failure of Marxism to liberate the masses and generate socialism in either the Soviet Union or the United States, many radicals began to question their faith in fundamental change. The Red Scare attack on Communism and any radical politics only made matters worse. Some activists gave up on the revolution completely. Others carried on by searching for alternatives to the moral bankruptcy they perceived in the Communist Party. Foremost among them were New York intellectuals, leftist writers, and radicals, including Irving Howe, Lewis Coser, and Dwight Macdonald, who had become sickened by amoral state and party power. In 1944, Macdonald founded *politics* magazine with the intent to express a new vision of socialism, stripped of its doctrinal baggage. Two years later, in 1946, he wrote a seminal essay, entitled "The Root Is Man," on the topic of a moral reckoning for the Left.

In "The Root Is Man," Macdonald addressed the fundamental problems he found in Marxism: its scientific certainties, bureaucratic collectivism, historical abstractions, and, above all, ethical shortcomings. Speaking on behalf of "renegade Marxist[s]," Macdonald declared, "We feel that the firmest ground from which to struggle for that human liberation which was the goal of the Old Left is the ground not of History but of those nonhistorical values (truth, justice, love, etc.) which Marx has made unfashionable among socialists."[1] Marxism, according to Macdonald, lacked a human pulse and therefore could not resonate with the rhythms of daily human life. It was impersonal, amoral, and thus obsolete. Yet the failure of Marxism did not mean, for Macdonald, a rejection of socialism as a lost cause. Instead, he considered his disillusionment with Marxism as a reawakening to the possibility of building a socialist society, but this time on deeply rooted, moral grounds—into the heart and soul of "man" himself.

Democratic socialist Irving Howe, despite his frequent disagreements with Macdonald, shared a similar mission to realign the American Left around a new paradigm of what he called "democratic, humanist and radical values." In 1954, five years after *politics* folded its publication, Howe founded *Dissent*, dedicated to forging a "third-way" path around the weeds of liberalism and Communism and resurrecting the moral core of socialist belief. In the opening issue's introduction to readers, the editors described *Dissent* as a forum to discuss "what in the socialist tradition remains alive and what needs to be discarded or modified." Totalitarianism, for one, was out, as was Communism. The commitment to socialism, however, remained strong, though unorthodox. As they made clear from the beginning, they hoped to revive "not the 'socialism' of any splinter or faction or party, but rather the ethos and the faith in humanity that for more than 100 years have made men 'socialists.' "[2] Howe too was searching for roots.

Notably, Macdonald and Howe, though atheists, pointed to religious activists and writers as the primary exemplars of the kind of spiritual socialism they were looking for. Macdonald gave Simone Weil, the French religious philosopher, a podium in the pages of *politics*. In the 1950s, he also wrote favorable essays about Dorothy Day and the Catholic Worker movement, extolling their virtues as practical yet utopian visionaries for the Left. And both Howe and Macdonald celebrated the spiritual socialism of Italian novelist Ignazio Silone, whose disillusionment with Communism and Marxism matched their own. "No more . . . than Silone could avoid the subjects that had chosen him, could I avoid his work once it had chosen me," Howe recalled in his memoirs. "His questions were also mine."[3]

The pressing questions for many disheartened, "homeless" radicals in the 1940s and 1950s came down to this: how would they revitalize the ethical basis of socialism, make it practical, and build a "New Left" movement flexible enough to maneuver around the impasse of anti-Communism? Silone, in novels such as *Bread and Wine*, and essays such as "The Choice of Comrades," provided the theory. Socialism, he deduced, presupposes democracy; democracy depends on community; and community grows from the simplest human actions, such as caring for the sick, breaking bread, and sharing wine. These gestures of love and compassion, Silone contended, also defined Christianity—not supernatural, institutional, or doctrinal Christianity, but a kind of sacred experience inherent in the practice of social solidarity. "What remains then is a Christianity without myths, reduced to its moral essence," Silone wrote. "In the Christian sense of fraternity and an instinctive devotion to the poor, there also survives, as I have said, the loyalty to socialism. . . . I use it in the most traditional sense: an economy in the service of a man, not of the State or of any policy of power."[4] Expressing his hope that socialism would endure the traumas of the 1920s and 1930s, Silone concluded, "I do not think that this kind of Socialism is in any way peculiar to me."[5]

Silone's religious approach to radicalism was not unique to him, and his message resonated with scores of American leftists at midcentury, who believed that the spiritual dimensions of the human condition needed more attention. Howe, Macdonald, and many socialists throughout the world received Silone's work as a harbinger of a New Left shift toward values and morality. But there were already activists in the United States putting the essence of Silone's thinking into practice. Spiritual socialists, such as Sherwood Eddy, A. J. Muste, Dorothy Day, Myles Horton, and Staughton Lynd, had recognized the moral dearth of Marxist politics well before the 1950s. Through community building and direct action, they offered an alternative to secular Communism and religious conservatism that ended up reshaping the American Left and American religion by the mid-twentieth century. Their focus on community, cooperation, peace, and individual dignity softened the state socialism of Communist-affiliated organizations and created a discourse of human values and democratic activism that would define the New Left movements of the 1950s and 1960s. Spiritual socialism was, they could claim truly, an organic American tradition and not a subversive foreign import.

Leftists at midcentury needed such claims. After the collapse of the Communist Party in the late 1950s, radicals of the "Old Left" were at a crossroads, and those associating with the "New Left" coalesced from across the radical spectrum, including pacifists, anti-Stalinist democratic socialists, former fellow travelers, and community activists with a shared interest in nonviolence and decentralization.[6] Spiritual socialists, however, do not figure prominently in these accounts as a comprehensive tradition that predated the crisis of Communism in the 1950s and circumvented the confusion, for the most part, unscathed. That is, they were able to maintain a vision of moral social change despite the criticisms of anti-Communists and serve as a vanguard for the New Left as it developed out of the turbulence of the Red Scare.[7]

At a pivotal time of realignment for the Left and religious revival, generally, spiritual socialists offered American radicals the theory and practice that would reshape socialism in the mid- to late twentieth century. They made moral and even religious values relevant for leftist discourse, and, crucially, they broadened the Left's agenda. No longer tied exclusively to Marxism or the "labor metaphysic," as C. Wright Mills would later call it, spiritual socialists addressed the whole person as a sacred agent of God.[8] Accordingly, issues of oppression were extended to include race and gender and state-sponsored violence, in addition to class. The spiritual socialist vision made progress on these fronts (in fact, on all fronts of oppression) a theological and practical necessity. In other words, the only way to cultivate the Kingdom of God was through careful attention to root, structural problems that obstructed human dignity and harmony in any way. It is not surprising then that spiritual socialists were able to influence and dovetail with emerging social movements on civil rights, pacifism, and New Left politics in the 1950s and 1960s. They shared similar values and objectives. For example, white supremacy, a glaring problem in the United States, had no place in the Kingdom of God. It had to be overcome in order to achieve God's will for the nation and the world. Marxism, though still relevant for many spiritual socialists as an economic analysis, offered little help with these broader, cultural issues of race and religion. Consequently, spiritual socialists turned to the Bible rather than *The Communist Manifesto* for answers and inspiration.[9]

This story has not been told. While some historians have addressed the history of religion on the left,[10] the narrative remains fragmented, and the popular perception still envisions the conservative "religious Right" as the voice of politicized Christianity.[11] Excellent work has been done on religion and liberalism, but most scholars, let alone the general public, have little information about the religious Left or its rich history.[12] Even many historians of the "long civil rights movement" have sidelined religion in favor of more secular sources of black radicalism.[13] Yet religion was not antithetical to the Left or merely tolerated as a supernatural sideshow to serious political activism. Instead, religious activists, especially spiritual socialists, helped bring the Left back to its moral baseline and projected a new hope for the future of radical change. The impact of the religious Left on secular radicals like Howe and Macdonald in the 1940s and 1950s makes this clear.[14]

Midcentury is an important moment in time for understanding how socialism evolved from a labor-oriented European doctrine to an Americanized moral project of democratic community building and values.[15] To do so, we must uncover the tradition of spiritual socialism. Americans need to know what the rest of the advanced industrial world figured out long ago: that socialism has many forms and should not be relegated to a rigid definition. Nations can and must find their own version, cultivated organically from their own political culture. It is also important for understanding the revival of democratic socialism today. In an era when concepts like "ownership of the means of production" have little meaning, and top-down bureaucratic systems have little appeal, it is crucial to educate the public about how socialism can be made to work for them and their values in their daily lives. Socialism today is no longer the "dirty word," as one activist put it, that it was in the mid-twentieth century.[16] Instead, it has become heralded as a viable democratic, moral alternative to traditional politics. To trace that transformation, we must analyze the role of the religious Left and its relationship to socialism.

The narrative of spiritual socialism reveals the social thought of left religious radicals who refused to measure progress on a scale of issue-oriented political gains, church attendance, or denominational conversions. Their tradition must be traced along a much longer arc of continuous struggle for socioreligious renewal throughout the mid-to late twentieth century. Socialism, in the minds of these activists, did not fail in either the United States or the world; it simply had not been afforded the time required for it to take root and permeate human relations. Socialism as a spiritual project, they predicted, could take millennia to achieve.[17] Their patience, however, had political consequences, making them less apt to compete for sensational media headlines on hot-button topics such as abortion and affirmative action. What's more, their message of a selfless life lived for others was much harder to advocate than the individualistic and sometimes materialistic peddling of the religious Right.[18]

The figures in this narrative are fairly well known, but not necessarily in the context of socialism. Some spiritual socialists, including Muste and Day, fall under the label "pacifist," and accordingly they have been afforded passing mention in studies on nonviolent direct action. They receive more thorough treatment in scholarship on the history of American pacifism, but such distinctions fragment the tradition, especially because spiritual socialists were not always staunch pacifists.[19] What is more, the issue of violence was *not* the central problem of the twentieth century for these activists. Nonviolence, even for Muste and Day, operated as a practical means to a higher end: the building of the Kingdom of God on earth. By this they generally meant the gradual process of establishing God's will for the world. More specifically, spiritual socialists envisioned a future, utopian society that reflected the teachings and practices of Jesus. They believed that the Kingdom of God on earth, when brought to full fruition, would be a society of perfect peace, cooperation, and equality among all persons. This amounted to their spiritual interpretation of socialism, another word they used to describe the Kingdom come. As such, Christian nonviolence was, for them, an interpretive religious means for building a socialist society of peace, equality, and fellowship. It was not an end in and of itself. By studying these activists exclusively as pacifists, then, we miss the multidimensional aspects of their larger, eschatological project.[20] Spiritual socialists went beyond pacifism, channeling it toward a completely new society. Not only did they espouse antiviolence and antiwar principles in a negative sense; they also projected a world of complete equality and cooperation. Direct action, for the absolute pacifists in this group as much as for the self-proclaimed "pragmatists," was geared toward demonstrating alternatives. It was not about just preventing and disrupting immoral actions. It was also about making moral action seem possible and practical.

Neither were spiritual socialists mere "religious radicals," broadly understood, threading their way through the rise and fall of the American Left, and serving as prophetic voices. Scores of activists in U.S. history offered a social interpretation of religion.[21] Yet this study of spiritual socialists goes deeper into the historical significance of a tradition that carved a special space in the psyche of the American Left. Spiritual socialists were serious socialists, who spoke as and to socialists, often identifying themselves as such, though qualifying the term to avoid confusion with the forms they sought to contest. These radicals did not tout a traditional, political conception of socialism, and that made all the difference to independent leftists like Macdonald and Howe. Rather than encouraging centralized power politics, they promoted small-scale, local organization from the bottom up. Instead of privileging the proletariat or some special vanguard, they embraced the inherent dignity of all individuals. And, instead of dogma, they spoke of values and moral behavior. They showed that religion could be revolutionary and not just reactionary, and they gave hope to the disillusioned, an important role they played since the 1920s, when their distinctive thought and practice began to find traction, after the Great War caused many radicals to lose faith in progress. The religious Left, many believed, was on the wane. However, a study of spiritual socialism shows that the religious Left has never disappeared from American politics or culture. It remained strong among progressives throughout the twentieth century and continues to shape political and social action today.

Back in the early twentieth century, before the Great War, left-liberal religious activists believed they had good reason to proclaim their confidence in the coming Kingdom of God on earth. For one, foreign missionary work was thriving, impelled in part by what John Mott, the Student Volunteer Movement (SVM) coordinator for the Young Men's Christian Association (YMCA), called an "unprecedented development of missionary life and activity among young men and young women." Writing in 1900, Mott reinforced the ambition among Protestant missionaries to "evangelize the world in this generation" by spreading the Christian gospel into every uncultivated corner of the globe.[22] At home in U.S. cities, advocates of the social gospel, a mission to apply Christian values to social problems, were also projecting high hopes. They marshaled their evidence of a rapidly advancing Christian society from progressive political policies, laws, and social relief agencies that had been instituted in little more than a decade. The spirit of God seemed to be moving mankind inexorably into a modern, moral dispensation that would soon reflect all the qualities of heaven unto earth. Muste, remembering the optimism of the time years later, wrote that "there was a general feeling . . . that the Kingdom of God was pretty close at hand here in the United States. At any rate, we were going to make steady and almost automatic progress towards its realization."[23] Former-minister-turned-secular-leader Norman Thomas, the longtime leader of the Socialist Party of America, also characterized the early twentieth century as an era of hope. "I vividly remember my own youthful conviction that all the great victories essential to the onward march of man had already been won; what was left was but to press onward toward that far-off divine event to which the whole creation moves."[24]

World War I, according to most historians and contemporaries, challenged these lofty assumptions.[25] At best, the wartime crisis arrested the momentum of progressive politics in the United States. At worst, it produced a patina of disillusionment among many reformers who could no longer profess a faith in the steady, moral development of civilized nations. The war, in this sense, did not so much destroy the movements of left-liberal and social Christianity as it deflated the general spirit on which such idealism had found buoyancy. The Great War dealt a major blow to facile predictions, as social missioners realized that the baser instincts of human nature were more entrenched and intractable than they had previously thought. As Thomas put it, "No one—certainly no American—who grew to maturity in the years before World War I could in his wildest nightmare have imagined the horrors which have become commonplaces of the daily news since 1914."[26] If progressive religion was going to survive the demoralization the war had wrought, radicals had to reevaluate their assumptions and approach to social change.

Faith in the possibilities for world peace and brotherhood, in the end, was not all lost. Between 1920 and 1970, a new expression of religious activism, what I call spiritual socialism, developed among a variety of historical actors who insisted that the process of constructing a truly humane world in which the spirit of God infuses every social relation would take more time, require more radical methods, and demand more concentrated attention at the local level. Spiritual socialists, including Muste, Eddy, Day, Henry Wallace, Horton, Martin Luther King Jr., and Lynd, all returned to the fundamental elements of their faith, believing that simple acts of caring for the sick, tired, hungry, and exploited members of one's community would eventually change the world. Creating the Kingdom of God on earth, they understood, was not a matter of political expediency, but a long-term process of social cultivation that must address both spiritual and material needs in local cooperative communities. For these activists, the recurring social setbacks and political failures of leftist movements did not shatter their sense of mission; instead, it radicalized them.

The intellectual tradition of spiritual socialism is crucial for understanding the remaking of the American Left after World War I. By emphasizing religious and democratic values as crucial components of modern life that had gone missing in Marxist theory and practice, their unorthodox perspective on the spiritual and cultural meaning of socialist principles helped make leftist thought more amenable to Americans, who associated socialism with Soviet atheism and autocracy. Spiritual socialists, in short, reconstructed an American Left based on religious values and democracy that became relevant to mainstream politics. Emphasizing the "social" side of socialism as a religious way of life, spiritual socialists held that the most basic expressions of religious values—caring for the sick, tired, hungry, and exploited members of one's community—created a firm footing for a socialist society. Traditional Marxists, they contended, neglected these human values in their focus on violent and immediate revolution implemented by the party or proletariat. By insisting that people start treating each other better in everyday life, spiritual socialists transformed radical activism from political policymaking into projects of local, grassroots organizing.

Spiritual socialists used religious values to reformulate leftist thought into a moral project relevant to mainstream American politics, but they also made religious values more acceptable to American radicals. For example, civil rights activists in the 1950s and 1960s used Christian values to couch their claims for social change. The emerging New Left movement of the 1960s picked up on this radical rhetoric and proclaimed to "speak American" in their demands for democracy, individual dignity, and equal treatment. Many leftists, in fact, promoted a spiritual, not just material, understanding of social progress and exhorted Americans to think of socialism as a moral imperative. The tradition of spiritual socialism provided the American Left with a moral foundation and language that made religion and radicalism congruent, not antithetical.

To be clear, when these figures referred to "religion" or the "spiritual," they did not mean formal religion or its theology and observances. Each spiritual socialist brought their own personal beliefs and Christian content to their activism, but they could agree with Thomas that religion reduced to basic human values. As Thomas wrote, if "religion is a deep sense of values transcending quantitative measurement, then I think religion is necessary to the good life and to the good society."[27] Spiritual socialists wanted to liberate religion from doctrinal dead-ends and give its essential values, including equality, human dignity, peace, and cooperation, a live option in daily practice. Equating the coming Kingdom of God on earth with a socialist society, they insisted that religious values were necessary elements for building a new world order, since they had the substance and power to transcend both narrow-minded materialism and petty human selfishness. Yet spiritual socialism remains an overlooked tradition of left radicalism, one that has continually put pressure on liberals, conservatives, and Marxists to address the interplay between morality and social justice. They put the human spirit back onto the political agenda in the mid-twentieth century and the social work back into socialism.

By understanding the unique vision of spiritual socialists, who believed they could create the foundation for a better world, historians may break out of the standard "rise and fall" declension narratives that have dominated politically centered studies of both the American Left and U.S. religion.[28] Spiritual socialists conceived of socialism as a decentralized, religious way of life, not as an economic system or political program for proletarian revolution. Consequently, they regarded political "failures" to achieve power or affect policy as temporary setbacks. They also regarded campaigns for political power during World War I, World War II, the Cold War, and within the Communist Internationals as misapplications of moral values. They focused instead on the much longer struggle to build small socialist communities that would prefigure the coming Kingdom of God on earth, which they understood to be an ideal, spiritualized state in which socialist values—equality, peace, and cooperation—become normative social practice.[29] Their approach to international relations, therefore, offers an alternative to the recently renewed interest in conservative religion and liberal Christian realism. They did not all advocate absolute pacifism, but they did believe, contrary to conservative evangelists like Billy Graham and Christian realists such as Reinhold Niebuhr, that human virtues and moral values could reshape international relations and redeem a sinful world.[30] They argued that a religious way of life learned in small, local, cooperative communities would eventually transform the global landscape through cultural reconstruction.[31]

If spiritual socialists have not found a footing in the historiography, it is in large part because they had a hard time finding a definitive place among their contemporaries. They were activists in limbo, deemed too radical for Christians and too religious for many on the left. The very nature of their thought and practice also kept spiritual socialists from claiming a more visible role in national circles. Having accepted the fact that their eschatological objectives to produce a new world order outstripped their capabilities at the global level, spiritual socialists opted for building socialism from the bottom up in cooperative communities, rather than channeling their energies toward topical solutions at the national or international levels. They did not abandon high-level politics completely, but they knew that their writings and speeches amounted to empty rhetoric without the accompanying work of constructing a new social order.

Dissatisfied by the unethical trade-offs of mainstream politics, they continuously returned to the most fundamental social sources of their idealism and started again, just as Howe and a host of independent radicals began to do in the 1950s. Though the regrouping of independent leftists after the 1930s has been a slippery topic, the story of spiritual socialists offers a fresh perspective on the opportunities and failures of the American Left during this fascinating time of transition. They may not have escaped the noose of the Red Scare completely, but their religious convictions gave them a certain measure of credibility among Americans. And their coolness toward Communism allowed many of them, though not all, to sidestep the internecine battles among radical sects that only added to the ideological exhaustion of the Left by midcentury.

The unique thought and practice of spiritual socialists made them politically less visible, but no less influential. In the 1920s, for example, YMCA missionary Sherwood Eddy began publicly identifying himself as a socialist, intent on preaching a message of grassroots democracy and building alternative institutions in the United States, such as his Delta Cooperative Farm in Mississippi. Around the same time, radical journalist Dorothy Day cofounded the social Christian program that became known as Catholic Worker in New York City, and Myles Horton established the Highlander Folk School in Tennessee. Peace activist A. J. Muste also advocated a revolution in daily communal practice, which, as he told his labor comrades at the alternative institution Brookwood Labor College, was the only rational means to radical ends. In 1948, Henry Wallace, the former New Deal administrator and vice president, ran for president on a spiritually infused platform that called for prioritizing spiritual socialism at home over military crusades abroad. Historians tend to see his loss to Truman as an example of the futility of national strategies on the left. Yet Wallace ended up inspiring a generation of spiritual socialists, including New Left historian Staughton Lynd, to change the world through local to global community building and cooperative diplomacy aimed at the spiritual, not just political or material, needs of nations and their peoples.

Notably, these spiritual socialists came from different religious backgrounds and experiences. Eddy grew up as a Congregationalist; Muste gravitated from the Dutch Reformed Church, to Congregationalism, to Quakerism, to the nondenominational Labor Temple within the span of two decades; Day remained a staunch and lifelong Catholic after her conversion in the late 1920s; Horton grew up Presbyterian; Wallace experimented with an array of religions including Presbyterianism, Theosophy, and Native American mysticism; and Lynd attended a Jewish Reformed school and later identified as a Quaker. In later years, Pauli Murray became an Episcopal priest, Cornel West was raised Baptist, and the Reverend William Barber currently preaches for Disciples of Christ. Jews, however, are not strongly represented in this story, though they did find common cause with spiritual socialists from time to time. There were exceptions to the general rule, and perhaps some residual religious sympathy, but Jewish leftists, by and large, tended to make their moral claims in secular, ethical language.[32] Howe and Coser, for example, appreciated spiritual socialism on moral and practical grounds, but they never subscribed to a theology.

Despite the diversity of their denominational affiliations, however, spiritual socialists all shared an ecumenical commitment to the same basic religious values that they believed any Christian should practice and apply. Instead of specific dogma, they emphasized the social message of Jesus, who repeatedly told his disciples to love and care for each other and the members of their community through simple acts of compassion and cooperation. Eddy, Muste, Day, Horton, Wallace, and Lynd took this commandment for community building very seriously, a point of convergence that marks them as fellow spiritual socialists with a common cause. Instead of working for social reform through top-down policy or political activity, they all insisted that the best (and perhaps only way) to build the Kingdom of God on earth was through local, social work in small groups, towns, and neighborhoods where people interacted face-to-face.

This radical *social* approach of spiritual socialists in their response to national and international problems, in fact, distinguishes them from religious reformers of the past—that is, before World War I. Socially concerned Christians, such as Walter Rauschenbusch, Jane Addams, Shailer Mathews, George Herron, Francis Peabody, W. D. P. Bliss, and Harry Ward, certainly promoted and even practiced ideas of the cooperative community and social responsibility, but they filtered their Christian ethics through a Victorian-era worldview laced with the assumption that moral suasion, legislation, and policy reforms, managed and directed by a political and religious leadership, would change society in the near future.[33] These "social gospelers," as the historian Robert Handy acknowledged, "were not so much activists as they were preachers, proclaimers, and educators."[34] Spiritual socialists, on the other hand, learned from their experiences during and after World War I that incremental, piecemeal reforms had limited any effect on the real sources of social and economic problems, including capitalist exploitation, poverty, and health care. Political victories, for them, amounted to *hollow* victories if unaccompanied by concurrent changes in social values and interpersonal relations in the long-term overhaul of an immoral, fundamentally flawed system.

Muste was one such activist for the religious Left who, in the wake of World War I, began to think differently about the possibilities of achieving both a socialist society and the Kingdom of God on earth—twin visions of a future state of peace, equality, and human cooperation. He carried on the social gospel faith in postmillennial social salvation, but blatantly rejected their methods of mechanical, political management of society. He favored instead the organic, internal cultivation of an entirely new social order. "The difficulty with the late 19th and early 20th century," Muste explained in 1944, "was that people were obsessed with mechanism, with the machine, and derived from that obsession a conception of life which led to the idea that the problems of the social order could be met by changes in the external arrangements of life." According to Muste, the Victorian conception of social crisis as a problem of "mechanics" and "social engineering" neglected the human soul as the most primitive and important source of social behavior.[35] Social gospelers of that time, he believed, wasted their moral vigor applying Band-Aids to a social cancer of violence, competition, and greed that really required complete eradication from the inside out. They righteously worked on behalf of the coming Kingdom of God, but with flawed, futile methods of reformism and propaganda. "The liberal Christians were never, in my opinion, wrong in cherishing this vision," Muste made clear. "Their mistake, and in a sense, their crime, was not to see that it was revolutionary in character and demanded revolutionary living and action of those who claimed to be its votaries."[36]

The term "social gospel" or "liberal reformer," then, does not adequately represent spiritual socialists who belong to a lost lineage in leftist religious thought and action. In fact, the use of the term "social gospel" has become historically problematic. For one, it is discussed most often in the context of a declension narrative, marked by its emergence at the turn of the twentieth century, by its climax as a progressive reform movement in the years just before the outbreak of World War I, and then by its decline, if not complete disappearance, since the early 1920s.[37] Some historians have noted that a new manifestation of the social gospel seemed to coalesce in the 1960s as civil rights protestors, New Left activists, and liberal clergy once again expressed their political and social views as an extension of social Christian belief.[38] Yet the religious Left, as this study shows, did not disappear from history in the years between 1920 and 1960, even if it went missing in the historical narrative. By focusing on the tradition of spiritual socialism instead of the social gospel, we may complicate declension narratives of twentieth-century religion in America.

One reason why historians have had trouble recognizing the endurance of left-liberal religion pivots on the problem of categorization. The term "social gospel" is either tied to Progressive Era politics or employed as a broad and inclusive term referring to liberals, legislators, imperialists, anti-imperialists, radicals, reformers, social conservatives, and theologians. Therefore, the term holds very little tangible substance, especially when trying to trace its significance along the contours of social movements. My hope is that the term "spiritual socialist" cuts through this confusion by identifying a particular type of activist, one who equated socialist and religious values and called for the cultivation of the Kingdom of God on earth in small-scale communities. They identified themselves as revolutionaries on the left, not as liberal reformers, but as small "s" socialists with a serious radical program for fundamental political and economic change by way of social and cultural reconstruction.

The term "Christian socialist" also fails to accurately describe these activists, not only because the concept carries connotations of continental communal philosophy and a turn-of-the-century mind-set about mechanical social engineering, but also because Christian socialists were too tied to class struggle and Marxist analysis.[39] Spiritual socialists moved beyond Marx to consider multiple forms of oppression, including race and gender. Calling them Christian socialists also undermines our understanding of the profoundly ecumenical inclusion that spiritual socialists advocated. Although they took their cues from the gospels, spiritual socialists cared more about applying social ethics than they did about their particular religious source. Theologically, spiritual socialists shared a belief in the immanence of God, working in history through human agents toward postmillennial salvation in the coming Kingdom on earth, which they conflated with a socialist society. But they purposefully kept it vague in order to connect with as many people as possible. In fact, spiritual socialists used phrases like "Kingdom of God," "cooperative society," or "socialist society" so interchangeably that their religious philosophy often resembles a vague, conceptual shell game without concrete substance.

This problem of imprecision is exacerbated by their common tendency to reject biblical literalism and liturgy in favor of lived religious experience, actively applied in real-life situations. Beyond the basic principles of social Christianity, spiritual socialists did not concern themselves with theological doctrine, a point of pliancy that made them more open to religious and cultural diversity throughout the world. The spiritual socialists profiled in this book all happened to express their social vision in ecumenical Christian terms with Christ's basic social message as the driving imperative for their activism. However, they were not interested in converting radicals to Christianity or Christians to socialism. They wanted people to put the morals that underlay both Christianity and socialism into practice, generally recognizing the importance of a humanitarian deed over any fixed creed, as long as that deed demonstrated a religious quality to bind people together in cooperation, fellowship, and love. Buddhists, Hindus, Jews, and even secular socialists who applied Jesus' message of goodwill were all welcomed as co-creators of the Kingdom of God on earth. As Lynd explained, "We [believe] that there [is] a common religious experience that different persons might use quite different words to describe."[40] Underlying this respect for religious pluralism, spiritual socialists' abiding belief in a form of personalism or the dignity of every human being as an equally valued child of God framed their ecumenical acceptance of diverse perspectives.

Such spiritual open-mindedness did have its disadvantages though, especially when it left them vulnerable to accusations of watered-down, impractical utopianism. When pressed to define their vision more explicitly, spiritual socialists often fell back on idealistic, romanticized notions of love, cooperation, and the Kingdom of God. Their significance in the history of American radicalism, therefore, lies more in their understanding of means rather than ends. Though they did not offer a clear blueprint for the future, they did maintain a faith in concrete Christian acts, however small, that they believed would contribute to the Kingdom's slow-going construction. Jesus' social program and the model of primitive Christianity, practiced in local communities, contained enough spiritual power to transform the world, they claimed.

Just as spiritual socialists dismissed religious dogma, they also discounted the political doctrines that secular socialists typically wielded in sectarian debates. Spiritual socialists took an active interest in issues of social justice, and many of them, such as Muste, Day, Horton, and Lynd, participated directly in the labor movement. They agreed, for example, with the basic Marxian premise that industrial capitalism operated as a corrupt and corrupting system based on monetary gain rather than human values. Yet their opposition to capitalism emanated from religious reasoning—it was incompatible with the new world order, not because it contained economic contradictions that would inevitably hasten its demise, but because it contained ethical contradictions that hindered the spiritual development of humanity. The problem with capitalism, as practiced in the twentieth century, was that it encouraged people to express and act on their most selfish impulses, a culture of behavior that could never exist within the Kingdom of God. If people could learn instead to suppress these base instincts and follow the example of Christ in their relationships with others, then over time a revolution of practical religious values would transform the world into heaven on earth.[41]

Spiritual socialists' version of socialism deviated from orthodox Marxism in a number of other significant ways. They did not subscribe to dialectical theories of inevitable progress, violent programs for achieving political power, or a secular vision of an ideal society centralized around top-down state authority. Neither did they advocate overthrowing the government and establishing a centralized workers' state. Instead, they went to work on behalf of all exploited peoples without singling out a particular class or group (such as the proletariat) as the exclusive vanguard of a new world order. Workers in the ideal, socialist society would have democratic access to the means of production, but only by virtue of their identity as respected and valued children of God, not because of their privileged proletarian status. For these reasons, most spiritual socialists did not herald the Socialist Party, or any secular organization, as the best vehicle for achieving the Kingdom of God. They may have appreciated and even joined them for a time, but more often than not, they became disillusioned with the myopic focus on materialism and political expediency in these national groups as well as the general rejection of religion that the Socialist Party, for one, espoused.

With their ethical resolve regarding radical politics, spiritual socialists projected a unique vision of religious redemption for both the industrial-capitalist system *and* secular alternatives to that system. They demanded that the means to the ideal society prefigure that society, or, in other words, that a future world based in peace, love, and honesty could emerge only from the deliberate practice of those principles. Their experiences with secular radicals, who often encouraged violent and unethical tactics in the quest for a socialist state, revealed to them the futility of rationalizing immoral strategies for moral objectives. That is why they were often wary of identifying with the term "socialism" and all the negative connotations it conjured. Instead of a workers' state, spiritual socialists heralded the Kingdom of God. Instead of venerating proletarian heroes such as Joe Hill, killed in Utah for his radicalism in 1915, they identified Jesus Christ as the most relevant model for left-labor revolution. For spiritual socialists, the struggle for revolution amounted to a social process of practicing moral principles, not merely a political project for establishing power.

Neglecting the cultural and social substance of socialism has caused Americans to underestimate the lasting influence of leftists who have worked for long-term changes in small communities. On the social side of socialism, religion becomes much more important. Spiritual socialists insisted that only changes in the hearts and minds of men and women could create a new culture of social behavior. Concomitantly, they believed that only religious values possessed the power to initiate and sustain such changes. Jesus commanded the disciples to love and take care of one another; and for spiritual socialists, this simple decree underscored all social action in the here and now. It meant healing the sick, feeding the poor, housing the homeless, sharing wealth, and respecting the dignity of every person as an equal member of the human family in the image of God. These gestures of fellowship and compassion formed the fabric of the Kingdom of God on earth—in the practice of social solidarity and essentially socialism. The coming Kingdom of God on earth, then, *was* the ideal socialist society, in which peace, love, and justice become practical realities, first developed in local communities and then extrapolated to more complex social environments at the national and international levels.

Spiritual socialists all shared this belief in common; they spoke of religious and socialist values as one and the same; they dreamed of the Kingdom of God and a socialist society in tandem. By deconstructing socialism down to its fundamental roots in human experience, they recognized a naked moral impulse, a spiritual source so primal that it contained universal meaning. However, none of the spiritual socialists in this book claimed to know the political dimensions of the Kingdom of God on earth, a blind spot in their vision that often made the entire concept seem vague and illusory. They talked in terms of its social *process*, but not as much in terms of its fully fledged structure and operation in a complex world. As Muste acknowledged in 1954, "We cannot foresee the society which is to be and we must finally accept the fact that we are dealing with a process and it is in the process that we find our success rather than in the realization of a static plan for society."[42]

Their method of practicing direct action in one's community (helping those in need and sharing resources) seemed like a far more powerful and realistic approach to social revolution than moralizing. Individuals would learn by doing good works, and society would change through the practice of fellowship. "What we do on our own street has a kind of reality that is not present in mere resolutions and therefore has more significance than much talk," explained Muste.[43] Essentially, however, spiritual socialists still relied on moral suasion to convince people that their interests were better served by cooperating with others. The social revolution might begin in the hearts and minds of men and women, but that kind of change called for nothing short of religious conversion, one person at a time. Spiritual socialists were aware of this matter. It is why they spoke of long-term cultivation measured by generations. In the interim, though, they continually confronted people's penchant for instant gratification. They also had to contend with a public polity responding to immediate threats from perceived enemies at home and abroad. The Progressive Party campaign of Henry Wallace in 1948, for example, faltered on this issue of practicality. Wallace could not convince voters to trust in his program of long-term, patient process while Truman was appealing to their sense of urgency and crisis. In an imperfect world full of danger and violence, it was far easier for people to vote according to their fears rather than their hopes.

It also proved much easier for people to accept the theological notion of individual salvation over social salvation and original sin against human perfectibility, a point that helps explain why conservative, fundamentalist churches have seemed more successful in their efforts to build a grassroots base of political power and influence in the mid- to late twentieth century. Conservative evangelicals, like their political counterparts, tapped into the fears and biases of their followers to great effect, emphasizing the negative features of human society and human nature and drawing acute lines of separation between the saved and the depraved. Wielding a message of biblically based discrimination in their Sunday sermons, conservative clergy have cultivated a grassroots movement against the grain of left-liberal efforts to foster ecumenical acceptance of cultural diversity and social equality.

This is not to say that left-liberal activists have failed to exert any influence on society, even if their presence as an organized constituency is less visible than that of the religious Right. Liberal and left idealists have had a significant impact on ideas of race, gender, and class differences in the popular consciousness.[44] Marshaling hard evidence of cultural and intellectual influence, however, is more challenging than a study of political polls and policy, making it difficult to determine the historical achievements of many left liberals. Yet by understanding the vision and grassroots activism of spiritual socialists, historians may appreciate more fully the importance of subversive, slow-moving social movements that operate at a cultural register less evident and perceptible than political movements. This book gives them a voice. It also invites scholars to reconsider the Left and its ongoing relevance to U.S. politics, including the democratic socialism of recent presidential candidate Bernie Sanders or the moral revivalism of Reverend William Barber. Spiritual socialists teach us that we cannot understand the Left in U.S. history without grappling with the ways in which religious values helped ground socialist theory in the mainstream currents of American political culture. They also help us understand socialism in a broader context. The word "socialism" has taken on multidimensional meanings over the course of the twentieth century, and, therefore, the history of socialism deserves multidimensional treatment, especially if we are to trace the ways in which radicals sought to claim a distinctively moral and decentralized form that has survived the Cold War and the ideological battles of the twentieth century.

CHAPTER 1

Reconstructing Socialism in the Wake of World War I

In a 1936 essay, "Return to Pacifism," labor leader A. J. Muste summed up his short-lived and disappointing experience with dogmatic Trotskyites who vainly hoped that an immediate, if violent, revolution would midwife a utopian new world order: "The necessary saving conclusion that a moral and religious spirit must be infused into . . . every relation of life is now drawn," Muste wrote. "Until it is, I believe that the movement will be cheated of its goal."[1] The goal, a classless society reflecting peace and justice, would never emerge, in other words, if activists abandoned their principles for the sake of immediate power. After years of witnessing Marxists muddle means to justify ends, Muste realized that any durable social revolution must be built from the bottom up, by practicing basic spiritual values in the midst of daily life, rather than commanded from the top down by any party, pundit, or labor union.

Reconciling his religious and radical vision around a new post-Marxist plan of action, Muste was speaking the language of spiritual socialism, a left-wing intellectual tradition that emerged from the religious and political context of the early twentieth century, when Christian socialism, progressivism, the social gospel movement, and Communism had offered idealistic designs for an imminent and inevitable utopia. By the end of World War I, however, many leftists and liberals realized that the path to a society of peace, equality, and human dignity was not paved by good intentions. Public policy and moral rhetoric from on high did not transform social behavior or human nature, as the horrors of the war had illustrated. In the wake of these atrocities, spiritual socialists were among the disillusioned, at least to a certain extent. They no longer held faith with the left-liberal traditions that had pledged to change the world in one generation. Unlike many Progressive Era reformers, however, they did not fall into despair and defeatism. Instead, they began to search for a new and practical means of fostering fundamental social change. In the 1920s, spiritual socialists were beginning to distinguish themselves from both liberals and Marxist radicals by advocating a grassroots approach to building a new world order. A revolution in human values, they argued, had to emerge through daily interpersonal relations, different cultural norms, and varied institutions, remodeled to reflect the Christian maxim: love thy neighbor as yourself. Spiritual socialists took to the task. They developed, in theory and practice, a new religious political tradition that carried on vestiges of prewar idealism, but with a postwar sensibility about the long-term potential for creating the Kingdom of God on earth.

Spiritual socialists, in short, were attempting something new in the 1920s. They returned to the very foundation of their political and religious beliefs, rooted in values, and insisted that activists must work from there, from the ground up. Distinguishing themselves from Communists, traditional Marxists, and social gospelers, radicals such as Muste and Young Men's Christian Association (YMCA) missionary Sherwood Eddy carried the dream of a socialist society and the Kingdom of God across the proverbial battlefields of World War I and into the so-called conservative decade. They reformulated socialism into what they considered a more realistic approach, and they did so without sacrificing their ideals. In fact, they expanded the ideals and the agenda of socialists of the past. While traditional socialists and Communists focused almost solely on class, labor, and economic exploitation, spiritual socialists began to call attention to other forms of oppression, including racial and cultural forms that kept humanity from realizing the Kingdom of God on earth. This holistic approach, they asserted, needed a new methodology, namely democratic community building and the attention to pluralism that made communities organic, genuine, uninsulated from the world. For spiritual socialists, the 1920s did not signal a return to "normalcy" or isolationism, but presented a new and exciting challenge for experimenting with international ideas and sustaining American socialism in communities of fellowship. They were not part of the "lost generation," set adrift on winds of despair. Instead, they became *recollected* around a new vision of heaven on earth.

To be sure, the lessons of the Great War changed activists like Muste considerably, though the path to spiritual socialism was not always linear. From his participation in a precedent-setting strike at Lawrence, Massachusetts, in 1919, to his election as general secretary of the Amalgamated Textile Workers (ATW), to his involvement with the experimental school for workers' education known as Brookwood College, and to the chairmanship of the Conference for Progressive Labor Action (CPLA), founded in 1929, Muste searched for ways to keep the hope of revolution alive. He even inspired a following among "Musteites," who preferred broad-based and inclusive industrial unionism over the restrictive trade union cliques of the American Federation of Labor (AFL). Muste offered an innovative method to the labor movement through organizations such as the CPLA and American Workers Party (AWP). He and his followers, as one historian has argued, "attempted to 'Americanize' Marxism by placing praxis at the center of organizing and revolutionary activity."[2] However, Muste's mission to Americanize socialism did not begin or end with the CPLA and AWP. It was a lifelong project, preceding the 1930s and enduring into the 1940s. And while it is true that Muste helped Americanize socialism through praxis, he did so with a specific emphasis on religious values at a time when many radicals praised the atheistic, materialistic Soviet style and dismissed religion as reactionary.

Muste saw something of value in the Soviet experiment and the following it had sparked in the United States. Yet he became frustrated with the perverse environment of contention, coercion, and conformity that he experienced in the labor movement in the 1920s and, later, the sectarian infighting of Communist organizations he joined in the early 1930s. Throughout these decades, as he suffered a series of disillusionments with the possibilities of building a beloved community or Kingdom of God in the crucible of party politics, Muste confronted and refined the values at the core of his calling. He could no longer justify radical action by 1936 without adherence to the basic Christian principles of integrity, nonviolence, and brotherly love that he had learned and preached in the Dutch Reformed Church of his youth. Revolutions were hard to accomplish, but the formula for social change, he realized, was simple: peaceful input produces peaceful outcomes while violence begets violence. Perhaps the positive results were not always readily apparent, given the complexity and corruption of society and human behavior. But Muste had learned his lesson. The envisioned ends of a new world order or the Kingdom of God on earth, he concluded, must match the means needed to get there, even if it took more time and demanded more discipline.

Seen from this angle, Muste becomes someone else in our history, not only a pacifist aberration from the norm of leftist viciousness, as he is often portrayed.[3] His pacifism amounted to more than principled acts of conscience. It functioned within his overarching ideology of social change as a way of life and as a crucial means for creating a socialist society worthy of the will of God. Muste's forays of direct action, moreover, were not limited to marches, pickets, and sit-ins, important as these deeds were. To understand his significance for the Left, we must also acknowledge his participation in community building for the Kingdom of God as a form of radical activism that has not been fully explored in the scholarship.

By spearheading new institutions in the 1920s, spiritual socialists like Muste and Eddy made the transition from a prewar to a postwar climate of thought and practice. They believed they were building grassroots communities that would reshape American thought and social behavior. They also believed that an adherence to religious values set their form of socialism apart from traditional organizations on the left. Eddy, for example, used his early twentieth-century experiences in Christian evangelism to create a new education project in 1921, the annual American Seminar, which took travelers around the world to learn about the latest developments in science, culture, and public policy. That same year, Muste helped found and manage Brookwood Labor College, an alternative institution that offered American factory workers a chance to discuss labor theory. In an era known for U.S. isolationism, these activists were internationally engaged, especially in their attempts to understand and learn from the Soviet Union. They wanted to open American minds to radical experiments in social change, but they did so by tempering Communist theories with American principles of freedom, democracy, and religious fellowship. Through these new grassroots institutions, spiritual socialists hoped to demonstrate to the world that a third way between American liberalism and Soviet Communism was possible.

Muste's own path to radical activism began conservatively enough in the Dutch Reformed Church, the "center of social life and culture" for his family and larger community. In fact, religion reigned so predominantly in Muste's upbringing that he never considered becoming anything other than a minister, a vocational calling he pursued first at Hope College Preparatory School in Michigan and then at New Brunswick Theological Seminary, a

Dutch Reformed institution in New Jersey. It was near there, during his practicum placement as a supply preacher in the summer of 1908, that Muste was confronted with the seedier side of the "city of man" in New York's tenement districts. The "fetid smells and unceasing raucous noise" that Muste found difficult to endure represented the first real illustrations of poverty that he had ever witnessed, an experience that influenced his growing interest in social problems and the social gospel.[4]

At seminary, Muste had been exposed to some of the social gospel ideas that were popular among liberal theologians in the early twentieth century; but it was during the philosophy lectures he attended at New York University and Columbia University where thinkers such as William James and John Dewey "exercised a profound influence on [his] intellectual life." Arthur Cushman McGiffert's course, at nearby Union Theological, in particular, covered the history of Christian dogma, and it broke down the barriers of belief on which Muste had been raised. Remembering them as an "intellectual and spiritual experience," Muste credited McGiffert with opening a "new approach to the study of religion and new historical vistas" beyond the conservative doctrines of the Dutch Reformed Church. A few years earlier, while still studying at Hope College in Michigan, Muste had stumbled across a volume of Ralph Waldo Emerson's *Essays*, which the would-be minister later claimed as the "most seminal influence of all on [his] thinking," an intellectual encounter that no doubt opened Muste's mind to ideas of immanent divinity, existing within nature and extending to all areas of human life. Now, in New York City, the inquisitive seminarian was continuing to challenge his preconceived notions about biblical literalism, God, man, and the church both in and out of the classroom.[5]

The appalling poverty of the East Side piqued Muste's conscience; but he also bore witness to the activism of people who were trying to do something about it. Young Muste had come to the Northeast at a very volatile time in U.S. history. Every day, it seemed, the exploited factory, steel, and mine workers of the modern American industrial order fought their employers for better pay, shorter hours, and healthier living conditions. "These were the years of mushrooming sweatshops[,] . . . of the strikes which marked the founding of the garment trade unions, and, in Paterson and more distant places, of the turbulent I.W.W. organizational campaigns and strikes," Muste recalled.[6]

In 1909, when the newly ordained minister began preaching in a Dutch Reformed church in Washington Heights, William Howard Taft had just been elected president by the moneyed interests of the Republican Party. Progressives, however, were not giving up on their vision of a fairer, more humane kind of capitalism. Among them were religious liberals hoping to apply Christian principles to improve social relations and ameliorate social shortcomings. Pastors such as Walter Rauschenbusch, who had received his baptism into the world of poverty in the so-called Hell's Kitchen of New York City a few years before Muste, began to proclaim a social gospel of compassion and cooperation. As Christ had gone to the poor, helped the lame, and healed the sick, proponents of the social gospel believed Christ's disciples should follow suit. "No man shares his life with God whose religion does not flow out, naturally and without effort, into all relations of his life and reconstructs everything that it touches," Rauschenbusch wrote in his 1907 polemic, *Christianity and the Social Crisis*. "Whoever uncouples the religious and the social life has not understood Jesus."[7]

Essentially, Rauschenbusch and other leading social gospelers of the time were exhorting Christians to act on their beliefs and apply their values in daily life. Muste was already predisposed to agree with such arguments, as is evident in his 1905 Hope College commencement address on the functions of an active faith. Progress, Muste assured his listeners, only occurs when people channel their natural discontent with life and the world into effective purpose. "The deep unrest of [one's] soul is a divine call to battle. Let him plunge boldly into the conflict then." According to the vigorous valedictorian, nothing could be worse than to waste one's life on contemplation or philosophy. "Character is built by action rather than by thought," he frankly stated. The same held true for enacting God's plan and building the Kingdom of God on earth. The passive pursuits of theory left God lifeless and frozen in abstraction. Through activity, however, humans could unleash His energies. "The God of experience is Personality, Power and Love," Muste wrote. "In the stress and agony of conflict we feel his living presence. At our side in the battle rides a sustaining power."[8]

Muste's speech rang with many of the notes that would underlie his thinking as a spiritual socialist, particularly the idea that small, seemingly mundane acts could eventually change the world. "Out of the elements of the daily struggle we mold at last conceptions of justice, parity and truth and build that temple of morality which is the chosen seat of true religion," he avowed. Given his tender age and the blatant confidence of his tone, it is tempting to qualify Muste's enthusiasm for this "wise and simple" plan of action within the context of his generation's general buoyancy and optimism about reform.[9] Like Eddy, Muste grew up in an age of assurance that positive efforts in proselytizing and policymaking would yield positive results, whether in the mission to evangelize the world in one generation or the call to cure social problems with religious values and social science.

By the 1912 presidential election, however, Muste's political outlook had taken a turn toward the left, toward a more radical approach to social restructuring. Earlier that spring and summer, during the presidential primaries and the nominating convention in Baltimore, Muste had followed the Democratic Party proceedings with "intense interest." "I felt this was a great victory for progressivism and, of course, [I] looked forward to casting a ballot for [Woodrow] Wilson [in the fall]," he remembered. On Election Day, however, Muste voted for Socialist Party leader Eugene V. Debs, a clear illustration, he wrote, of "how rapidly [his] social and political orientation was changing."[10] Muste's immersion in the slums of New York and the theories of the social gospel no doubt nudged his politics farther left, but it was the young minister's own penchant for due diligence that carried him into the socialist camp. Wilson was offering legislative adjustments to ameliorate the miseries of industrial capitalism. Debs, on the other hand, promised to do away with the old system altogether. Given the choice between reformism and revolution, Muste sided with the latter, identifying with socialism before he made his wartime turn to pacifism. He never voted for a candidate in either of the two major parties again.

The climate of global warfare would radicalize Muste even more, though he did not immediately espouse a pacifist position. In the fall of 1914, at his Fort Washington Church service to commemorate Spanish-American War veterans, Muste even preached what one would later call a "just war" sermon, rationalizing military defense as a necessary evil, duly exercised whenever democracy and religion are threatened. "I had never been given an inkling that there might be such a thing as a pacifist interpretation of the Gospel," he confessed in his memoir. A year later, however, Muste was reading the peace testimonies of Quakers such as Rufus Jones and seriously wrestling with the inconsistencies between Christian values and the call to violence. As he explained, "I could not 'bend' the Sermon on the Mount and the whole concept of the Cross and suffering love to accommodate participation in war."[11]

Muste, during these years, was making major changes in his life based on the demands of his conscience. In late 1914, he had decided to break with the Dutch Reformed Church on the grounds that he could no longer adhere to its assertions of biblical literalism and Calvinist dogma. In 1917 at Newtonville, Massachusetts, where he had accepted a ministry at the Central Congregational Church, he faced another moral dilemma. The war, as he put it, had "backed [him] into a corner," both theologically and politically, forcing him to decide whether to stay and sermonize on the virtues of warfare, in which he no longer believed, or leave his church once again over ethical scruples. Muste chose to go. "It was a problem which I could not evade because I had been brought up to take religion, specifically the Biblical teaching and Gospel ethic, seriously, and to abhor the sham which enables a person to preach what he does not try desperately to practice," he recalled. Devoting himself to antiwar activism, Muste joined a recently founded Christian peace organization, the Fellowship of Reconciliation (FOR), and "thus became publicly identified as a Christian pacifist."[12]

It was a bold and courageous move at a time when anyone critical of U.S. intervention faced repressive measures. For the duration of the U.S. involvement in World War I, Wilson and his administrators put progressivism and civil liberties aside in their crackdown on dissidents, especially through the Espionage and Sedition Acts (1917–18), which prosecuted American citizens for wartime disloyalty in language, action, and even thought. Federal agents banned left-wing literature from the mails if it contained content critical of the war or draft. In 1918, they also arrested and imprisoned Debs, who had earned Muste's support in 1912. Public voices, including those of many religious leaders, sounded the call for patriotic duty, making it difficult for pacifists and conscientious objectors to speak out without censure. Muste was among those in the vocal minority. He began to find common cause with antiwar activists in groups such as FOR, organized to promote peaceful conflict resolution as a primary Christian responsibility.

Muste, however, did not approach pacifism as a single-issue panacea for all the world's problems. Instead, he considered it part of the broader vision and the deeper *persuasion* for begetting the Kingdom of God on earth. "Persuasion" is the operative word here, especially given Muste's views on human nature. Unlike many religious liberals of his day, Muste found it difficult to entertain illusions about the innate purity and innocence of mankind. The "solid . . . dose of Calvinism" he had received in the Dutch Reformed Church had left within him a "strong conviction about human frailty and corruption."[13] Yet he did believe that people could change, just like he had changed, when confronted with the challenge to practice what they professed to believe. The problem, for Muste, pivoted on convincing Christians that their own moral integrity and the moral outcomes of their actions were more important than money or power. It was about persuading people to keep their baser instincts in check. According to Muste, the envisioned Kingdom of God on earth would not emerge as a place of peace once people were no longer prone, inherently, to greed, jealousy, or other sins. That, he doubted, would ever happen. The Kingdom of God would emerge only after fundamental social and cultural change—when society no longer tolerated hypocrisies that separated moral belief from moral action.

Muste realized, of course, that such transitions would take time, but he believed that the initial steps could and should start immediately. The mistake of most liberal humanists of the early twentieth century, he argued, was that they assumed such changes had already taken place or were about to take place. They were "imbued with optimism and a rosy view of human nature," as Muste put it, giving them a false sense of security. Then came the war, the brutalities of which sent shock waves through the progressives' patina of certainty and effectively shattered the glass houses they had built on shallow beds of idealism. Determined to reclaim the moral high ground, progressives, by and large, became war crusaders, employing "means which they had felt deeply to be stupid and revolting . . . against such [German] monsters." For Muste, these actions reflected the deep trauma of disillusionment on the part of "a people who believed their country had passed beyond war" and now "had to overcompensate in order to silence their inner resistance and to assuage their hurt."[14]

The war also convinced Muste that the primary culprit of local, national, and international misery was capitalism, a system that perpetrated greed, injustice, and, subsequently, war itself. Years later, Muste expressed his cynicism about the true motives of the First World War. "We learned we had actually been fighting to help Great Britain and France hold their colonies against the Central Powers; to save the loans of our bankers; to try to escape a depression from the collapse of the armament boom after we had got our industries all geared up to making good for the Allies," he said in 1937. "Democracy was not saved but raped." In the 1940s, Muste would warn against making the same mistakes again. He boldly stood for "spiritual power," the strength to stick to one's values and serve as a moral, constructive model for the world, over the "military power" that the United States marshaled in the global conflict.[15]

The First World War prompted Muste to analyze the capitalist system more closely, both to understand its power and to identify its weaknesses. At the international level, capitalist enterprise had free rein, but it remained vulnerable at its most basic level of operation—the shop floor. A labor-force walkout could cripple production, leverage negotiating power for the union, and draw attention to the abuses of the industrial system. Muste went to work here, during and after the war, by joining and supporting nonviolent picket lines. His participation in one such strike, at Lawrence, Massachusetts, in early 1919 would change his life and his identity. He became, thereafter, a labor leader.

Muste might have dodged the nearly debilitating postwar despair of the "lost generation," but that is not to say he never felt lost after the war. The global crisis had provided many outlets for activism, from civil liberties cases to the cause of conscientious objectors to peace marches. After the armistice and the Treaty of Paris had been signed, however, the erstwhile minister needed to find new ways to apply his values in an age of "normalcy." He was not alone in his search. In Providence, Rhode Island, where he had become actively involved in the community's Quaker meetinghouse, Muste began to build a network, from Boston to New Haven, of postwar pacifists who "were wrestling with the question of how to organize [their] lives so that they would truly express the teachings and spirit of Jesus." The circle of friends, composed of more than one former minister who had lost his post because of his pacifism, called themselves "the Comradeship," a sort of "left wing" of the FOR, who felt camaraderie for each other as morally estranged outcasts from mainstream society. These outcasts, however, did not want to live as recluses, cut off from the world and its problems. The idea of creating an "intentional community" or commune where they could practice their values in peace held little appeal. As Muste recalled, "We were all agreed that we did not want to shut ourselves off from the struggle against war, and for economic justice and racial equality, in the competitive society."[16] They wanted to build the Kingdom of God within the world, not away from it. Muste's efforts to push the FOR further to the left, toward a more comprehensive socialist mission, shows that he had not joined the group for pacifist reasons alone. He had a bigger picture in mind.

Participation in the 1919 textile-mill strike in Lawrence convinced Muste of the power of nonviolent, moral means in tense, real-world situations. During a sixteen-week standoff against violence-inciting management and local police, Muste lent his support to thirty thousand striking workers, many of them immigrants, who demanded a forty-eight-hour workweek and improved labor conditions. The animosity surrounding the strike made it difficult for Muste to convince many of the mill's workers to resist a no-holds-barred proletarian revolution, but he considered it crucial for their strategy and survival. "Strikes in those days," Muste explained, were not unlike "jungle warfare," in which planted labor spies and club-wielding policemen intentionally provoked the workforce to react with rage and, thus, disorder. "It was hoped that the strikers would resort to violence and that thereupon the strike could be discredited and broken." Muste and his coterie of pacifists from the Comradeship implored the picketers to stay the nonviolent course and keep the moral high ground. "I told them," Muste recalled, "that our real power was in our solidarity and in our capacity to endure suffering [for what is right]." Once the workers realized that the plan, though peaceful, meant militancy rather than passivity, "they changed their attitude toward us." Ultimately, the plan worked. After a few months of intense and exhausting resistance, the workers broke the resolve of the mill owners and negotiated an acceptable contract. The strikers promptly returned to work the next morning and, as Muste put it, "that was that."[17] It had been a long struggle, but, looking back, Muste realized that the painstaking method of applying steady pressure had been the only way forward. Any supposed shortcuts, including sharp, violent insurrection, would have led to counterproductive dead-ends. The peaceful course, though difficult, had yielded the best results.

The strike also opened doors for Muste, personally and professionally, within the labor movement. In the fall of 1919, he was offered the position as general secretary of the recently founded ATW union, a task he undertook for two arduous years, making a "desperate effort" of fashioning solidarity in such a "chaotic industry." He resigned in 1921, and the ATW folded shortly thereafter.[18] Union organizing may have been new and daunting to the former minister, but the episode exposed some of Muste's limitations as a spirited revolutionary. For all of his talk about building a new world order or the Kingdom of God through painstaking struggle, bit by bit, he too lost heart and felt frustrated with the persistence of daily contention. Muste, at age thirty-six, already needed a break from picket lines and union battles, though he wanted to remain active in the labor movement in some way.

A directorship at the experimental Brookwood Labor College in Katonah, New York, opened a new opportunity for Muste to put his passions to work. The school, owned by pacifists William and Helen Fincke, offered workers an education in economics, public speaking, and the history of labor, so that men and women could contribute more effectively to the collective struggle in their home unions and workplaces. Part of a postwar wave of progressive education, institutions such as these became increasingly popular experiments in social reform. Professor John R. Commons at the University of Wisconsin–Madison, for example, made it his mission to apply Christian values and social science to communities and labor unions for the sake of a more democratic industrial order. Labor schools throughout Europe also caught the attention of activists in the United States. The founders of Brookwood were influenced by these sources, hoping to build a better world through local intention. Dedicated to trade union clientele, it was the first of its kind, though a similar school, the Commonwealth College in Mena, Arkansas, also opened in the early 1920s. The Wisconsin School for Workers and the Highlander Folk School would follow suit in the 1930s.

Endorsed by over a dozen unions that promised to provide funding and scholarships for attendees, Brookwood received about twenty adult students in its opening year in 1921. Muste was there from the start, and he remained there for the next twelve years. The college, in many ways, offered fertile ground for Muste's fundamental mission to build the Kingdom of God on earth. At Brookwood, he helped to foster nonviolent cooperation in the labor movement, to transform the class consciousness of both faculty and students, and to create a wide-reaching network of dedicated, *spiritualized* socialists. As he recollected, "We were, of course, affected by the revolutionary ferment of the times, as well as by the visions of the prophets of a new heaven and a new earth. We were also imbued with the idea . . . that we should order our lives today as if the Kingdom were already here."[19] As historian Kip Kosek put it, Brookwood "tried to set a pattern for a new kind of labor movement that was at once a new kind of human community."[20]

Brookwood, in short, operated as an intentional community, a place where idealists could practice their values of cooperative living.[21] The fact that it remained tied to labor unions and the struggles of the working class clinched Muste's commitment. He convinced himself that his involvement in the school amounted to serious socialist action, not the kind of passive isolation he had disparaged in the past. "My activity," Muste insisted, "has been in the labor movement . . . seeking to effect changes in society, or a part of it, rather than to build an image or nucleus of a more ideal community with the larger society."[22] Muste was consciously trying to avoid the sectarian tendencies of leftist organizations, and he did not envision Brookwood as a commune or cult. Instead, he wanted to demonstrate to visitors and staff the kinds of behavior—sharing and cooperating peacefully as equals—that prefigured the socialist society and the Kingdom of God. "Muste also remained a socialist," his most recent biographer, Leilah Danielson, affirmed, "and he viewed utopian experiments as . . . not ends in themselves, but rather part of a larger effort to democratize and demilitarize the politics of the left."[23] Such is true, but Muste envisioned more than a reform of the politics of the Left. He intended his intentionally socialist praxis as a method of transforming the entire world into the Kingdom of God on earth. The school for him represented a seed, not a sect.

Yet the assignment to serve as director of a small college tucked away in the woods of upstate New York did represent a sort of retreat for Muste, a much-needed respite from the daily grind of vanguard activism. As biographer Jo Ann Ooiman Robinson wrote, Brookwood "would remove Muste from the grueling and essentially hopeless ATW battles and allow something of a return to a reflective mode of life."[24] Muste, of course, did not see it that way. His disdain for the "reflective mode of life" kept him busy fundraising among unionists, contributing to field action whenever he could, and, eventually, giving more of his time and attention to organizations such as the CPLA that he considered more militant and revolutionary than Brookwood. Though Muste talked about the importance of concentrating political action within a "specific social context" and the arduous process of creating alternative institutions, his experience in labor education and small-community building during the 1920s increasingly roused his impatience with the slow pace of social change, a personal shortcoming that he would confront in the mid-1930s.[25]

In 1921, however, Muste was eager to teach socialist theory in an environment of socialist practice. Characteristically, he threw himself into the new project with gusto. In fact, one staff member, Cara Cook, recalled that the director had a tendency to involve himself too often in the "petty details" of mundane decision making, everything from cleaning duties to curriculum plans. This hands-on approach, Cook admitted, became aggravating at times, when staff and faculty felt they needed to seek Muste's input on all matters, large and small. His reluctance to delegate did not seem dictatorial, however, at least not to Cook. Instead, she considered it symptomatic of that combination of "practical realism and idealistic faith" inherent in all of Muste's actions. The director of Brookwood was, according to Cook, "a dreamer of dreams, indeed—sometimes [dreams] so far beyond hope of immediate achievement that all sight seems to have been lost of the here and now." But then, she continued, Muste would pull back to the reality of practical necessity and assume "some immediate, petty task, unnoticed or shunned by others, but the accomplishment of which is an unmistakable next step toward the greater goal."[26] If, as the saying goes, the devil is in the details, for Muste, so too is God's design.

Cook could also understand Muste's ambiguities regarding the balance between slow-moving social reconstruction and dynamic political commitment. Before arriving at Brookwood in 1926, she had been involved in union organizing and strike action in Washington, D.C. There, she could do her own thing and choose her own friends, those who shared her values and worldview. She felt the certainty of her opinions. At Brookwood, however, life was different. The school community, containing a diversity of people in an isolated area, "demonstrated how relative were [our] values, and how transitory [our] 'absolute' convictions," Cook explained. "Every day brought new ideas and contacts to modify those concepts, keep them in constant flux, and push one forward to a new synthesis."[27]

Cook's students, mostly poorly educated adults with working-class backgrounds, challenged many of her previously held convictions as well as her formerly self-assured identity as an "intellectual radical." Their real-life experiences complicated her assumed theories. Their thinly veiled disdain for any elitism also complicated formal classroom instruction. By default, as much as design, the school operated with an open, democratic forum of student-teacher give-and-take. "Every course taught at Brookwood," Cook remembered, "was inevitably colored by the point of view of the one who taught and the one who learned . . . in an atmosphere of perfect freedom. The flow was in both directions, as I learned from my own experience." This mutual, cooperative approach to education and activism, what later New Leftists such as Staughton Lynd would call "accompaniment," also precluded any attempts by Brookwood faculty to propagandize from the lectern. Bias toward labor rights notwithstanding, the institution's literature took pains to assure the public that "Brookwood is not a propagandist institution. It seeks the truth, free from dogma and doctrinaire teaching. It believes that the labor and farmer movements constitute the most vital concrete force working for human freedom, and that by exerting wise social control they can bring in a new era of justice and human brotherhood."[28] The primary purpose of the labor college—to grant experience supplemented by knowledge and theory, so that workers would become better equipped to solve problems and improve social relations nonviolently in their daily lives—guided Muste and his staff. As Muste asserted, "The school did not have a body of economic and political doctrine to inculcate. We deliberately sought to stimulate intellectual controversy."[29]

The school certainly caused controversy beyond its campus gates by the late 1920s. Organized as Local 189 of the American Federation of Teachers, Brookwood fell under the auspices of the conglomerate union, the AFL. At first, the AFL association seemed beneficial to Brookwood because it drew recruits from established trade unions to serve its mission to the larger labor movement. In 1928, however, some officials of the AFL, including its vice president, Matthew Woll, began to take issue with what they considered a Communist-leaning, antireligious curriculum at the school. Concerned about keeping their liberal and even conservative political connections in an age of Communist paranoia, the AFL made moves to disassociate itself from Brookwood and the radical atmosphere it found "antagonistic to A. F. of L. policies."[30]

As educational director and chairman of the faculty at Brookwood, Muste naturally stood at the center of the maelstrom. His anticapitalist views, however, did not help his case with Woll and the executive committee of the AFL. While teaching a course on the history of the Russian Revolution, for example, Muste had praised the Soviet Union as a worthy, though imperfect, experiment in the search for economic and social alternatives in modern times. "Even if it fails, it will still remain a beautiful and holy thing," he apparently told his students.[31] At this point, the Bolshevik Revolution was a relatively new phenomenon, and though it had been born of violence, Muste was unwilling to dismiss the Soviets' first brave steps into a new world order.

Given the chance to respond to Woll's charges, Muste clarified his position, insisting he remained critical of antidemocratic and antireligious Soviet policies as well as many Communist activities in the United States. Brookwood, he stated, was not a Communist-front institution, especially considering that actual hard-core Communists dismissed the labor school as "a cloak for the destructive policy of the reactionary labor fakers."[32] While the AFL accused Brookwood staff of irreligion, Muste insisted that he heard Communists charging the opposite, referring to him as being "as far from Communism as a pious Jew from pork."[33] The school's emphasis on religious values, in fact, made it suspect among traditional Marxists' groups. This did not mean that Brookwood socialists abhorred the Soviet Union as an evil entity. Muste had indeed referred to Soviet Communism as a historically significant and "holy" experiment in restructuring human relations, points he refused to retract for the sake of AFL solidarity. "I still stand by that statement without hesitation or qualification," he declared in a press release in early 1929.[34] But, when confronted with charges of Communist sympathy, Muste, as many spiritual socialists would do, defended himself by emphasizing his religious values.

Muste stood his ground against AFL censorship of the school and its faculty, along with many Brookwood defenders, including Christian socialist Harry F. Ward and political philosopher John Dewey, who directed their criticisms at the Woll committee. During an address on the subject to the American Federation of Teachers, Dewey brought attention to the hypocrisy of the AFL's claim to liberalism. "The Executive Council of the A.F. of L. have taken an action that is very much like betraying the ideals for which we have all been fighting in common," he charged. "Do they want us in the movement? Are we . . . a really organic part of the labor movement?"[35] Muste had similar concerns. In fact, his indignant demeanor throughout the controversy signified that, for him, there was much more at stake than just academic freedom. His defiant motivations were really about defending Brookwood's contributions to the building of a radically different society. In what Cook called a "brave and uncompromising" speech in the spring of 1928, Muste made his intentions clear to the AFL leadership. He and his fellow faculty members at Brookwood were going to continue opposing capitalism and "struggling through to a new social order." "If that be treason to the American labor movement, let them make the most of it," Muste challenged. "We are going to stand for these things; we are going to fight for these things!"[36]

It is not difficult to detect a hint of delight in Muste's assumed role as a persecuted radical. The more militant, mostly Communist, organizations considered him reactionary in politics and religion, despite his contempt for capitalism. The AFL's accusations, however, painted the former minister as a dangerous and subversive element in American society, proof positive that he was stirring up some turbulence in the prevailing system. Moreover, Muste realized he had built up an influential network of intellectuals and activists, such as Dewey and Ward, willing to take his side in a battle of principles against the powerful mega-union. That battle was short-lived. Within a year, the controversy calmed down; the AFL executive committee never officially published its damaging report against Brookwood, and the case never went to hearing. Yet the incident did have a lingering effect on the school. Some staff members favored caution as well as a more conservative public image, especially after October 1929, when the developing economic Depression sent the labor movement into a frenzied state of militancy. Muste may have felt like a vigorous, if beleaguered, radical in 1928, but throughout the next five years he became increasingly worried that his quiet life at Brookwood rendered him a passive spectator in the unfolding "civil war" of Depression-era politics.[37]

The mission at Brookwood certainly had its virtues as a prefigurative, working model for the Kingdom of God on earth and the principles of spiritual socialism. Given the diversity on campus and the passionate convictions of nearly all involved in the enterprise, residents at the school had to learn to dwell "amicably with others" in an "intensive community life." Essentially, this was the kind of concentrated social environment perfect for applying Christian values as if the Kingdom of God were a living reality. The school's small, rather manageable context, moreover, made cooperation seem more possible and less frustrating than in larger, urban settings. As Cook put it, "The democratic basis on which the school functioned, and the self-contained character of its social and intellectual life, made it an intensely stimulating yet comprehensible little world, in which one could see some tangible result to his particular contribution."[38] Muste had claimed, for years, that his purpose in life was to help create durable social, rather than transient political, change in small Christian-based communities. Brookwood had given him the opportunity to do so. The national crisis exploding in the early 1930s, however, made Muste's decade-long struggle at the labor college seem diminutive and moderate. He grew impatient with the coming Kingdom of God and felt tempted by the apparent shortcut of political radicalism in the national arena. The Christian community-building efforts he had believed in now seemed out of touch with the more pressing work of Communist organizations.

In 1932, Muste's dilemma came to a head, though not on terms of his choosing. That year, the more conservative faculty members took the director to task, expressing their concerns that he was spending more time and energy on national organizing than on Brookwood-related duties. They were especially nervous about Muste's involvement in the CPLA, an organization founded in the wake of the AFL dispute that was intended to serve as an alternative base for progressive laborites caught between moderate, mainstream unions and Communist Party insurgents. Determined to develop a national presence, members of the CPLA proposed a series of national objectives, everything from an end to racial discrimination to the creation of social security to the formation of a Labor Party like that in Great Britain. They also published a periodical, *Labor Age*, appealing to a mass readership. Muste contributed regularly to *Labor Age*. He also became chairman of the CPLA, while remaining director of Brookwood, a situation that caused anxiety among some faculty who were fearful that the school would become subsumed under CPLA authority.

Muste did not have any clear intentions of making formal ties between Brookwood and the CPLA, but neither did he make a clean division between them. In fact, he saw his work for the national labor organization as a natural extension of Brookwood's mission. "We have always wanted to turn out revolutionists at Brookwood. That has always been our urge," Muste reminded his staff in October. "Therefore," he continued, "Brookwood must be under the control of people with a general CPLA point of view." No doubt, such statements offered cold comfort to those who wished Brookwood to remain unaffiliated. A few days later, the conservative faction at Brookwood recommended that Muste resign as director, though they invited him to serve as an advisor for the school.[39]

Muste did not go away quickly or quietly. In early 1933, he was still trying to convince his more conservative colleagues at Brookwood that they had lost sight of their main purpose: to serve the larger labor movement. From Muste's point of view, he and his activist-minded adherents were staying the course while the rest of the faculty had taken a rightward turn out of fear of reprisal. Clearly, though, the director failed to consider the possibility that it was he who had changed or that his priorities had shifted. Brookwood had been intended, from its very beginnings, as an integral part of social and industrial revolution. The school trained trade unionists to contribute more effectively to bucking the system from below and from within. Yet Brookwood residents, including Muste, had always defended the school's integrity as an independent educational center, containing intrinsic value apart from revolutionary politics. The community they were building, in other words, was long regarded as an end in itself. As times changed, however, so did the radical intensity of some of Brookwood's staff. The AFL controversy had made Muste and his supporters more self-conscious and insecure about their place in the movement. The onset of the Great Depression directly thereafter also added urgency to the task of building a new world order.

Muste's frustration, in particular, was palpable. "Much as we may love Brookwood, its dear associations, its history, we have absolutely no right, especially in such a period as the present, to regard an institution as a fetish, an end in itself," he cautioned in 1933. His entire tone, in fact, made it clear that Muste now considered the educational errand into the wilderness as isolated, useless child's play, especially given that a much more serious game, requiring more militant methods, was ensuing across the country and the world. "We have decided to do rather than merely to teach," Muste explained on behalf of Brookwood's radical faction. "We have taken a more definite and concrete position on issues in the labor movement. We have gone to the workers in concrete struggles, have found it difficult to draw the nice line between educational and organizational work, and have taken sides, as in actual life one always must." For a man supposedly dedicated to cooperation, love, and fellowship, Muste did not mince words in his challenge to colleagues. They were timid, he said, while he was courageous. They were passive, and he was active. They were wrong; he was right. "It is a betrayal of the workers to make such a swing to the right at a time when the economic system gives signs of crashing around them," he stated bluntly.[40] When he finally did decide to resign from Brookwood in February 1933 along with nineteen (out of twenty-eight total) faculty members who decided to go with him, Muste was not magnanimous. His closing statement read, in part:

> Because organizations and institutions are carried on by individuals or groups it may happen that a psychological situation is created which makes it impossible for some of them to continue to work together. . . . In our opinion that stage has arrived at Brookwood, that whatever our views in regard to individuals, we cannot continue to work with the other group in the Brookwood faculty. We lack confidence . . . in the ability, judgment, disinterestedness, courage, militancy and working-class loyalty of the group.[41]

Like so many left-of-center organizations in the 1930s, the fellowship at Brookwood had cracked apart along factional lines of discord. Much as Muste had hoped to avoid the sectarianism of the Left, he did not. In fact, he seemed to embrace a militant position in the early 1930s as a sign of his purity in theory and praxis.

The next month, March 1933, Muste sent a short update for the Brookwood newsletter, brimming with enthusiasm for his new life of activism in places such as Philadelphia. "I am out in the field! It is grand!" he announced. "[I] have seen the work of Eddie Ryan, Jean Bloom, John Godber, Larry Heimbach, Mike Demchak etc. at first hand in the past few days. They *are* building the American labor movement. Yours for intelligent, militant action, A.J."[42] Despite its notes of conceit and condescension, Muste was truly expressing his excitement for the opportunities he now had to participate, unfettered from administrative responsibilities, in labor radicalism. This was his chance to join the vanguard and make a direct strike against a vulnerable social and economic system. If, as Cook claimed, "Brookwood had its share of self-appointed messiahs," Muste was among them. Cook, however, did not begrudge her mentor for moving on. In fact, she left Brookwood in protest with him, one of the nineteen staff members to do so. The move seemed, to her, in line with Muste's overall mission: "his search for the cooperative commonwealth of mankind." "He has sought to bring about his 'heaven' here on earth, and to find his deity in the release of mankind's own divine possibilities," Cook explained. The workers, during the Depression, needed the most help, so Muste naturally went out to struggle alongside them, even if it meant leaving the Brookwood "family" behind. Years later, while writing her memoirs, Cook could forgive the uncompromising idealist his lesser faults in light of this greater scope of vision. "For A.J. Muste, I am convinced, the goal is still unsullied, and the man himself still uncorrupted."[43]

Yet Cook could not have predicted in early 1933 just how quickly this messianic move to the barricades of labor radicalism would lead Muste away from his Christian and pacifist convictions. Cloaked in crisis mentality, Muste kept moving, along with the CPLA, toward increasingly radical means for immediate revolution. "The CPLA became steadily more political-minded," Cook recalled. "Its Socialist members withdrew—they already had a party, they said."[44] Muste's former seminary colleague, Socialist Party leader Norman Thomas, who had been involved with the CPLA at its inception in 1929, was among those who severed his connections to the group. Muste did not mourn that loss, especially since he considered those members insufficiently militant. He had voted for Socialist Party candidates during elections, but now deplored their narrow party politics. In a 1933 article in the *New Republic*, for example, he had dismissed them in no uncertain terms, saying, "I do not blush to confess that the war and the postwar history of the Social Democracy has made me one of those who do not believe that the party is or is likely to become an effective revolutionary vanguard."[45] The flight of the Socialist Party members from the CPLA, however, left an ideological vacuum in an organization on shaky and shifting political ground. "New, more leftward elements, came in: including a large number of unemployed," Cook wrote. Caught up in the fast pace of the times, "labor institutions of all shades everywhere were restless, and poor, and scared."[46]

They were also more vulnerable to Communist takeover, which is exactly what happened to the once progressive-oriented CPLA. The organization changed its name to the American Workers Party, merged with the Communist League of America in 1935, and then became Workers Party U.S.A., an offshoot of the Trotskyist Fourth International. Muste made the Trotskyist turn too. His reading of Marxist literature in the late 1920s and early 1930s had predisposed him to accept many of the revolutionary concepts now popular among his new circle of friends. Above all, these radicals seemed imbued with a kind of "religious" zeal for building a new world order that was largely unheard of among *actual* religious activists. "The Left had the vision, the dream, of a classless and warless world," explained Muste. "This was a strong factor in making me feel that here, in a sense, was the true church. Here was the fellowship drawn together and drawn forward by the Judeo-Christian prophetic vision of 'a new earth in which righteousness dwelleth.'" In other words, Muste followed his dream of the Kingdom of God on earth and found it expressed among revolutionary atheists. "The Communists are those who today are able to convince vast multitudes that they do cherish the ancient dream of brotherhood realized on earth and have the determination to make it come true," he wrote.[47]

Decades earlier, liberal Christians, including social gospelers, had envisioned the Kingdom but lacked the radical commitment to realize it. They believed that a new world would unfold almost inevitably with only a few adjustments and reforms here and there. After World War I, those Christians advocating a neo-orthodox theology of never-ending evil and sin denigrated the liberal utopia as naïve and fantastic. Muste did not go that far. He continued to keep faith in the coming Kingdom; but he believed that it would require much more radical methods than previously thought. "The liberal Christians were never, in my opinion, wrong in cherishing this vision," Muste made clear. "Their mistake, and in a sense, their crime, was not to see that it was revolutionary in character and demanded revolutionary living and action of those who claimed to be its votaries."[48] This level of radicalism marked the difference, Muste implied, between Christian socialists before and after the war.

The Communists' commitment to radical change, their propensity to put words into action, and to build dreams on deeds made them appear all the more practical to Muste and so unlike the Christians and pacifists who, he felt, lacked a working method for bridging the real and the ideal. In an era when Gandhian nonviolent tactics were still developing in India, and had not made a significant impact in the United States, pacifists did not apply leverage to the extent that their more radical, though violent, counterparts were doing in the early 1930s. "Pacifism was mostly a middle-class and individualistic phenomenon," Muste wrote. "The churches certainly were not giving the illustration of spiritual force, of true community, which might have had a nonviolent but transforming influence."[49]

Muste was caught between two imperfect choices: the sufficiently radical but hopelessly violent Communists, and the spiritual but passive mainstream churches. The problem was that Muste did not fit the mold of either of these camps, not traditional Marxism or traditional religion. Instead, he operated as a spiritual socialist in a world where spiritual socialism had not taken root. His frustration with this fact helps explain the leftward turn he took with antireligious Communists in the early 1930s. Always open to experimentation, Muste was willing to try methods of violence to achieve a social revolution, even while acknowledging that such methods were anti-Christian. In 1936, however, the prodigal son dramatically declared his "return to pacifism" and the Christian values he could no longer deny. The shortcut of revolutionary violence, he believed, had proved a dead-end. "The proletarian movement is the philosophy of power, the will to power, the desire to humiliate and dominate over or destroy the opponent, the acceptance of the methods of violence and deceit, the theory that 'the end justifies the means,'" he stated.[50] He still wanted a revolution, but not the immediate, violent kind. And he refused to accept that pacifism precluded revolutionary change. To the contrary, Muste insisted that the only way to a socialist society characterized by peace, equality, and cooperation was through the praxis of these values in small acts and the small ways of saying "no" to an immoral world. Direct action, for him as well as his fellow spiritual socialists, was not limited to marches, pickets, or sit-ins, but also included the daily social behaviors that defined community building.

Muste's return to the religious Left, in fact, was a reconciliation of means and ends, a freshly refurbished conviction that to create a socialist society of love and brotherhood, revolutionaries must act accordingly. "Since it is precisely to love, to the apprehension of our unity with mankind, to the kingdom of God, that we are won," he wrote, "we must carry this dynamic and method into every relationship." Such lofty proclamations to Christianize the social order were not much different than those made by social gospelers and Christian socialists in the early twentieth century. The methodology, however, had changed since the Great War. Instead of top-down solutions, Muste insisted that only grassroots cultivation in one's own social backyard could change society. "We must, after the example of Jesus, work from within and not without, though it lead to crucifixion," he advised.[51] Throughout the next three decades, until his death in 1967, Muste continued to agitate as a spiritual socialist, participating in localized acts of conscience that had global implications. Whether protesting U.S. intervention in World War II, Korea, and Vietnam, marching in labor strikes, or disrupting the buildup of nuclear weapons, Muste never made a secret of the religious values that undergirded his radicalism. His notion of "spiritual force" in foreign relations, for example, sought to challenge Cold War militarism and religious thinkers such as Reinhold Niebuhr, who justified hard power as a necessary evil in the fight for justice (see Chapter 3).

The relationship between religion and radicalism was also on the mind of Eddy, who followed a trajectory similar to Muste from Christian liberalism to spiritual socialism during and after World War I, though never to the point of absolute pacifism. By January 1931, when Eddy addressed a crowd gathered in New York City to celebrate his thirty-five years of service with the YMCA, he was ready to make his spiritual socialist convictions clear. His speech, coming at the end of the commemorative evening, outlined his ongoing mission. He intended, he said, echoing Muste, to continue building the Kingdom of God on earth and to "Christianize [the] social order" "by the intelligent application of love in every relationship of life," a statement typical of many Christians who believed in progressive, religious reform.[52] Eddy's next words, however, gave his spiritual vision a hefty dose of political substance, even as it set him apart from many of his Christian colleagues. "I am not a Communist; I am not a Capitalist; I am a Socialist," he announced.[53]

It was not exactly a surprising revelation. Eddy had been making radical speeches about the evils of capitalism throughout the 1920s, ever since he had returned to the United States from service as a chaplain in World War I and founded his global travel program, the American Seminar, which took clergy and laymen abroad each year to learn the latest techniques in social democracy. Like Brookwood Labor College and, later, the Highlander Folk School, Eddy's American Seminar used education as a means to foster socialist theory and practice. Participants traveling from nation to nation were exposed to new ideas and methods that they could then implement in their own communities back home. This international exchange of ideas was exceedingly important to Eddy, a longtime missionary in India and China. In fact, it was during his time in India that Eddy first began to think about the value of small, localized cooperatives as a basis for a socialist society and the Kingdom of God on earth (see Chapter 2). No longer intent on imposing Western culture and authority over indigenous villagers, as he had done in the late 1800s, Eddy, by the 1920s, had learned the importance of cross-cultural education. He founded the travel seminar to reproduce, in a way, his experiences for more Americans, insisting that the United States had as much to learn from other countries and other peoples as it had to dispense. In a supposed age of isolation, Eddy retained a dynamic internationalism via the American Seminar. In a supposed age of left-liberal disillusionment, he also kept his radical religious idealism alive. The American Seminar represented Eddy's attempt to find new methods of socialist practice that could dovetail with his Christian values and international interests. "To be creative, revolution must be religious," he affirmed, stating the truth that Muste had also learned to embrace.[54]

Eddy certainly hoped his outspoken socialist values would spark a revolution in American religion; however, he also intended religion to revolutionize American socialism into a moral project aligned toward the Kingdom of God on earth. This is a point that scholars have neglected. Centering their studies on theology or mission culture, they do not address either Eddy's importance as a religious voice for the non-Communist Left or his identity as a socialist. The oversight is unfortunate, because it underestimates the impact of religious thought in radical political and social movements of the time period. Eddy's missionary experience was significant not just in terms of the liberal, modernizing shift in Protestant evangelism, but also in the history of the American Left.[55]

Religion became an integral part of Eddy's mission because, at an early age, he had a chance encounter with Dwight Moody during a college retreat. Eddy, the man who would later rail against the evils of capitalism, had been born into a family of significant wealth in Leavenworth, Kansas, on January 19, 1871. His father's work as a wholesale druggist had made him "one of the [most] successful businessmen" in town, bequeathing a significant fortune to his eldest son upon his death in 1894. Eddy remained financially independent for the rest of his life, never accepting a salary for his work for the YMCA.[56]

Enrolling at Yale College in 1888, Eddy intended to pursue an engineering career geared toward accumulating more wealth. "I believed that money was power," he recalled. A single weekend, however, changed his mind and his life. Invited by a classmate to attend the Dwight L. Moody Northfield Student Conference in upstate New York, Eddy decided to go, if only for the promise of swimming and dancing at the rural summer resort. "I dropped into a back seat at the first meeting, hoping that it would soon be over and I could go out for tennis." Then Moody, "huge and homely," took the stage. "He was the most dynamic human being I had ever met—terribly in earnest," Eddy wrote. The sermon had a powerful effect on the would-be entrepreneur, who "felt shriveled in selfishness" at the thought of his own privileged and cynical ambition. Eddy had grown up attending a Congregationalist church, but he had never intended to devote his life to religious work. The conference changed his course. "Before [Moody] had finished," Eddy remembered, "I saw myself as I was—no good to my college, to my country, to man, or to God." That night, Eddy dedicated himself to a life of service, "the making of men instead of money," as he put it. He began teaching Bible classes back at Yale, and, after graduation in 1891, he joined the staff of the Twenty-third Street Branch of the YMCA in New York City.[57]

Like it had for Muste, Eddy's year in New York City introduced him to the "raw" social problems of an urban environment. For the first time in his life, he encountered masses of unemployed, poverty-stricken, and mentally ill supplicants, searching for food or shelter, revealing to him the need for an acute application of religious values. He had learned piety but not practice in the liberal Congregationalist church of Leavenworth; his small-town upbringing had not prepared him for the enormity of the social crisis. Faced with the beggars and thieves he had read about in Scripture, the young YMCA volunteer felt, firsthand, the pulse of living religion. Eddy wanted more; he wanted to learn more and do more, especially for the needier areas of the world, where he believed Christianity could most dynamically and dramatically transform lives. Soon after, Eddy signed the declaration card of the YMCA's Student Volunteer Movement, pledging to serve as a foreign missionary.[58]

As a YMCA secretary in Asia, Eddy felt the first stirrings of what would later develop into strong socialist convictions (see Chapter 2). But it was World War I more than any event or experience in his life that quickened his transition from Christian liberal to spiritual socialist. "The war broke upon our complacent, ordered, evolutionary world as a brutal fact, like Vesuvius in sudden eruption," he stated vividly in one of his memoirs.[59] Though he had promoted a social gospel sensibility before 1914, the war radicalized Eddy's worldview. Christianity, he concluded by war's end, could not coexist within the paradigms of evil that capitalism, and subsequently imperialism, cast on the world. He realized that the roots of capitalist culture ran deep, requiring the creation of an entirely new social order in its place. Insurmountable as it seemed, the difficulties of social revolution did not deter Eddy, but instead they motivated him to get to the bottom of humanity's moral problems. "I ceased to be a liberal asking alms of capitalism; I became a radical demanding the justice of socialism," he wrote of his experiences during wartime.[60]

Eddy initially supported the Allied cause and its rhetoric of democratic defense against Prussian militancy. In this sense, he was one of many liberal, progressive Protestants who formed a support network for the preservation of democracy and religious freedom, grafting notions of spiritual warfare between forces of good and evil onto the military crusades in Europe. In 1916, once he got to France, where he served as a YMCA chaplain to British soldiers, Eddy began to change his mind. There, he witnessed firsthand the degenerative effects that combat had on ordinarily moral men. Gambling, prostitution, and violence were common within the camps, even as Eddy struggled to remind the soldiers of God's commandments against such vices. Instead of blaming individuals for their depravity, as he had done when he first arrived in India, the forty-seven-year-old lay minister looked at the larger picture and realized that human behaviors reflected the social context. The atmosphere of war, in this case, shaped interpersonal relations in such a way that once-sinful activities no longer seemed amiss.[61]

This got Eddy thinking. If the conditions of combat made decadent behavior more tempting and even normative for individual men, then, he thought, there must be a systemic set of factors that had generated the world conflict—conditions that made it more tempting and normative for nations to engage in violent and destructive acts. As Eddy explained, the war "drove some of us to think deeper into the causes of the great catastrophe to find what was radically wrong with the world and to enter upon a new pilgrimage of ideas."[62] While pacing the shores of France and "wrestling with the most difficult moral problem of [his] life," Eddy came to some life-altering conclusions.[63] Capitalism, he pinpointed, created a competitive global system that continuously brought nations into variance over limited resources. World War I, therefore, was no random conflict, sparked by an assassin in Serbia. It was symptomatic of a particular economic system, which, Eddy now claimed, amounted to "fundamentally a war system."[64]

Struck by this revelation, Eddy could no longer cast sole blame for the recent rise in militarism on the empires of Germany and Austro-Hungary. The Entente powers, including Great Britain, France, and, later, the associated United States, had set the stage and were now playing their roles. In a letter to his mother, describing his visit to Canterbury Cathedral in southern England, Eddy made the connections:

> In the great nave hang the battle flags of the modern world war, which marks the failure of the church in social or corporate Christianity. Good men they were and there are good men today, but they and we alike have failed to Christianise the political order, the social order and the industrial order. Our politics is selfish, materialistic and pagan; our society is selfish and unchristian; our commerce and industry is too often greedy and unmoral. The saddest thing is that as yet we do not seem to have learned the lesson of war. Every day I am praying for eyes to see, to penetrate beneath the crust of things and see things as they are, as God sees them.[65]

Eddy had believed that Christianity, in the West and increasingly throughout the wider world, would gradually pave the way for a more cooperative society and the Kingdom of God on earth. Progress toward that end, he now realized, stood stalled by the horrors of war, "forced upon humanity by a godless materialism, while the Christian Church stands by impotent."[66] The Great Church had failed to prevent the Great War, Eddy lamented. Continuing his line of thought in another letter to his mother two days later, he reflected on "fifteen centuries of personal piety and the failure of social Christianity." "Should it not search our [religion] like a refining fire?" he wondered.[67]

For Eddy, the experiences on and near the battlefields of Europe did illuminate a new direction in his religious thinking. The war had given him ample "evidence of a sick and envenomed social order" in need of an antidote. Christianity, as always, was Eddy's answer; but after the armistice, his prescription changed significantly. "I came to the conclusion that henceforth I must live a social life, proclaim a social message and help to organize a socialized society," he wrote.[68] Fortunately, Eddy assured, Jesus proclaimed a social message, and a very clear one at that. The Sermon on the Mount and other passages in the book of Matthew rendered all the tenets one needed to build a Christian society; but essentially the message amounted to a command to love one's neighbor as God so loved them.[69] Jesus' words, Eddy speculated in the wake of the war, obviously had been lost on a generation engaged in mass destruction and genocide. The rapid pace and immensity of modern life had not enhanced morality; instead, it had worked to smother interpersonal communication, understanding, and cooperation. Eddy knew he had to reaffirm these basic values in order for the Kingdom of God to stand a chance in the postwar world.

In the years immediately following the 1918 armistice, the dregs of destruction littered much of the European landscape. The war also shattered the spiritual landscape—the hope and optimism of millions of people, who had once believed in the inevitable progress of modern civilization. "The war . . . destroyed the faith of the old world," Eddy wrote of the nihilistic mood he noticed nearly everywhere.[70] He found it much harder to assure his audiences that God's divine plan still operated amidst such devastating evidence to the contrary. At times, disillusionment nipped at Eddy's heels too. "The war did something to me," he freely admitted. "I could never be quite the same again. Like a bursting shell or the upheaval of a mine, it shattered the easy, optimistic complacency of my previous ideas of a fictitious evolutionary social development toward millennial utopias."[71] In other words, he had realized that there were no easy panaceas for humanity's spiritual sickness. It had to be cut out, completely, as one would treat a cancer. The task was daunting and seemingly out of Eddy's range of experience. "I had specialized in retail sins," Eddy stated, "but knew little about the wholesale brand."[72]

Like Muste, Eddy began to analyze means and ends. An interpersonal and localized approach to spiritual and social work, he knew, had done wonders in the villages of rural Asia. Perhaps, he hoped, this primitive process of working with small groups of people, and striving to understand diverse points of view, would open up promising paths to change. Such a painstaking approach would take more time—more than one generation, certainly—but Eddy firmly believed that his collective socializing method was more realistic and ultimately more effective in the long run than topical solutions to social problems.[73] "Some of our most cherished dreams . . . banged into reality with a repercussion which made us realize that we had to think in terms of a longer time-span than we had hoped," he wrote.[74] If the present social order was stifling spiritual values, then Christians needed "to supplant [it] by one which more nearly approximates the Kingdom of God on earth."[75]

There was considerable fluidity between liberals and leftists in the early to mid-twentieth century, and Muste and Eddy both represent fitting examples to underscore this phenomenon.[76] All spiritual socialists, at one point or another, recognized and commented on their unique position between liberalism and the Left, and they felt misunderstood by both sides. Liberals, they knew, could appreciate their emphasis on religion, democracy, cooperation, gradual progress, and the sanctity of the individual, even as many leftists dismissed these values as bourgeois. On the other hand, liberals could rarely understand what socialism had to do with religion and individualism, while many socialists failed to grasp the importance of spirituality to the masses. Muste and Eddy, however, dissolved these dualisms in their concept of spiritual socialism. They did not consider religion, democracy, cooperation, and individual dignity as bulwarks of liberalism, but as harbingers of a socialist society. If people actually practiced their values, they believed, then fundamental, structural change was bound to follow, if slowly.

By the 1920s, Eddy was equating socialist and Christian values as indistinguishable, especially when practiced in the small, intimate settings of daily life: caring for the sick, hungry, and exploited members of one's community. Socialism, Eddy concluded, had picked up the religious dream of social idealism and made it secular.[77] Now, in the wake of the war, he was determined to revert it back to its spiritual source. The real work of spiritual socialism, Eddy insisted, would take place in communities, where social behavior was learned and reinforced. It was a lesson he had learned during his career as a missionary. It was a lesson he hoped to impart to the American people. In 1921, he helped found the Fellowship for a Christian Social Order, an organization dedicated to building the Kingdom of God on earth. That same year, he took the first contingent of the American Seminar on a tour throughout Europe.

Promoting an interpersonal approach to foreign affairs, the group-travel enterprise he founded brought potential activists from the United States into contact with activists abroad. Ignorance of other cultures and perspectives, Eddy knew from his initial forays into foreign missions, formed the seedbed of exploitation, violence, and war. He hoped to break down barriers of race, culture, and creed by fostering a network of open-minded activists who would make international politics more social, more personal, and thereby more peaceful. As detailed in Chapter 2, Eddy confronted racism as an obstacle to the Kingdom of God in the U.S. South in the 1930s. But he started out opening Americans' minds to a greater appreciation for diversity with the American Seminar in the 1920s. The groups each year were small, consisting of about thirty to fifty people, including ministers, students, writers, labor leaders, and missionaries, who expressed an interest in learning about the social and political life of foreign nations. Though associated with Eddy and the YMCA, religious content remained veiled. The 1923 contingent, for example, spent the summer visiting with German and British labor leaders, touring the slums of Berlin, and exchanging ideas with literary giants such as Bernard Shaw and H. G. Wells.[78] Yet Eddy's religious agenda was hidden in plain sight, in the very act of bringing small groups together to discuss social problems and share solutions. The Seminar presented the perfect opportunity to cultivate the kind of interpersonal communication and social cooperation he had found wanting during the war years. It was also a way to break down the barriers of isolationism and prejudice that kept many Americans in the 1920s from engaging with non-American ideas and values, especially those associated with socialism and Communism. In fact, Eddy's penchant for publicly commending the Soviet Union's experiment in social reconstruction provoked the ire of many colleagues within the YMCA.

Eddy had first traveled to Russia in 1910, while the imperial state still operated under the dictates of the czar. After the war, Eddy was eager to return to the country again, this time to witness the considerable changes that the Bolshevik Revolution had initiated. He got his chance in 1923, when the Communist leadership finally accepted the travel request of his American Seminar. In some ways, Eddy was impressed with the social improvements he favorably compared to the "hideous" czarist regime that had existed a decade earlier. Corruption and the suppression of civil liberties still prevailed, but he hoped these were merely residual features of the old system that a more thorough commitment to social and spiritual values would eventually correct. "The government is making a tremendous fight against graft and bribery, under the inherited traditions of the old regime of abysmal corruption," Eddy wrote. "Conditions are . . . still bad. Nevertheless, despite these failings Russia constitutes an economic and industrial challenge, wherever ruthless capitalism exists in the world." The Soviet system was far from perfect, he acknowledged, especially in its disregard of religious and civil liberties. At least, however, this complex society was attempting to grapple with the economic sources of its own corruption. "When a state . . . tries the boldest social experiment in all history, it must be reckoned with," he concluded.[79]

Eddy hoped to impart the message that the Soviet system appeared less threatening up close than the filtered image of its evilness and corruption that was in the minds of most Americans. He had seen it in person, and he wanted others to follow his example, because more interpersonal relations between Americans and Soviets, he assumed, would help both sides develop into more humane societies. As an outspoken advocate of radical reform, Eddy, like Muste, could not hide his interest in the Soviet Union's new social order. In the letters he sent home from Moscow in the fall of 1923, his voice rings with excitement, noting how "profoundly impressed" he was by the "demonstrations for the peasants in methods of farming, modern community centers, social welfare" and affirming his "sympathy with much of their economic policy." He seemed particularly intent on banishing rumors of Soviet duplicity. "I went anywhere . . . with perfect freedom . . . chose my own interpreters, selected the factories to be inspected, saw everything and talked with everybody I wished, whether friends or foes of the present regime," he reported with some pride.[80] Russians, he insisted, had something to teach Americans about social and economic equality, if only Americans were willing to listen. "Whether as a menace, or as a challenge to set our own house in order, or as a vast experiment which may in time work out some values that may be of use to the rest of humanity, we ought to know what is going on in that section of the world," he implored in 1931.[81] Eddy's American Seminar, in fact, was organized for that very purpose: mutual exchange and cross-cultural understanding.

The first American Seminar visits to the Soviet Union occurred in the 1920s, before the full story of Stalin's crimes became public knowledge for radicals in the United States. However, even in those early years, Eddy did not turn a blind eye to Communist corruption. The top-heavy central government, its suppression of civil liberties, and its use of unremitting violence, he realized, stood as fundamental obstacles to the socialist society he promoted. Instead of criticizing these features as inherently malicious symptoms of the Soviet political and social program, as many Americans assumed, Eddy saw them as the unfortunate effects of the current regime's rejection of religion and the spiritual essence of socialist values. On this issue, the radical preacher remained most critical, even going so far as to challenge Russian leaders to a debate on the topic during his visit in 1926. Eddy got his wish, and on August 22, he blasted away at Soviet religious intolerance for five hours in front of a standing-room-only crowd of one thousand or more. "The door is apparently open now for a series of religious meetings whenever I go back to Russia," he stated in a letter to his mother and brother.[82]

Such displays of fault-finding showmanship, however, did not satisfy many of Eddy's critics, who accused him of overlooking the regime's most obvious crimes against democracy and humanity. Perhaps they had a point. Though Eddy wrote two books in the 1930s offering a balanced assessment of Communist Russia, he failed to denounce the establishment, completely, for its autocratic brutalities.[83] In July 1932, for example, Eddy penned a telling letter to Josef Stalin. Referring to himself as "a friend of the Soviet Union," the frequent visitor said that he wrote not to reproach the Soviet dictator for his suspension of basic freedoms, but to inform him that "your tourist business for foreigners is very badly run."[84]

It was difficult for many of Eddy's friends and colleagues to determine where his loyalties lie, and the outspoken socialist's scathing comments about the evils of capitalism quickly generated discord between himself and many of the YMCA's corporate donors, who demonized him as a Soviet subsidized agitator. Even Eddy's brother and financial manager, Brewer, warned him of the damage his radicalism could wreak on his reputation. "You won't win these important men, who control wealth, by radical or threatening speeches," he chastised in a letter.[85] Brewer, the more conservative of the two brothers, especially took umbrage with the "underlying assumption that capitalism is all wrong and . . . a victory for the workers . . . is right." As he chided, "Nothing could be further from the truth in my opinion. These sentences are the most superficial and least balanced and safe-guarded that I have ever heard you utter or seen you write . . . [and they will] will stamp you as a crank and not as a Christian leader."[86]

Eddy, again resembling Muste, refused to back down. As far as he was concerned, the great philanthropists of America, men like John D. Rockefeller, were part of the social problem, not its solution. They doled out trivial pledges for humanitarian organizations, but refused to part with the bulk of their privileges for the sake of any meaningful social reconstruction. "Charity as a substitute for justice was bound to fail," Eddy concluded.[87] He no longer wanted any part in courting half-hearted largesse. Yet he worried about the harm his radical rap might cause the YMCA. Faced with the dilemma of pulling his socialist punches or maintaining his freedom as an independent thinker, Eddy submitted a resignation as early as 1920 to the organization he had served since college. At that point, the YMCA rejected his offer to disassociate himself from their fold. Still, the controversy, fueled by threatening complaints from important donors, continued to surround the spiritual socialist for years. In a June 1924 letter to Brewer, Eddy noted his concern that "a dozen *big* business men made a drive against my Indianapolis address." He did not know how long his friends in the YMCA would withstand the public pressure to cut him loose. "[They] are standing by me loyally but the end is not yet," he acknowledged.[88]

The quarrels with capitalists convinced Eddy that he needed to practice what he preached, lest he add charges of hypocrisy to the arsenal of his opponents. Consequently, he announced in 1927 that he would relinquish the trappings of his own life of luxury by selling his comfortable suburban home and moving into public housing on the outskirts of New York City. "Was I to withhold and cling to these special privileges for myself and my family, or to share with those who needed them here and now?" Eddy rhetorically asked in his controversial book of that year, *Religion and Social Justice*. In the book, Eddy again made his case against capitalism, which, he claimed, impeded the growth of the Kingdom of God on earth. Hoarded wealth and materialism only exacerbated the problem, distracting otherwise good-hearted people from their spiritual responsibilities to self and society. "The teachings of Jesus," Eddy reminded, "clearly and repeatedly forbids the selfish accumulation of wealth. . . . Could any warning be more solemn than his that it is well-nigh impossible for a rich man to enter or have part in a Kingdom of family love whose whole spirit [is] mutual sharing?"[89]

The American Seminar had served Eddy's mission to build a socialist alternative to both American capitalism and Soviet Communism, all the while projecting an international agenda to restructure human relations into the Kingdom of God on earth. At decade's end, however, the world was facing another major catastrophe, the global Great Depression, when unfettered capitalism collapsed in a heap of broken confidence. In response, Eddy did not join militant socialist organizations, as Muste had done. Instead, he seized the opportunity to practice his spiritual socialist beliefs by launching a radical, cooperative farm in the Mississippi Delta.

Eddy first heard news of the October 1929 stock-market crash in a letter from his brother that he received while in India, recovering from malaria. "I wish you could have lived through this last week here in America," Brewer wrote. "It is invaluable to live through a great market collapse. . . . It has been a time of very great worry, in which we had to use good judgment and not sell under panic conditions."[90] Eddy did not panic. To the contrary, he hardly gave the economic catastrophe any attention at all, at least initially. He had expected it, even predicted it in a number of essays, including a 1926 pamphlet, *Danger Zones of the Social Order*, that he co-wrote with his pacifist colleague Kirby Page. Overproduction, they warned, was creating a vicious cycle around a hollow, collapsible core, making the wealth and luxuries of the present system precarious castles in the air. "If the love of money is indeed the root of all kinds of evil," the pamphlet stated, "then we shall certainly reap an abundant harvest of trouble from the seed-sowing now in process."[91] In 1929, however, the outspoken socialist did not seem to grasp the enormity of the crisis. When Eddy finally got around to responding to his brother's concerns about finances, his tone carried a note of indifference: "We take our losses as they come. I am not at all afraid but that these stocks will come back. We can afford to lose."[92]

Thousands of miles away in India, Eddy certainly felt detached from the news he received about the American economy. He was also in an optimistic mood. Everywhere he traveled, there were promising signs and positive trends that marked a "tendency toward the growing articulation and integration of human life in ever wider unity and cooperation." Imperialism, he reported, was in "steady retreat," while the demands for peace and democracy swelled within the most subjugated regions of the world.[93] Events in India, for example, inspired Eddy considerably, as he witnessed the power of love and nonviolence that one man, Mahatma Gandhi, had leveraged against the British Empire. Elated by the opportunity to meet the famous saint of the subcontinent in December 1929, Eddy did not even mention the deteriorating economic situation at home. "I am writing from the Ashram of Mr. Gandhi on the third day of our stay here," he informed his mother. "I have met many presidents, prime ministers and statesmen but this was the most remarkable interview of my life with this most unique man."[94]

Six years earlier, Eddy had published an "interpretation" of Gandhi in *Christian Century* magazine. The article praised the unassuming leader as the one person possessing the ability to unite the diverse population of India, break down barriers of inequality, and weaken the repressive grip of the British imperialists, all by means of nonviolence and the force of love, which he had learned, in part, from the Christian gospels. "If he succeeds," Eddy speculated, "he will have demonstrated the moral power of vicarious sacrifice and the spiritual application of the sermon on the mount to practical politics, as more potent than all the guns of Prussia, than all the ships of Britain, than all the dollars of America." In other words, Eddy believed Gandhi demonstrated the practical power of spiritual socialism. Small, simple acts in local communities, based on interpersonal communication and cooperation, had revolutionary potential, just as Jesus had shown in his own day. "Jesus himself launched the greatest spiritual revolution known to history and was [considered] a revolutionary" by the Pharisees, Eddy reminded, defending Gandhi's image as a "rebel" and "disturber of the peace."[95]

Gandhi's revolution, however, was not only anti-imperialist and pacifist. He was building communities and cultivating a new culture, a process that took time and patience, not because the Indian people in particular were ill-prepared for social democracy, but because the *human race* was ill-prepared for social democracy, given that it demanded a fundamental transformation of base, competitive instincts. Eddy called it the "long fight" for liberty and justice, a struggle not only for political freedom from foreign rule, but also for harmony among one's neighbors and countrymen. Gandhi had it right, Eddy affirmed. With "far-sighted sagacity," combining "high idealism with practical realism," the humble Hindu was leading his nation and the world toward the Kingdom of God on earth.[96] So was Eddy's American contemporary, A. J. Muste. However, Eddy's admiration for the Gandhian method and his hope for the "Gandhian moment" were not confined to his interest in pacifism.[97] Eddy never was an absolute pacifist anyway. He lionized Gandhi, instead, for putting pacifism to work on behalf of building a radically new society, not merely a peaceful one, but a just and equitable one as well.

Visiting the ashram in 1929, Eddy felt encouraged by the progress that Gandhi's method, the spiritual socialist method, had made in less than a decade. Small acts of moral conscience, home crafts, and alternative communities transcending barriers of race, caste, and creed had challenged the entire imperialist system. No doubt, Gandhi's social methods of moral dissent (more so than his absolute pacifism) inspired Eddy to support cooperative communities in the United States a few years afterward. "Not from a Christian to a heathen nation is the searchlight turned, but upon us at home," he asserted.[98] At the dawn of a troubling new age, he stood poised with a wealth of practical knowledge from his international experiences to begin the process of building spiritual socialism and the Kingdom of God at home in the United States.

CHAPTER 2

The Kingdom of God in the City and the Country

The Great Depression that began in the fall of 1929 did not give many Americans a sense of optimism about the future. Sherwood Eddy was a rare exception. "I am no longer a liberal even though I am still an optimist," he wrote in 1934, after witnessing the promising results of spiritual socialism in the 1920s, in India and also through his American Seminar traveling program.[1] While planting churches abroad in India and China in the early twentieth century, Eddy had discovered a method that would set him apart from most traditional socialists: small-scale community building that he believed reflected the Kingdom of God. In the 1930s, he returned home to the United States, eager to apply it. During a time when many left radicals strategized to overthrow the government and seize power, Eddy and a cadre of spiritual socialists started an experiment in cooperative farming in Mississippi, a project that stemmed directly from his experiences as a missionary in Asia and his abiding idealism, even during times of intense economic and social crisis.

The 1930s, of course, were rife with serious economic issues, but Eddy put racial injustice at the forefront of his socialist mission. He and other spiritual socialists like Howard Kester worked to integrate workers in the Southern Tenant Farmers' Union (STFU) and the Delta and Providence Cooperative Farms. Their efforts demonstrate that religious socialists, particularly white socialists, were not indifferent to racial oppression, even while many radicals had their eye on the precarious economic system. They took up the challenge of black radicals such as W. E. B. Du Bois and Reverdy Ransom who posited the race problem as the test for any genuine socialist or Christian conscience.² Many African American activists operating on the radical fringes of the social gospel movement or the black church certainly saw racial discord as central to social Christianity, and they helped push these issues onto the agenda of the Left during the mid-twentieth century.³ But spiritual socialists, including Eddy, Kester, A. J. Muste, Myles Horton, and Staughton Lynd, also recognized racism as a source of crisis for achieving the Kingdom of God on earth.⁴ All spiritual socialists, whether black or white, were reading similar texts, such as the writings of Walter Rauschenbusch, and networking with like-minded scholar-activists at universities and seminaries or through the Young Men's Christian Association (YMCA). They may never have met, but they shared a commitment to bringing the Kingdom of God to earth by eliminating racism and inequality.

That sense of crisis also pervaded the Bowery district of Lower East Manhattan, where a former Communist fellow-traveler and an itinerant lay preacher founded the first Catholic Worker hospitality house to help the poor, hungry, and mentally ill of New York City. Like Eddy and her personal friend A. J. Muste, Dorothy Day believed that "the little way" of spiritual socialism offered the best means to transform the social order. "It is the living from day to day, taking no thought for the morrow, seeing Christ and all who come to us, trying literally to follow the Gospel, that resulted in this work," she explained.⁵ "It [is] in these simple, practical, down-to-earth ways that people could show their love for each other."⁶ These simple acts of altruism, however, were not intended solely as demonstrations of personal piety, but as truly world-changing deeds, when applied for the sake of social salvation. As Day put it, "Going to the people is the purest and best act in Christian tradition and revolutionary tradition and is the beginning of world brotherhood."⁷ Everyone, according to Eddy and Day, deserved inclusion.

In the 1930s, spiritual socialists such as Eddy and Day faced the Great Depression with a revolutionary commitment to community-based cooperation. The stakes of social change in the 1930s were high, but whereas the federal government went big with the New Deal, and the organized Left went big with centralized party militancy, spiritual socialists went small, emphasizing grassroots organizing and local relief efforts even more than in the 1920s, when they were still transitioning from progressive-era political culture. Eddy applied his spiritual socialist beliefs at the Delta Cooperative Farm in Hillhouse, Mississippi, which he helped found in 1936 to offer displaced tenant farmers a chance to experiment with cooperative living and communal agriculture. Day, a recent Catholic convert, cofounded the first Catholic Worker hospitality house in New York City in 1936. Both programs operated as decentralized, localized alternatives to New Deal relief or the Communist Party. While the disorder of the decade fueled the fires of secular organizations, spiritual socialists fought for the Kingdom of God in the city and the country, through peaceful fellowship. They consciously set out to demonstrate that a spiritualized, decentralized form of socialism could yield more fruitful results than conventional institutions, whether party, church, or state.

The aversion of spiritual socialists to the party or state sets them apart in the history of the American Left, especially during the Old Left era of the 1930s. The near collapse of capitalism and the urgency for revolution sparked a frenzy among radicals who became caught up in the dogmatic dogfights that splintered the Left. The Communist Party maintained its strict discipline and boosted its membership, but such rapid success came with a price. The top-heavy organizational style, the Soviet loyalty tests, as well as the tendency toward violence and deceit, typical among most left sects, turned off radicals like Muste. Muste learned to distrust party and state bureaucracy by 1936. But Eddy and Day recognized the crux of this problem early on in the decade. In a way, the cannibalism of the Old Left and the inadequacy of the New Deal gave spiritual socialists a negative example to oppose, a condition to hasten the development of a viable alternative: a democratic, spiritual form of radicalism that began to coalesce among post-Marxists in the 1930s. In the 1950s, independent radicals such as Dwight Macdonald and Irving Howe would search for a New Left politics dedicated to democratic socialism and the spiritual needs of individuals.[8] In the 1930s, however, Eddy and Day were already attempting to live it. Eddy, a self-identified socialist, eschewed the Socialist Party, though he was willing to work with members such as Norman Thomas on grassroots, community-building projects such as the Delta Farm. Eddy's distaste for centralized planning, however, was never as pronounced as that of Day, who criticized the state welfare apparatus for failing to inspire religious responsibility among its citizenry.

Unfortunately, and in spite of her popularity among intellectuals, Day has not been thoroughly folded into historical accounts of leftist social activism. Most biographies and profiles are written by scholars associated with Catholic institutions. They trace her conversion from Communist sympathizer to Catholic radical, but downplay the ongoing significance of her socialist identity. When she is discussed as a leftist, scholars, like her contemporaries, have had a hard time placing her on the radical spectrum. She associated with those of the Lyrical Left in the 1920s, challenged the Old Left in the 1930s, and associated only loosely with the New Left in the 1960s. Lost in left field, Day's core ideology, the fundamental motivation for her work as both community organizer and pacifist spokeswoman, goes missing. The confusion on this point is somewhat understandable—Day has been called an anarchist, a libertarian, a radical, a Communist, and a Catholic saint. Moreover, her rejection of state power and bureaucracy has tempted some scholars to place her within a conservative or libertarian, rather than liberal or leftist, tradition. Others have criticized her for a lack of political commitment to social justice in electoral or legislative channels as well as her apparent failure to forge connections to the labor movement.[9] Analyzing Day as a spiritual socialist, however, cuts through this tangle of misinterpretations without marginalizing her religious values or radical identity. Creating the Kingdom of God was always her goal, as it was for Muste and Eddy. Spiritual socialism, the kind of interpersonal care that Macdonald would praise Catholic Worker for in the 1950s, provided the means to that end.

As a college secretary of the YMCA in Asia, Eddy had learned how difficult it would be for the Kingdom to come. Assigned in 1896 to spread the gospel in India, he at first, not unlike many missionaries faced with culture shock, assumed a dominant, even arrogant, attitude toward indigenous peoples. His early writings from India, in fact, reflect a palpable disdain for native impiety. "Heathenism here is indescribable in its depths of degradation," Eddy stated bluntly in "First Impressions of India" in March 1897. To him, the subcontinent seemed nearly hopeless, heaving as it was with "dark-skinned, half-clad natives" who "clung" to superstition and the "worship of repulsive idols."[10]

But Eddy changed during his fifteen years in India, becoming less reproachful toward natives and more willing to work with them as cocreators of a Christian society. As historian Ian Tyrrell wrote, "In more than a decade as a YMCA traveling secretary he learned about the social and economic causes of conflict in India and became strongly attached to the country and its people."[11] The experience broadened his entire worldview, but not only in terms of missions and cultural exchange. He also began to think differently about society and politics. Rather than blaming individual sin for the natives' misfortune, Eddy pointed to other causes, such as the corruption of national and local leaders, describing the "Native State government" as "unspeakable" in its lack of social justice.[12] Saving souls remained important, but Eddy began talking about sanitation, education, and health care as social problems with fundamental social causes, not merely as symptoms of personal sin or mass heathenism. Whereas before Eddy assumed that individual conversions could correct social ills, he now realized that the whole of society needed Christianizing if individuals were expected to practice Christian values within it. Eddy's awareness of the deep-seated debasement of society increasingly led him to accept more radical solutions to spiritual problems. Other than wholesale, fundamental change, he argued, how else could society root out its immoral malignancies?

World War I deepened Eddy's commitment to radical change. However, it was Eddy's experiences in India and China that preconditioned his critical view of the war and his subsequent identity as a socialist. He read Rauschenbusch's version of the social gospel in books; but he experienced it firsthand in his relationships with the natives he encountered. In Asia, Eddy began to promote a specific kind of social gospel, marked by a belief in decentralization, local cooperation, and the equality of every human being as a child of God. Eddy's missionary experiences, in short, taught him the value of spiritual socialism, which he would later implement in the United States.[13]

By 1914, Eddy was speaking excitedly about a "new method" of Christian campaigning that he witnessed while working in both India and China.[14] Instead of trying to reach thousands of people at once, he now focused on a few promising, native individuals, who could then cultivate Christian values and customs in their own villages, on their own initiative. "The whole work is natural, indigenous, and spontaneous," Eddy wrote several years later.[15] He became convinced that this intense and concentrated approach to evangelizing proved more practical and effective. In a letter to his wife in 1919, he noted the difference: "In previous campaigns we worked from without, seeking to win enquirers, train them in Bible classes, and hand them over to the church but the churches often failed to care for them, unprepared as they were. This time we are starting within the church and working out. We begin with twelve men in the church and seek to vitalize them and get them going out and winning their non-Christian friends. The campaign this time was intensive, not extensive."[16]

A slow and personal method, he knew, would take more time, but Eddy remained confident that he had discovered the "true secret" to making

Christian reformations stick. "We are having smaller meetings but larger and more abiding fruit," he proudly reported.[17] With this new approach, missionaries acted as leavening agents, offering a new way to begin. It was up to the people themselves to build a new society, because true community building meant trusting residents to make moral choices on their own terms. To this end, Eddy devoted both time and resources. In 1916, he donated $1,000 for the founding of industrial "cooperative societies" in the villages of India, "similar to that of Hampton and Tuskegee [Institute] in America," that taught weaving, carpentry, and agriculture. These skills, he hoped, would help poor natives escape the cycle of debt and dependence on corrupt state officials. Moreover, the little commonwealth taught villagers values of cooperation, equality, and mutual respect—crucial components, Eddy believed, of any successful, long-term Christian community.[18] Eddy, in short, was pushing the social gospel to its most socialist extensions. "Our task, then, was not only to win or change individuals, all-important as that was, but to Christianize the whole of life and all its relations, industrial, social, racial, and international," he wrote.[19]

After twenty years traveling throughout Asia, Eddy returned to postwar America to do just that: to build a new social order and "spiritually reconquer America."[20] Eddy realized that his plan signified a radical departure from the prevailing climate of liberal reform, but he accepted the charge with relish. "The liberal seeks reform within the present framework of society. I as a radical must seek to build a completely new order," he explained.[21] Earlier in his life, Eddy admitted, socialism had been "only a distasteful word" to him, associated as it was with secular and violent revolution.[22] The more he thought about it, though, the more he turned to socialism as the nearest political approximation to his ideals.[23]

There is no doubt that Eddy took his socialist identity very seriously, but his meaning may seem unorthodox to those who associate socialism with top-down, centralized planning or secular radicalism.[24] Eddy's embrace of the term to describe his worldview thus complicates our understanding of socialism in the twentieth century. Rather than define it strictly as a state-centered political program or economic system, Eddy and others saw socialism as a democratic and spiritual method of molding communities into the Kingdom of God on earth. Socialism, for these religious activists, was never relegated to party politics, though Eddy, like Muste, did vote for Socialist Party candidates such as Eugene V. Debs and Norman Thomas. In fact, Eddy and Thomas would join forces as cofounders of a cooperative farming experiment in the mid-1930s, determined to test socialism as a social and spiritual, not just political and secular, project.

Eddy and Thomas were responding to the gaps in the New Deal's 1935 Resettlement Administration, which offered a small measure of assistance to displaced farmers in places such as Dyess, Arkansas, and Tupelo, Mississippi. These modest efforts, however, did not reach everyone affected by the crisis. Hundreds of thousands of sharecroppers, many African American, remained homeless, jobless, and hungry, with few options to improve their lot. When these desperate men and women tried to organize to demand fair pay from their employers, they faced eviction and even violence.

Confronted with the need to organize in their own interest, freelance farmworkers, both black and white, who had been evicted from plantations in Arkansas formed the STFU in 1934 as a means to exert collective leverage against the unfair treatment they received from landowners. The sharecroppers were not entirely alone in their struggle; they had gained the support of friends in high places, especially in the Socialist Party of America. Dr. William R. Amberson, a professor of physiology at the University of Tennessee Medical School and a member of the Memphis chapter of the Socialist Party, brought the matter to the attention of Socialist Party president Norman Thomas, who encouraged the exploited and evicted workers to organize. Other members of the local Socialist Party network, including H. L. Mitchell, Clay East, and Howard Kester, exposed the plight of sharecroppers through their writings and personal contacts. Kester approached Protestant heavyweight Reinhold Niebuhr, who lent his support to the STFU. Amberson also reached out to a former YMCA missionary, Sam Franklin, who was visiting Memphis for a speaking engagement. After Franklin toured the countryside and witnessed the deplorable conditions of poor agrarian laborers firsthand, he contacted his friend Eddy, who made two trips to the region in 1936.[25] Eddy was appalled by the situation and determined to help. He bought a 2,138-acre parcel of cotton soil in Mississippi, and soon thirty families of former sharecroppers, twelve of them white and nineteen black, moved onto the property and began producing their own food and building their own homes. They named the place the Delta Cooperative Farm, later called Rochdale.

Unlike the New Deal programs in Dyess and Tupelo, which funded independently owned farm parcels, the Delta Farm operated as a collective enterprise from the very beginning. At least, that was the intention of the founders, who hoped they could demonstrate the viability of socialist-inspired alternatives to private, capitalist production. Eddy, for one, had high hopes that the farm would develop into a cooperative community and, as such, give practical expression to his mission to build socialism from the bottom up. Though he did not live and work on the property directly, he served on the board of directors, offering financial and moral support, and generating publicity for what he called "a new type of life" and a "movement" for "a non-violent, Christian cooperative endeavor."[26] He hoped that the black and white farmers could show how common interests and efforts could transcend racial barriers and selfish individualism.

Despite a rough learning curve, the organizers considered the experiment a success in the making. Members cooperated in the cotton fields, orchards, sawmill, and barns and their work kept them busy, financially solvent, and fed through all four seasons. By the end of the first year, the farmers (and Eddy) could boast of a "respectable profit" as well as capital improvements. The initial production yield of the little "experiment" in cooperative farming even impressed federal officials, who visited the property in 1937. A stunned administrator of the nearby Tennessee Valley Authority called it "a miracle." First Lady Eleanor Roosevelt and Secretary of Agriculture Henry Wallace also gave the project a stamp of approval.[27]

Not everyone was impressed. One contemporary critic named Jonathan Daniels considered the cooperative economy a sham, stating that its "one dependable cash crop is rich Yankees of soft heart." Though more radical in its ideals than the New Deal projects, the Delta Farm, he wrote, did not represent a true "test of the cooperative plan," especially given that its budget remained supplemented by donors such as Eddy. "It still hangs dependent upon capitalistic philanthropy and, as long as it does, it does not rest upon the cooperation in brotherhood of the common man," he concluded.[28]

To Eddy, however, the Delta Farm amounted to more than its crop yields and cash earnings. It operated as a community, complete with its own store, school, medical clinic, and dance hall. Residents could also attend a formal church, offering worship services, Sunday school, and Bible studies. But for Eddy, the spiritual benefits of the community went beyond organized religion. He wanted what he called a "realistic religion as a social dynamic," in which the spirit of the Christian message infused every aspect. "Many of our people are not consciously religious," Eddy explained. "Indeed some of them have a frank aversion to certain traditional forms of religion ... which had so little bearing upon practical life. But they are building a type of life that is both spiritual and practical and that is what we mean by religion."[29] In fact, for Eddy, it seemed *impractical* to attempt to build community without some kind of religious mainstay, "a uniting bond or tie which binds man to the center or Source of life, which we may call God, to himself in achieving a unified, integrated personality, and to his fellow men in the cooperative endeavor of the community to build a new social order."[30] This was the value that spiritual socialism, and thus the Delta community, had over its secular counterparts, whether in the form of private or federal projects. Religious values had the power to inspire members of a community to exercise their best virtues, to keep their base instincts in check, and to live out their highest ideals. In this way, members of the farm did not just practice their religion on Sundays; they strove to implement religious principles every day of the week.

Ideologically, Eddy found like-minded company to launch such a venture, as most of the investors and organizers of the project pledged their commitment to a combination of socialist and Christian values at the farm. Kester, a divinity-school graduate and member of the Fellowship of Reconciliation (FOR), echoed Eddy in his regard for the cooperative as "the first step toward the Kingdom of God on earth," a place where people could live and work together in racial and economic harmony. The affiliated STFU, composed of many African American "preacher-leaders," also supported the religious mission, while religious activists dominated the farm's original five-member board of trustees, including Eddy (secretary-treasurer), Franklin (resident director), and Niebuhr (president). As scholar Jerry W. Dallas wrote in 1987, the "long-range objectives" of the Delta Farm "were to create an example of interracial Christian harmony and to demonstrate that a collective cooperative farm was a better system of labor relations than the oppressive landlord-tenant arrangement."[31] In short, the diversified operation was intended to provide for the material and spiritual needs of its member-residents. Materially, the farm's poor soil failed to make things easy on the farming entrepreneurs, a disappointing truth that led Eddy and the trustees to approve and finance the purchase of a second property in 1938, situated eighty miles from Hillhouse. Reflecting their religious hopes, they christened this new enterprise the Providence Cooperative Farm.

Implementing idealized concepts such as cooperation and equality, however, proved difficult from the outset. Franklin, who remained on the Delta property as resident director for two years before moving on to the

Providence Farm, admitted as much in his memoirs. "We had no guidelines," he wrote. "Obviously what [we] had in mind was not another plantation, run paternalistically, or a set of little, separate farms." The organizers wanted to pursue, instead, a radical cooperative in which member-workers shared everything, not just tools and machinery, but the entire productive capacity of the land, held in common. Unfortunately, none of the associated members or organizers came equipped with practical experience in cooperative production or, for that matter, agricultural business. Daniels noted that "the staff of the plantation is better grounded in social and religious doctrine than in agricultural science." The families, accustomed to following planters' orders, did not know how to manage a farm; neither did the paid staff or volunteers. This deficiency, Daniels wrote, represented the "tragic flaw" of the farm and its potential to serve as a model for similar projects.[32]

There were certainly problems to overcome, as Eddy readily acknowledged. "It is not a panacea and it leads to no utopia," he wrote.[33] It was not, in the most traditional sense, fully socialist either, especially in terms of inclusion. Members were chosen and sometimes dismissed based on their ability or willingness to adapt to the system. Three of the original families at the farm, for instance, were asked to leave the property within the first year of operation for refusing to cooperate. As Eddy rationalized rather coldly, "Any Cooperative that is to succeed must be able to eliminate the unfit."[34] Acceptance and fellowship at this community of God, he implied, was conditional.

Inequality of pay on the farms also seemed at odds with socialist values. As overseer Sam Franklin stated, "We were not proceeding on the basis of 'from each according to his ability, to each according to his need.' We believed in differential rewards depending upon the nature of the work."[35] In other words, the farm members agreed to a graduated compensation scale in which skilled managers were paid at a higher rate (nearly three times as much) as unskilled field hands. "So far the determination of this rating [system] has constituted no serious problem," Eddy wrote.[36] According to Franklin, however, the situation was more complicated than Eddy assumed. "Determining these ratings and revising them in the council consumed time and energy," he remembered. As such, the system of inequality presented members and management with a "perennial problem" that also seemed to undermine the stated socialist values of the entire enterprise. "Our experience," the former director summarized, "pointed upon the difficulty of the problems that face all socialist efforts to reorganize industry and agriculture. How [to] reconcile democracy and efficiency? How [to] combine self-interest and group-interest."[37] The pay differential may have helped organizers dismiss frequent charges of Communism, but it did little to establish the socialist ideal of economic equality.

In its political structure, the Delta Farm also fell short of full democratic equality. Members elected a council of five with the stipulation that no more than three representatives could belong to the same race, a policy that reflected the importance of racial integration to the mission of spiritual socialists. This usually meant that three white men and two black men made decisions for the entire cooperative. Actions of the council could be overruled by two-thirds of the farm membership or by veto of Franklin, who, as Dallas discerned, "ran the Farm in a benevolent but strictly paternal fashion," a serious charge to level against a project meant to correct the patronizing tendencies of mission culture.[38] While in India, Eddy had discovered the benefits of empowering local, native leaders to edify Christian teachings among their peers. This model, however, was not replicated at the Delta Farm. Eddy still kept his distance from the daily decision making, despite his role as secretary-treasurer and financial patron of the program. But his friend Franklin served as salaried director, a leadership choice comparable to the top-down missions' structure he had rejected abroad.

This rather negative appraisal of the Delta and Providence Farm cooperatives has persisted as commentators continue to note the discord that existed among members and organizers over issues of democracy and socialism. Major disagreements along these lines certainly erupted, most notably when one of the project's original founders, William Amberson, resigned in protest in 1939, accusing the director and board of trustees of operating the farms in an irresponsible and undemocratic fashion. A secular socialist, Amberson found the "ecclesiastical approach" to cooperative farming a detriment to "the scientific search for knowledge" pursued by true Marxists.[39]

The problem with this viewpoint stems from a misunderstanding of spiritual socialism and a false dichotomy between Christian and Marxist activists or religion and politics at the farms. It must be remembered that Amberson was not the only organizer with Socialist Party ties. Eddy, Thomas, Niebuhr, Kester, Mitchell, and Franklin had all belonged to or been affiliated with the party before and/or during their participation in the cooperative project. They did not take structural economics lightly, despite their interest in adding a religious component to their assessment of social problems. In fact, Eddy argued repeatedly that economic conditions, particularly capitalism and its corrupting power, made it much more difficult for people to choose ethics over fiscal interests. He recognized the primacy of structural change as a driving force behind cultural change and remained convinced by personal experiences during World War I that moral and immoral behaviors were influenced by one's environment.

STFU cofounder H. L. Mitchell concurred with many of Eddy's convictions. The son and grandson of preachers, Mitchell believed that the cooperative spirit contained both spiritual and material benefits, since the lack of cutthroat competition would empower members to produce more efficiently, creatively, and harmoniously. As a young radical, he had sought a middle way between flame-throwing Communist revolutionaries and the Social Democrats, who preferred the ballot box and political coalition-building for achieving a socialist society. "Most of us younger members," Mitchell recalled, "believed that the 'Cooperative Commonwealth' of the future could not be attainted through the ballot box. . . . [I]t could be brought about by organization of a class conscious labor movement and the use of the general strike to topple the capitalist system."[40] The Delta Farm, he felt, satisfied both conditions. Its members associated as victims of class exploitation, and they chose to work outside the prevailing capitalist and cultural framework. If the cooperative failed to compete with private enterprise, it had more to do with poor farming conditions and the nature of experimental methods than any deep discord between ideological factions. Daniels, in rare exception to his criticisms of the project, gave some credence to this point. The organizers, he conceded, took "some of the most difficult land ever farmed in the Delta" and went "further than anyone had any right to think toward successful farming."[41] The project, however, did not last as a permanent community. In the wake of the 1954 Supreme Court decision on desegregation, members of the Providence Farm faced mounting pressure from white supremacists, using intimidations of violence to destroy what they considered an unholy and unnatural communion between the races. Such backlash finally drove members and staff away from the cooperative in 1956, after twenty years of operation.

Improving race relations was a preoccupation of spiritual socialists in the 1920s and 1930s. Though racial injustice represented one spoke in a multifaceted program of building the Kingdom of God on earth, the flagrant discrimination and violence against African Americans made it impossible to ignore as an obstacle to Christian cooperation. Those concerned with promoting a brotherhood of man, human dignity, and social equality recognized American racial discord as diametrically opposed to the cooperative commonwealth. Eddy and the organizers of the Delta Farm hoped to demonstrate that whites and blacks could work together in harmony. But, given his universalism, Eddy did not limit the purpose of the project to issues of race. Instead, he approached the participants of Delta Farm as complex human beings with multidimensional problems: social, economic, political, and spiritual. In the 1950s, the civil rights movement moved racial issues to a higher point on the progressive agenda. And, in the 1960s and 1970s, activists such as Pauli Murray would argue that African Americans were not only racial types, but also, in many cases, workers, women, gays and lesbians, parents, and children, with numerous needs. She theorized more explicitly the kind of multidimensional approach to individual problems that spiritual socialists practiced in earlier decades, though with more attention to the neglect of women in social justice movements. The organizers of the Delta Farm, however, fought racism in their community so radically that it triggered a strong response from white supremacists in the region who eventually succeeded in shutting the project down.

Eddy understood, since his days as a missionary in Asia, that even the most radical changes in social structure were bound to produce only "fractional modest achievement[s]."[42] The Kingdom of God certainly took time to cultivate, dependent as it was on human efforts in an imperfect world. "Because it is human, it will remain imperfect, but it will bring more good to humanity than in the past. And, it will surely come," he affirmed.[43] For Eddy, it was socialism that offered the most plastic, experimental, and primal program of action for building a new social order. For it was socialism, as he understood its essential religious implications, that best expressed the teachings of Christ's Sermon on the Mount and, in nascent form, that exemplified the Kingdom of God on earth. "For the extension of any cause," he wrote, "I have believed all my life and have tried to practice the three-fold technique of the spoken word, the printed page, and the organization of men first in small, intimate, vital groups and later in national or international bodies."[44] Such was his notion of spiritual socialism.

Eddy died in 1963, at the age of ninety-two, not long after the closing of the Providence Cooperative Farm. Eulogies for the late Christian activist sounded a common theme: images of small, but ever-expanding deeds for making the world a better place. Senator Paul A. Douglas of Illinois referred to Eddy as the "Johnny Appleseed of social justice during the last forty years of his life."[45] A booklet memorializing Eddy also said, "As a pebble dropped into a pond ripples to the edge so was Dr. Eddy's work extended to the far corners of the earth."[46] These contemporary admirers understood that Eddy's legacy endured in the little ways he contributed to the coming Kingdom of God on earth and the spiritual socialist methods he championed as Christian mission.

In New York City in the early 1930s, Day was also searching the gospels for a program to match her radical beliefs. It did not take long for her to realize that Christianity and socialism could coincide, at least at the most basic level. "The Sermon on the Mount answered all the questions as to how to love God and one's brother," Day determined.[47] Compelled to continue her work as a social activist, she was relieved to find a way to reconcile her religion and her radicalism rather than compromise one for the other. "Her conversion was a newly sanctioned continuation of her way of thinking rather than a dramatic turning away from a former viewpoint," Day's acquaintance, Robert Coles, summarized.[48] As Day herself put it in a 1938 diary entry, "My early religious fervor . . . underlay my radicalism and finally saved me."[49] Devoting oneself completely to the poor, the weak, and the lost souls of the world was a requisite not only for fostering a socialist society, Day now realized, but also for advancing the Kingdom of God on earth.

Day knew traditional socialist theories well. Before becoming a Catholic in 1927, she had found fellowship among hard-line Communists, mostly atheists who regarded religion as a tool of oppression. She wrote exposés on labor conditions and political persecution for the *Call* and the *Masses*. She was arrested with a group of suffragists protesting U.S. participation in World War I. She lived with her boyfriend, had an abortion, and steered clear of the organized, institutional Christianity that she and her radical comrades criticized for its neglect of the poor. "I felt that my faith had nothing in common with that of Christians around me," Day recalled.[50] In her opinion, the pious prayed and attended services on Sundays, but then failed to apply Scripture to the social needs of their neighborhood.

By the time she and cofounder Peter Maurin opened the first Catholic Worker hospitality house in the Bowery District in downtown Manhattan, Day had changed her mind about the potential for religious radicalism. "A personal conversion," she wrote in her 1938 memoir, "was necessary before any revolution could be successful" and "it is only through religion that communism can be achieved."[51] Like Eddy, Day believed that regime changes of political power were not enough to revolutionize the world. Instead of political solutions, she advocated a fundamental social revolution, one that transformed society by making spiritual values the normative mode of practice in daily life. Only religion, she and Eddy insisted, was radical enough to get to the roots of humanity and transform lives. Inspired in part by Saint Thérèse of Lisieux, Leo Tolstoy, and Peter Kropotkin, Day called it "the Little Way," a method of enacting religious values of love, compassion, and cooperation in the midst of daily activity. For her, Christianity amounted to an ongoing, lived sacrament that she practiced in the New York–area hospitality houses of Catholic Worker, offering works of mercy—food, shelter, and fellowship—to any poor and demoralized supplicant. "Her sanctity—if one wishes to call it that—was expressed not just in heroic deeds but in the mundane duties of everyday life," wrote Day's archivist, Robert Ellsberg.[52]

Ironically, the woman who would be remembered as "the most significant, interesting, and influential person in the history of American Catholicism"[53] as well as the "inventor" of Catholic radicalism[54] spent her formative years growing up in a nonreligious environment. Born in Brooklyn on November 8, 1897, Day was one of five children in a Scotch-Irish family that was frequently on the move. Her father, John Day, who wrote columns as a sports journalist, relocated his wife and children to Oakland, Chicago, and then back to New York City within the span of twelve years. He had been raised Congregationalist and his wife (Dorothy's mother) had grown up Episcopalian, but they did not seem interested in providing their children with any religious edification. None of the Days were baptized, and they did not attend church regularly. When young Dorothy did participate in religious activity during those years, she did so sporadically and independently from her parents.

Day was exposed to religion primarily through neighbors and friends, who occasionally invited her to Sunday worship services or weekday prayer meetings and, later, sponsored her baptism and confirmation in the Episcopal Church on Fullerton Avenue in Chicago when she was twelve years old. For all of this, Day went willingly. "I, too, wanted to do penance for my own sins and for the sins of the whole world, for I had a keen sense of sin, of natural imperfection and earthliness," she wrote. "It was as though each time I heard our Lord spoken of, a warm feeling of joy filled me." Day experienced a similar exhilaration after hearing a Catholic friend recount the life of "some saint," a story that left her young heart "almost bursting with desire to take part in such a high endeavor."[55] A voracious reader, Day loved stories and words and the ways they could stir the emotions she usually kept suppressed around her detached and dispassionate father. She picked up a copy of John Wesley's sermons at age thirteen and remembered being "strongly attracted to his evangelical piety." She also spent time reading the Psalms, which she said "became a part of my childhood" as an "outlet" for any "joy or grief."[56]

Upon entering college, however, Day found other, more secular outlets for her intellectual and emotional enthusiasms, spending most of her time among atheistic radicals, who convinced her that organized religion was nothing but a corrupt and exploitive enemy of proletarian liberation. "I was very caught up in socialist convictions," Day said, in reference to her years at the University of Illinois, where she enrolled in 1914 at the age of sixteen on a $300 scholarship.[57] While Socialist Party meetings at Urbana were too "dull" and "doctrinaire" for Day, she gravitated toward the direct action approach of the International Workers of the World (IWW) and the passionate immediacy of anarchism.[58] "I was hopeless of gradual change," Day recalled. "The incentive [was] to revolt rather than to sow patiently and build slowly."[59] If radicals were going to create a revolution and change the world, Day wanted to take part in it.

Accordingly, in 1916, Day moved from Chicago to New York City and took jobs as a writer-reporter for the socialist newspaper the *Call* and, briefly, as assistant editor of the *Masses* with Max Eastman and Floyd Dell. The work proved satisfying in that it put Day at the center of the struggle for the laboring poor, attending strikes, peace protests, food riots, and rallies, as both observer and participant. Yet radical journalism also left her with some early stirrings of discontent. "My job was always to picture the darker side of life, ignoring all the light touches, the gay and joyful sides of stories as I came across them," she later said.[60]

The work could also become dangerous, as Day discovered when she was arrested in Washington, D.C., with a group of suffragists in November 1917, a particularly difficult time for radicals targeted by Woodrow Wilson's exhaustive wartime crackdown on dissent. While Day marched in a contingent of picketers outside the White House gates, she felt the odium of the gathering crowd that soon turned violent. Young boys hurled stones at the women, and sailors moved on them, trying to tear their banners down. "I had to struggle for my own banner too, with a red-faced young sailor, before a policeman took me by the arm and escorted me to the waiting police van," Day wrote. The suffragists were released and arrested in a tiresome process for the next three nights, until on the third night they were kept in detention after refusing to post bail. Receiving a sentence of thirty days, Day joined a hunger strike with the other women, who were demanding fair treatment of political prisoners. The lack of food, warmth, and privacy, however, soon took its toll. "I lost all consciousness of any cause," she admitted. "I could only feel darkness and desolation all around me." After a few days, the guards delivered to Day the Bible she had requested on her second night in the prison. The book became her constant companion throughout the ordeal. "I clung to the words of comfort in the Bible as long as the light held out," Day recalled. "I read and pondered . . . and prayed."[61]

This was not the first time Day had sought solace in the Bible. Stirred by the power of "spiritual truth" and longing for a sense of "spiritual adventure," Day had often turned to the word of God during the otherwise unreligious years of her youth.[62] Looking back on her life at the age of eighty, in fact, Day could still "remember it clearly" the first time she held a Bible at the age of seven, "picking up the Scriptures from a desk in the attic of [a furnished house we rented in Berkeley, California,] and holding it in my hands. It was my first contact with the Book."[63] From then on, Day "read the New Testament with fervor."[64] Though she continued to appreciate the writings of radical writers such as Jack London and Upton Sinclair, who expressed a secular socialist's sympathy for the poor, Day was also drawn to religious literature, including the mystic meditations of Thomas à Kempis's *The Imitation of Christ*, a book that "followed [her] through [her] days," and the work of three Russian writers, Leo Tolstoy, F. M. Dostoevsky, and anarchist Peter Kropotkin.[65]

Day easily identified with these Russian writers and their sense of spiritual duty to the poor. However, finding such examples of socially conscious Christians in the United States proved difficult, because the Church offered few examples of the kind of zealous activism that she witnessed on the radical left. "I felt that my faith had nothing in common with that of Christians around me," she wrote.[66] For Day, organized Christianity in the twentieth century, mired by bourgeois pretense, lacked "vitality" and had "nothing to do with everyday life." Pious people prayed and attended services on Sundays, but then ignored the injustice and suffering in the world throughout the week.[67] In a letter she wrote at the age of fifteen, Day registered the artifice of typical Christian practice: "I have learned that it is rather hypocritical to be so strict on Sunday and not on every other day of the week. Every day belongs to God and every day we are to serve Him doing His pleasure."[68]

Social gospel advocates and some Catholics in the lower ranks of clergy and laity, of course, were involved in progressive politics, including Father John A. Ryan, who lobbied for social justice and welfare throughout the 1920s and 1930s, and Father John LaFarge, founder of the Catholic Interracial Council of New York. Day admired their efforts, but still felt something missing in methods tied to the political maneuverings of mainstream politics. She wanted to find, instead, a personal approach to social problems that involved real human contact and the communal practice of socialist values. Dostoevsky and Tolstoy inspired her to believe that Christians could resolve to fight for social justice, not in the name of abstract dogma or "the Church" as such, but in honor of human dignity and the redemptive power of God's love. As Tolstoy states in his philosophical treatise, "The Kingdom of God Is Within You," "Christianity in its true significance abolishes the state, annihilates all governments." And "revolutionary enemies fight the government from outside; Christianity does not fight at all, but wrecks its foundation from within."[69]

Indeed, secular revolutionaries fighting government and industrial elites also disappointed Day. "I was a Communist in sympathy but with reservations scarcely formulated," she wrote.[70] By the mid-1920s, those mild reservations had hardened into concrete criticisms, particularly on the issue of violence. "I did not look upon class war as something to be stirred up, as the Marxists did," Day recalled.[71] Her aversion to the revolutionary means of Marxism soon soured her taste for the entire Communist program of action, which, she believed, belied radicals' supposed values of brotherly love. Such hypocrisy, for Day, amounted to "a heresy" that made Marxism "a false doctrine," unfit for the fundamental work of building a new world order.[72] She recognized, even before becoming Catholic, that the aims of peaceful revolution would always falter on these makeshift paths of violence. Thus, despite her "scorn for [organized] religion," Day felt the need for a moral, even spiritual substance to buoy the aims of radical activists.[73] "I have said, sometimes flippantly," she explained in 1938, about a decade after her conversion to Catholicism, "that the mass of bourgeois smug Christians who denied Christ in His poor made me turn to Communism, and that it was the Communists and [their hypocrisies] that made me turn to God."[74]

Day's "turn to God" sharpened considerably when she became pregnant with her daughter in 1925. The news was unexpected, but not unwelcomed. Day had had an abortion six years earlier, and she assumed she would never have a child—a circumstance that brought her "sorrow" and a sense of being "incomplete." The prospect of motherhood, therefore, lifted Day's spirit on waves of joy and thankfulness, and, during her walks to and from her beachside home on Staten Island, she began to pray and recite the rosary compulsively. "I am surprised that I am beginning to pray daily," Day recorded in her notebook in November 1925. "I began because I had to. I just found myself praying ... and encouraged that I am praying because I want to thank Him, I go on praying," and I "am filled with exultation."[75]

Even before her daughter was born, Day had decided to baptize her as a Catholic—a ritual she hoped would help ground the newborn's life in purpose and meaning. "I was not going to have her floundering through many years as I had done, doubting and hesitating, undisciplined and amoral. I felt it was the greatest thing I could do for a child," Day explained.[76] Day's selection of the Catholic Church as the ideal spiritual environment for her daughter was not a difficult one. The choice emerged, instead, as a natural extension of her long-held fascination with the mystical yet practical elements of that religion. As a young girl growing up in the tenements of Chicago, for instance, Day had witnessed her Catholic neighbor, Mrs. Barrett, praying on her knees in daily thanksgiving and communion. Through this act of faith, Mrs. Barrett, it seemed to Day, simultaneously transcended the poverty and misery of life in a "sordid little tenement flat" and found a source of happiness within it. "She had God, and there was beauty and joy in her life," Day concluded. Inspired by this "glimpse of supernatural beauty," Day had felt, then, her "first impulse towards Catholicism."[77] The masses, not only individuals, also influenced Day's decision, because the newly arrived immigrants and workers in Chicago and New York City were, more often than not, Catholics. As Day disclosed, "This fact in itself drew me to the Church."[78]

The birth of her daughter, Tamar Teresa, in March 1926 invoked an overwhelming need in Day to worship, overtly and without restraint. The miracle of creation "had awakened in [her] heart a flood of gratitude," the "final object" of which "was God." Indeed, Day recognized almost immediately that the incomprehensible emotions of motherhood must connect to a supernatural source. "No human creature could receive or contain so vast a flood of love and joy as I often felt after the birth of my child," she explained. "With this came the need to worship, to adore."[79] Little Tamar was baptized as a Catholic as planned, but Day was not satisfied with a vicarious association to the Church. She wanted to become part of it too. "I felt that Catholicism was something rich and real and fascinating, but I felt outside," she recalled.[80] Ready to finally embrace formal religion, Day began to consider her own plans for conversion.[81]

Closing the gap between her heart and religion, however, increasingly exposed the distance between Day and her radical friends, including Forster Batterham, her common-law husband and the father of Tamar. An atheistic anarchist and scientist, Batterham could not understand Day's sudden fascination with an institution he associated with oppression and mass deception. "He would not talk about the faith and relapsed into a complete silence if I tried to bring up the subject," Day remembered. For years, Day tried to persuade Batterham to overcome his aversion to ideas of religion and marriage. When he refused, a decisive break, she realized, was inevitable. "I could not become a Catholic and continue living with him, because he was averse to any ceremony before officials of either Church or state."[82] Torn between her love for Batterham and her love for God, Day chose the latter. In what she considered "the struggle for [her] own soul," Day could not compromise. She was baptized Catholic in December 1927.

"It had seemed like death, at the time, to become Catholic," Day recalled in an article for *Commonweal* in 1958.[83] Indeed, her conversion marked not just the end of her marriage and romantic attachments, but also, at first, the end of her involvement with the radical movement: "It meant also giving up a whole society of friends and fellow workers. It was such a betrayal of them, they thought. One who had yearned to walk in the footsteps of a Mother Jones and an Emma Goldman seemingly had turned her back on the entire radical movement and sought shelter in that great, corrupt Holy Roman Catholic Church, right hand of the Oppressor, the State, rich and heartless, a traitor to her beginnings, her Founder, etc."[84] It was not long, however, before Day began to feel isolated in her personal pursuits of prayer, Scripture reading, and churchgoing. She refused to forsake her spiritual commitments, but she longed for reconciliation between religion and radicalism. "How little, how puny my work had been since becoming a Catholic, I thought. How self-centered, how ingrown, how lacking in sense of community!"[85]

Studying the gospels, Day, like Muste and Eddy, found the solution to her dilemma. There, in the most basic principles of Christianity, Jesus confirmed her belief that to serve God, one must also serve others. In the Beatitudes, for example, Jesus speaks of those who will inherit the Kingdom of God: the meek, the poor in spirit, the persecuted, the peacemakers, and those who convey pure-hearted mercy. In sermons, Jesus instructed His disciples to give to the needy, love one's enemies, and forgive each other's sins. Day concurred with all of these so-called ethics of the kingdom, but she particularly appreciated the intensity of application that Christ commanded. Instead of lofty ideals, astounding and unattainable, He offered basic but demanding guidelines for righteous living, not intended for half-hearted parading, but for hard-wearing perfection. Day believed that such devotion to practicing Christian values dovetailed with her desire to cultivate social revolution.

While Day was working out this new philosophy of life in the early 1930s, the world economy crashed down around her. The U.S. stock market's dramatic fall in October 1929 had failed to recover, leaving many people out of work, out of money, and out of hope. For many radicals, the apparent failure of capitalism heralded the long-held promise of revolution. Droves of Communists and socialists, including the short-term Trotskyist A. J. Muste, set themselves to revitalizing organizations dedicated to overthrowing the old system and establishing a new political economy. Despite many factional and policy shifts, the Communist Party USA (CPUSA), for example, continued to organize the poor and working-class, sometimes in concert with liberals and sometimes in opposition to them. The Socialist Party also gained initial momentum in the early 1930s under the leadership of presidential candidate Norman Thomas, whose radical platform was co-opted in many ways by the Democratic Party and its New Deal liberalism.

None of these organizations appealed to Day, and over the next few years, she became increasingly moved and frustrated by the desperation and poverty caused by the Depression. Just as it had for many on the left, the economic crisis revitalized Day's sense of radical purpose; but she still needed to find an appropriate spiritual outlet for its application. Eager to practice Christian compassion, Day sought the guidance of God in late 1932, asking Him in a "special prayer" at the National Catholic Shrine in Washington, D.C., where she was on assignment to cover a Communist-initiated "Hunger March of the Unemployed," to reveal some opportunity "to use what talents [she] possessed for . . . fellow workers, for the poor."[86]

When she returned home to New York City, Day found the answer to her prayers.

Years later, Day always told anyone interested that her life really began when she met Peter Maurin in early December 1932.[87] However, her first meeting with the "French peasant" whose ideas would come to "dominate" her mind and spirit was a casual, even disruptive, occurrence.[88] Tending to Tamar, who lay sick with the measles, Day had little time to entertain visitors in the small apartment she shared with her brother, John, and his wife, Tessa. When Tessa welcomed a talkative, "ragged and rugged" stranger into their home one afternoon, Day was polite but distracted.[89] "In my mixed roles as cook, dishwasher, nurse, and mother, as well as writer, it was hard for me to grasp what he said immediately," recalled Day.[90]

Undaunted, Maurin continued talking, in his thick foreign accent, to anyone within earshot—even the doctor and the plumber who dropped by during the length of the evening. The thrust of his dialogue, however, was directed at Day, the woman he had been searching for over the previous several weeks. "I learned from Tessa that he had actually come to see me," wrote Day. "[He] had come a few times before to see if I was back from Washington." As Day understood it, the fifty-seven-year-old Catholic "agitator" first heard of her when an Irish Communist in Union Square told him about the articles she had written for *Commonweal*.[91] Thrilled to discover a kindred spirit in the quest for social justice and religious revolution, Maurin tracked down Day through the offices of *Commonweal* editor George Schuster.[92] Day's writings were headed in the right direction, Maurin thought; but he felt she needed a program of action. He had one to offer.

Maurin's program, as he described it to Day, consisted of three major steps: founding a newspaper for what he called "clarification of thought," opening houses of hospitality to feed and shelter the urban poor, and, finally, organizing agricultural communes to support self-sufficient, mutual aid societies—an idea inspired by Kropotkin, whom Day also admired. Like Kropotkin, Maurin held strong antistatist values, not because he rejected the need for social welfare, but because he took the obligations of social welfare so seriously. Federal relief agencies, according to Maurin, allowed people to evade their responsibilities to each other, because the state, acting as an enormous, remote intermediary, grievously altered the relationships of community. What once required interpersonal concern and attention now disappeared into the abyss of tax-and-spend formalities. Maurin was intent on readjusting the social structure back to its most primitive, personal roots. "[He] envisioned a twentieth-century version of the ancient notion of a hospice," explained Day, "a place where 'works of mercy' were offered and acknowledged in a person-to-person fashion, as opposed to the faceless, bureaucratic procedures of the welfare state."[93]

Maurin's emphasis on "works of mercy" reflected his French-Catholic education and his belief in the social mission of Christianity. As Day soon discovered, all the "old-fashioned prayer books list them," separated into spiritual deeds (instruct the ignorant, counsel the doubtful, admonish sinners, bear wrongs patiently, forgive offenses, comfort the afflicted, and pray for the living and the dead) and corporal deeds (feed the hungry, clothe the naked, harbor the harborless, ransom the captive, visit the sick, and bury the dead).[94] It was the latter that concerned Maurin the most, because priests, nuns and other members of the Catholic clergy tended to concentrate their ministry in the spiritual, instead of corporal, realm. Maurin insisted that the Church, no less than the state, remained a limited and lifeless institution unless it assumed its share of the social burden by "undertak[ing] their task in life, striving not only to love God and their brother but to *show* that love."[95] In the early 1930s, with the Depression, in particular, the needs of the poor and destitute seemed insurmountable. Yet Maurin had faith in the ability of people—not just Catholics and Christians, but all people—to practice the works of mercy, genuinely and selflessly, both in crisis and as convention.

The Franciscan ideal of voluntary poverty blazed as the "core of [Maurin's] message," the fundamental plank in his entire theological system.[96] Without a denunciation of personal privilege and wealth, he insisted, the works of mercy amounted to little more than charity: superficial, shallow, and sporadic demonstrations of Christian duty (much like its secular counterpart, the tax). On the "more or less" spectrum of social change, Maurin definitely had the more in mind. He wanted to transform individual lives, restructure communities, and, thus, revolutionize the world into a model of God's kingdom. "Peter Maurin always held before our eyes a vision of the new man, the new social order as being possible, by God's grace, here and now," wrote Day.[97] Indeed, for Maurin, the path to the new social order seemed simple and practical, especially when reduced to the clear-cut aphorisms he often repeated. "Be what you want the other to be," Maurin exhorted. "Be poor with the poor." "To give and not take, that is what makes men human."[98] Such mundane acts, he believed, were the measures of our humanity and the makings of "a new heaven and a new earth, wherein justice dwelleth."[99] Such was Maurin's vague notion of the Kingdom of God on earth, a society wherein people treated each other as family members and human beings, not as strangers or competitors. He hoped for a society in which "all men would be able to fulfill themselves" and feed themselves; he spoke of a society in which "it is easier for people to be good."[100]

In Day, Maurin found a ready recruit to join his ministry and help implement his vision of a Christian society. The two religious radicals certainly shared similar ideas about the social mandates of Christ and the primitive anarchism of Kropotkin. The program also accorded with Day's ideas regarding a revolution from below, by way of basic human interactions. Yet Day remained uncertain about how to convince others to take such radical steps.[101] "I can well recognize the fact that people remaining as they are, Peter's program is impossible," she acknowledged. "But it would become actual, given a people changed in heart and mind, so that they would observe the new commandment of love, or desired to."[102]

Day's faith in the potential for revolutionary changes in human behavior stemmed from the concept of cultivation, a recurring theme in her life and writings. In fact, it was the act of gardening that eventually convinced her to trust in God's process, even if slow-moving or unseen. Though she planted the seeds and carefully sowed them, the teleology of the product remained a mystery. "I *must* believe in these seeds," she wrote, "that they fall into the earth and grow into flowers and radishes and beans. It is a miracle to me because I do not understand it."[103] This analogy of cultivation came back to her, framing her Christian worldview and anchoring her confidence in revolution. "If we had faith in what we were doing, making our protest against brutality and injustice, then we were indeed casting our seeds, and there was the promise of the harvest to come," she explained.[104] Earlier in her life, Day had despaired of any gradual change, dismissing it as reformism and not revolution. Faced with Maurin's "long view" or "vision" of the coming Kingdom of God on earth, however, Day thought in terms of cultivation and rallied her faith in the potential for "a slow and steady bettering of conditions."[105]

From this perspective, sowing the Kingdom of God on earth seemed neither unreasonably utopian nor insufficiently reformist. Instead, Day understood it as realistic and *radical*, which literally means to "get at the root of things."[106] By operating at the most basic level of human fellowship and carrying out the works of mercy in a condition of voluntary poverty, Day and Maurin saw themselves as "getting at the roots" of the social order, building up the biblical "branches" for Jesus' "vine," and pruning off worldly values in order "to go and bear fruit—fruit that will last."[107]

During the early years of the Great Depression, the soil seemed most suitable for social experimentation. "The air of excitement, of impending social change" convinced many activists that this was "the time to try new things," Day recalled.[108] Initially, however, Day remained in the familiar territory of radical journalism, the first part of Maurin's program. "Among his ideas it was the one of publishing a paper which most immediately appealed to me," she wrote. "I was all for plunging right in. After all, I had a typewriter and a kitchen table and plenty of paper and plenty to write about."[109] Day also had years of experience writing and working for small, independent periodicals that aimed to expose the plight of the working class. Day raised money for the new enterprise by soliciting contributions from friends. "The rest of it," she wrote, "the editors squeezed out of their own earnings."[110] Once she had secured adequate, if inconsistent, financing, the project seemed easy enough to execute: "The thing was to find a printer, run off the first issue and go out on the streets and sell it. Beginnings are always exciting."[111]

On May Day in 1933, 2,500 copies of the first issue of the *Catholic Worker* were ready for distribution, priced at a penny each. Day walked over to Union Square, where a Communist rally was under way, and began selling her stack of papers. The idea that she was introducing a spiritual component to the typically secular Communist climate thrilled her. "Religion in Union Square! It was preposterous," she crowed.[112] Indeed, the first issue of *Catholic Worker* reflected the editors' self-conscious synthesis of radicalism and religion. They referenced past papal encyclicals related to social justice and called special attention "to the fact that the Catholic Church has a social program." In this area, they felt, their "little paper" was "filling a need" by addressing both the spiritual *and* "material welfare" of their readers. The novelty of this approach was not lost on Day. "Is it not possible," she pondered, "to protest, to expose, to complain, to point out abuses and demand reforms without desiring the overthrow of religion?"[113] In the 1930s, many radicals would have responded to Day's question in the negative, claiming that religious questions had little if anything to do with the urgency of overthrowing the capitalist system. By the 1950s, that would change, as disillusioned Marxists such as Howe and Macdonald, though atheists, began to consider religious questions as crucial components of a new kind of socialism. *Catholic Worker*, they recognized, had been well ahead of its time.

Stripped of its religious overcoat, however, the paper resembled any other labor-oriented publication, suffused with articles on union membership, strikes, workers' wages, and the exploitation of women, children, and racial minorities in industry. For Day, this amounted to standard radical fare; but for many Catholic readers it was too traditionally Marxist and, thus, subversive. "The very word 'worker' made people distrust us at first," Day recalled. "We were not taking the position of the great mass of Catholics, who were quite content with the present in this world." They thought "we were Communists in disguise, wolves in sheep's clothing."[114]

As conservatives accused the editors of latent Communism, many radicals on the left belittled the paper for its vague political stance. The editors of *Catholic Worker* definitely opposed the evils of capitalism and favored improved, humane industrial relations, but they did not delve into the issues that divided so many radical sects, such as the true nature of the Soviet Union or the dialectical inevitability of economic change or strategies for seizing political power on behalf of workers. Day was well aware of the difference. "Our paper . . . is not 'for' any line of political action and we get a great deal of criticism for it," she admitted to a Canadian Christian radical in 1934.[115] True to her values of decentralized, social communion, however, Day refused to yield to political pressure or involve herself with the affairs of state. "I should like very much to be able to throw myself into the work of a political movement, but I can't," she wrote. "The whole policy of our paper is against political activity." To participate in politics, she explained, meant sanctioning the power of the state and its secular approach to social and economic problems, a dangerous tendency that would lead to "fascism" or centralized socialism.[116] "When people seek to win the State, they are won by the State," she said succinctly.[117]

On these grounds, Day and Maurin took issue with both Communism and welfare liberalism as it existed in the 1930s. "*The Catholic Worker* stands opposed to Communism, Socialism and Fascism," they clarified in 1934.[118] This did not mean that Day rejected socialism, only the state-centric brand symbolized by the party and its many sectarian offshoots. The editors of *Catholic Worker*, in fact, did not wish to waste their energies engaging in the ideological warfare raging among radicals eager to overthrow capitalism and establish some form of workers' regime. "The state is bound to be a tyrant, a dictatorship. A *Dictatorship of the Proletariat* becomes again another dictatorship," Day explained years later.[119] The history of corruption within the Soviet Union only confirmed her doubts. Calling the Kremlin "a center of evil," she agreed with anti-Communists that the great Russian experiment in social engineering was ruled by ruthless tyrants concerned only with preserving their own power. "I knew how terrible Stalin was," she told an interviewer, years later.[120] On this point alone, *Catholic Worker* was also ahead of its time.

Catholic Worker also refused to sanction the liberal welfare state emerging from the New Deal, a political expression of social justice that other notable Catholics on the left, such as Father John A. Ryan, supported wholeheartedly. But for Day and Maurin, New Deal agencies functioned as non-Christian entities, "as though God were unknown," operating through cold bureaucracy like an impersonal machine, collecting taxes and redistributing resources without inspiring any sense of religious duty or responsibility among citizens.[121] This purely "materialist" approach left the nation spiritually as well as economically bankrupt, a point that Day drove home in her correspondence with the editor of the Catholic *Interracial Review*. "If they, the liberals and Communists, are trying to win adherents to their cause of materialist philosophy," she wrote, "we too are trying to win them in our Catholic philosophy, by spiritual and corporal works of mercy, and by a general program of propaganda." The New Deal or the *Daily Worker* might feed the poor and win their votes, but those involved with the *Catholic Worker* wanted to feed the poor and "win [their] souls."[122] Any state aid, legislation, or "parliamentary means" were, for Day and Maurin, just "makeshift ways to better a few of the average people's lot." "And little can ever come of, or from the State," they concluded.[123] Federal aid might become necessary in times of national emergency, and the Depression certainly qualified as such a crisis; but Day knew that many people fell through the cracks of federal programs, such as the displaced tenant farmers whom Eddy helped organize in the Mississippi Delta.

Day's and Maurin's central belief in a personal approach to social reform made questions of scale all the more important, lest Catholic Worker communities bear any resemblance to "unwieldy" state bureaucracy.[124] "We want to decentralize everything and delegate to smaller bodies and groups what can be done far more humanely and responsibly through mutual aid, as well as charity, through Blue Cross, Red Cross, union cooperation, [and] parish cooperation," Day explained in a 1949 *Commonweal* piece.[125] When pressed on the issue, Day always described her politics as *local* politics, *personal* politics, which consisted of pursuing community life "loyal to the teaching in the Sermon on the Mount" and extending a "neighborliness that is both political and spiritual in nature."[126] National and international lobbying efforts, she felt, were far less immediate, less effective, and thus less important to her mission. "I am not interested in politics or elections," she wrote bluntly in her diary in 1979, near the end of her life. Thus, Day rejected the process of voting as an empty endeavor to effect change. Noting her agreement with those such as John Ruskin who opposed bureaucratic democracy, Day wrote that people "would never get anywhere with the vote," since it was "the hearts and minds of men [that] must be changed."[127] Even as early as 1938, when writing *From Union Square to Rome*, she openly criticized Catholics "who trust to political activity rather than to Catholic action to further the Christian revolution."[128] According to Day, they needed to work on rebuilding the social realm before they could change the political realm. They needed to "seek first the Kingdom of God" within local communities and trust that "all these things will be given to you as well."[129] Such was the "real purpose" of *Catholic Worker* in its projection of "a Utopian ideal, an actual, Gospel view of life."[130]

Given its religious substance and anti-authoritarian tone, the *Catholic Worker* became, for its editors, a weapon of spiritual warfare in the fight against secular forms of statecraft in an age of crisis. Day, for one, realized the stakes were high. If industrial laborers could not relate to the *Catholic Worker*, then they would turn to the *Daily Worker* and its message of secular radicalism. The appeal of Communism for well-meaning people, she knew from firsthand experience, exerted a powerful pull. "It is because of the Communist party's ideals, not because of its essential anti-religious aspect; because of its love of the ordinary man, and not because of its hatred towards God, that so many young people are being attracted towards Communis[m]," she wrote in 1933. "And being attracted to what is good in their natures, and fervently embracing it as a cause, they come eventually to accept whole-heartedly all the party teaches."[131] Day feared that young people dedicated to social justice and solidarity with the poor were being duped by this "diabolic plot" to accept the antireligious and unethical aspects of Communism because they lacked alternatives. "We feel that Communism is gaining in this country, because Christian people do not protest against injustice as they do," she said in a 1935 letter to the New

York police commissioner.[132] Day hoped to provide a spiritual counterpoint to secular politics with the paper. The former fellow-traveler made her stand unequivocally in a 1934 issue: "Is it to be left to the Communists to . . . feed the hungry, clothe the naked, shelter the homeless—these corporal works of mercy are too often being done by the opposition, and to what purpose?"[133] Day believed that Christians, not Marxists, should undertake these acts of compassion, because they were central to Christ's message. "Our manifesto is the Sermon on the Mount," she once wrote, indicating that the *Catholic Worker* had a clear spiritual agenda derived directly from the Gospels.[134]

To mark the difference, Day called for a social approach from the bottom up, via small, local institutions that provided the intimacy of personal care and cooperation. "Immediate works of mercy shows what can be done now, not waiting for the revolution or the state," explained Day.[135] Such was "Christ's technique," "working from the bottom and with the few" to build the Kingdom of God upon pillars of men and women, living out love and mutual aid as brothers and sisters under God.[136] Utopia, in this sense, did not exist in some future, idealized world. It could exist only in the present, in the mundane manners of mankind. "The 'means to the end' begins with each one of us," Day declared.[137] Accordingly, she considered it a waste of time to wait for changed political conditions or economic structures before enacting a "revolution of the heart."[138] The method, simply, was to match means to ends. In order to achieve equality, people must treat each other as equals. To establish social justice, they must act justly, and to generate cooperation, they must stop competing for wealth and resources. The social revolution, in short, depended on a revolution in social relations. That was the kind of decentralized, personalized, and spiritualized socialism Day could and did support in the pages of *Catholic Worker*.

Though there were plenty of initial criticisms of the *Catholic Worker* among Catholics, Day and Maurin's unorthodox newspaper did garner praise from both clergy and laymen, who valued the Catholic perspective on social problems. Reverend Donald A. MacLean of Catholic University of America wrote in the summer of 1933, "God grant that your apostolic efforts . . . may prove successful in every way, and stay the onward rush of this militant atheistic movement in America."[139] The editors even received an early endorsement from *Commonweal*, which described the new periodical as "newsy, realistic and expressively Catholic."[140] The content and format may not have matched the slick periodicals that competed for its readership. Daniel Berrigan, for example, remembered the issues lying around his boyhood home as dense and high-brow. Composed of "uncompromising squads of close print, it languished there next to the livid hagiography of the Messenger of the Sacred Heart," he recalled. "My father read the *Worker*, and my mother. Period."[141] Something about the publication, however, was working. By the next May Day, after one year running, the editorial staff had increased circulation from 2,500 to 35,000 and growing.[142] By the end of the decade, it would claim 100,000 readers. Public confusion about the paper's political stance, however, continued, despite its popularity. In his two-part profile of Day in 1952, for instance, independent socialist Dwight Macdonald observed that "politically, the Catholic Workers are hard to classify. They are for the poor and against the rich, so the capitalists call them Communists; they believe in private property and don't believe in class struggle, so the Communists call them capitalists; and they are hostile to war and to the State, so both [sides] consider them crackpots."[143]

Given the nebulous nature of the independent Left, reshaping itself in opposition to Communism and traditional socialism in the 1930s and 1940s, it is easy to understand why Day felt somewhat alone and persecuted in her worldview, even going so far as to title one of her memoirs *The Long Loneliness*. She was a Catholic at odds with the established Church and a radical at odds with the traditional Marxist Left. She was a socialist, but not state-centric, a point that prompted Maurin to refer to himself as an "anarchist," though Day avoided the label, wary of the negative and confusing connotations it conjured, particularly the association with violence and destruction. "Blast the word," she once scribbled in her diary.[144] The term "libertarian," she noted, was "less apt to offend," yet it lacked the holistic substance of a way of life.[145] Whenever she did use the term "anarchism" to describe her politics, she insisted on a precise meaning that exposed the spiritual and social core of her ideology. "The whole point of view of the anarchist is that everything must start from the bottom up, from man. It seems to me so human a philosophy," she stated in an interview late in her life.[146] Day concurred with the anarchist's abhorrence to the state, but her odium did not erupt from the anti-authoritarian wells of individual autonomy. As H. A. Reinhold wrote of her in 1952, Day resembled "an anarchist of the heart rather than a follower of Bakunin or a bomb-throwing, church-burning . . . syndico-anarchist of the Catalan variety."[147] At the very least,

Day's occasional and qualified use of the term "anarchism" did not override her essential socialist worldview. She believed, above all else, that people needed to treat each other better, as equals, as God's inherently dignified children, as neighbors, and as family. That abstract and impersonal state could not provide this sort of community.

Instead, Day, much like Kropotkin, wanted to abolish the state so that people could relate to and rely on one another in communities, personally and socially, without the need for external, alienating, and spiritually repressive institutions. "The anarchist philosophy is that the new social order is to be built up by groupings of men together in communities," she explained. Borrowing a phrase of Martin Buber's, Day envisioned a "community of communities" linked together in loose cooperation that would one day replace state-centered compulsion.[148] She did not mind the term "socialism" to describe such a program, as long as it denoted decentralized, communal, and progressive action. In the late 1960s, for example, Day objected in her diary to *Commonweal*'s archaic description of *Catholic Worker* philosophy as "medieval socialist." "I prefer Martin Buber's term Utopian Socialists," she corrected without altering the root subject, evidence to the fact that she considered herself a particular kind of socialist.[149] Years earlier, she had also referred to Father Henri de Lubac's memoir, *The Unmarxian Socialist*, as a "great book."[150] Day identified with a certain kind of socialism *and* a certain kind of anarchism with precise meanings. She used the words "anarchism" to mark her rejection of the state, and "socialism" to specify the spiritual, interpersonal qualities of community building.

Day, in short, was redefining socialism away from its more recent connotations and reaffirming its essential denotation, a point of controversy that contributors to *Dissent* would debate in several issues of the newfound magazine in the mid-1950s. An editorial by French scholar M. Rubel in the debut copy pondered whether or not anti-Stalinist radicals could call themselves "socialists" without running the "great risk of not being immediately understood." Since the Russian Revolution of 1917, he reminded, the term had been captured and corrupted by the Soviets, imbued thereafter with overtones of authoritarianism, centralization, and undemocratic practice.[151] Norman Thomas added to the symposium in the summer edition with doubts that leftists could ever agree on a positive definition to resurrect the moral meaning of the concept, though he admitted that he too longed for a "new vocabulary" on the part of democratic socialists, who could announce in unity that "from henceforth we are using a newer and more precise term to describe ourselves in order to purge ourselves of the taint of the misuse of our old name, not only by communists and national socialists but by various heretics with whom we do not agree."[152] Founding editors Lewis Coser and Howe made it clear that they intended to reclaim the term "socialism" as a moral vision, all the while acknowledging that "to will the image of socialism is a constant struggle for definition, almost an act of pain. But it is the kind of pain that makes creation possible."[153] Though she may have appreciated the discussion within *Dissent*, Day did not overthink the onus of re-creation. She enacted a new definition of socialism in daily practice and daily struggle. Her pain helped make the re-creation possible.

The *Catholic Worker* staff kept busy offering workers a spiritual alternative to secular socialism in 1933, but the revolutionary program that Day and Maurin envisioned amounted to little more than words on a page. The newspaper's office on 15th Street and, later, Charles Street doubled as a soup kitchen and halfway house for the poor, but Day was eager to move forward, to contribute substantially to social reconstruction, and thus make *Catholic Worker* not merely a paper, but "also a movement."[154] The next steps, she realized, would be difficult. Maurin's theories about building communities in urban hospitality houses and rural farming collectives sounded deceptively simple when presented in "Easy Essays." Yet Day sensed that the application of these essays to an imperfect world would be anything but easy.[155] "He had lived alone for so long, had for so long been a single apostle, that he did not realize how grim the struggle was going to be," she said of her Catholic Worker cofounder.[156] Her mission, as she understood it, was the daunting task of transforming Maurin's theories into practice. "I considered of course that I was putting some flesh on his dead bones of thinking," Day confided in her diary years later. "It is one thing to dream of Utopias, it is another thing to try to work them out."[157]

Day was willing to make the effort. By November 1933, only six months after launching the *Catholic Worker* newspaper, she began talking seriously in her columns about the need for permanent houses of hospitality. The purpose was two-fold: to meet the current crisis of hunger and homelessness caused by the Depression, and to start building Christian communities for long-term reconstruction. Citing the "monastic ideal of service" and the "Franciscan spirit" of sacrifice, Day told readers that "a plan of action has been drawn up" and, "with the grace of God," a genuine, commodious Catholic Worker hospice would soon become operational.[158] These plans took some time to solidify, but in April 1936 the Catholic Worker staff finally found the space they needed in a dilapidated tenement building at 115 Mott Street on the Lower East Side. It would serve as their "revolutionary headquarters" for the next fourteen years, until moving to a larger space.[159]

The concept of Catholic Worker might have started with Maurin and his vision of utopian idealism, but the practical application of Catholic Worker socialism, in both word (the published paper) and deed (the hospitality houses) depended on Day. "Almost everyone agrees that Peter could have done nothing without Dorothy," wrote one analyst of the movement in 1966. "He is by all accounts, a most difficult man, impersonal, didactic, impractical, always lecturing and never conversing."[160] In 1952, Macdonald made a similar observation. "It is certain that without her practical turn of mind, Maurin would have remained an ineffectual eccentric," he wrote.[161] With Day's talents, the Catholic Worker movement, Macdonald continued, materialized as the mission of "practical fools," that is to say "fools on principle," who "try to live their everyday lives according to an ideal" that strikes most people as unrealistic and even impossible.[162] The enterprise to establish the first house of hospitality in New York City, for example, began as a leap of faith without much money or prior planning. "We [had] twelve rooms in the front house for women [and] . . . twenty-four rooms for men," Day described. "Four were used for laundry and storerooms. We did not use the basement because of rats and defective plumbing."[163] Staff and volunteers lived in voluntary poverty and practiced the corporal works of mercy by feeding and sheltering the poor, hungry, homeless, mentally ill, and alcoholics who had "no place to go."[164] In the mid-1930s, during the most desperate time of economic crisis, they offered free meals to over one thousand supplicants, sometimes two to three times a day. Obviously, the Catholic Workers were providing a much-needed service, and by 1938, twenty more hospitality houses, loosely affiliated with Day but calling themselves Catholic Worker sites, opened to the public in cities such as Buffalo, Milwaukee, and Philadelphia. Catholic Worker houses also sprang up in Canada and as far away as Australia.

In truth, Day had a hard time turning anyone away, since doing so, she presumed, would affront the spirit of Christ within each supplicant. Her strong belief in personalism, or the idea that a spark of God dwells in every human being and thus provides them with intrinsic worth and dignity, made it very difficult for her to set reasonable limits on the number of hungry and homeless that the Catholic Worker house served each day and night. The commotion of such compassion seemed impractical to outsiders, but Day did not see any alternative, especially given her meager resources and the sordid condition of her clients. "Instead of having plans and blueprints we have the actual people, the kind nobody wants, that the government will not help, the kind that are always being passed on," she explained, using the concept of personalism to make her case. "We've got to try to make the start of a Christian community and loving people because they are other Christs, and pray to be able to love them, and see Christ in them."[165]

Day applied this principle to everyone, including the atheistic Communists she pitted her paper against. "Inasmuch as they are creatures of God," she once wrote, "[they] are our brothers."[166] It also extended to all patrons of the hospitality house, no matter how rude, disruptive, or filthy. Describing one male resident in 1935, for example, Day painted a grim picture: "He sits at the lower window like a Cerberus and growls and curses everyone. . . . He hates us all, he hates this place. . . . He won't bathe, he won't dress. I have to ask one of the men to button him up." Yet Day refused to turn him out of the house. "He, after all, is Christ," she wrote with a reference to Jesus' mandate in the book of Matthew. "'Inasmuch as you have done it unto the least of these,' you know. It's the hardest problem we have yet."[167]

Day struggled with personal problems too, as many observers complained that she, an educated, well-read woman who took up voluntary poverty, seemed distant and even elitist in her relations with the poor, an image of inadvertent condescension that still haunts her otherwise "saintly" legacy. As one historian, Eugene McCarraher, wrote in his study of Christian dissidents, "the residue of culture and class" hung on to Catholic Workers such as Day, "whose literary skill and highbrow reading tastes marked her as a middle-class intellectual. Determined to be refugees from university and professional milieus, Catholic radicals found it difficult to make a home among the unlettered pursuers of happiness."[168]

Some of Day's contemporaries came to her defense on this issue. In 1952, H. A. Reinhold wrote that "her humility has prevented [Day] from becoming the kind of matriarch exemplified in those ancient and recent women heresiarchs" who kept a degree of separation between themselves and the poor. That same year, Macdonald also noted that, unlike most social workers, Day and her helpers lived a life of poverty alongside destitute residents, wearing castoff clothes, eating plain food, and sleeping on hard cots.[169] Day, however, was apt to agree with some of the critical remarks about educational and class differences that threatened to undermine a true sense of community. "I think that at the Catholic Worker we have high aims," she told interviewers in 1971. "But how much mingling is there, really, between the worker and the scholar?"[170]

Such divisions of class and intellect certainly caused discord in Catholic Worker communities; but this is not to say that Catholic Workers failed to support workers and their collective struggle against exploitation.[171] Day personally participated in strikes, parades, and other radical agitation efforts throughout the United States. Her Christian view of wage workers, however, clouded her understanding of them as a special class with specific needs in an advanced industrial environment. They were not, in her mind, the proletarian vanguard with a singular dispensation for advancing the new world order. Instead, they, like anyone else, were children of God, members of the Mystical Body of Christ, who deserved better treatment solely on account of their human value.

Day wanted a better way of life for workers in their homes and communities, not just on the shop floor. In a 1950 article for *Catholic World*, for example, the author made clear Day's "fiercely decentralist" ideas about labor and the means of production: "she wants decentralized factories, part-owned by the workers, and set in green fields, where every worker also should have his home, his garden, and ideally, his three acres and a cow." She wanted workers to grow their own food, make their own clothes, and practice a skill or craft that they could employ for personal purposes. If they must work in factories, Day insisted, they should operate as craftsmen who own their own tools (the means of production) as an extension of their creative potential.[172]

This "back to the land" vision was not unique to Day, Maurin, and the Catholic Workers. Followers of Catholic theorists G. K. Chesterton and Hilaire Belloc in the British "Distributist movement" also advocated ideas of a decentralized economy in the 1930s when people felt that urban life and enterprise had let them down. As mentioned earlier, a handful of spiritual socialists, including Eddy, had partnered to establish cooperative farms in the South. For many observers of the Catholic Worker mission, however, the pastoral ideal seemed antiquated, obsolete, and entirely impractical for addressing modern problems. "What she calls Christian anarchism is, I think, something fit for a pre-industrial society," Reinhold wrote in his 1952 *Commonweal* piece on Day.[173] The author of an article in *U.S. Catholic* in 1966 also noted that Catholic Workers seemed to combine "the social teachings of the Nineteenth Century anarchists" with "the kind of Christianity practiced by believers of the First and Second centuries."[174]

Day's work made more sense in the city, where she cared for, as one priest put it, "the offscourings of our industrial society, the flotsam and jetsam of the injustices arising from the overcentralization and maldistribution of our economic system." In this sense, she was regarded as "an apostle of the industrial age."[175] Out in the country, however, she seemed more distant from and less relevant to the search for moral methods to manage modern life. As McCarraher summarized, "Catholic Workers' implacable animus toward industrial technology proved injurious intellectually and politically." Instead of confronting the glaring injustices of the modern world, they "routinely retreated into a facile antimodernism" that "failed" to appeal to the working class.[176]

Yet Day did not think of her rural work as a retreat from the world. She considered the farming communes as an experimental engagement with new ways of life that people could adopt and then implement elsewhere, just as Muste initially intended for Brookwood Labor College or as Eddy projected for the cooperative farms. These were alternative institutions, acting as networking hubs for the dissemination of social change. "It isn't that we wish to isolate ourselves," Day explained in 1935. "What we are doing is trying to put our ideas *immediately* into practice, that is to live them." The mission, however, did not stop there. Catholic Workers created communities as living, dynamic forces of propaganda, not hermetic hideaways. "The great work which is to be done is to change public opinion, to indoctrinate, to set small groups to work here and there," Day continued. "From such [centers] we could send out missionaries of labor . . . we could send out these workers to live with people in factory towns, in lodging houses—to talk to them, to counteract the work of the Communists. They are working in just such a small way, sending out a few here and there, and their influence is everywhere felt."[177]

Macdonald, for one, understood Day's project as a special and effective type of socialism, whether urban or rurally based, as Day's daily activism dovetailed with his search for a moral radicalism rooted in communities and human values. In his essay "The Root Is Man," first published in 1946, Macdonald had stated his objections to Marxism, progressivism, and absolutism based on both a flawed reliance on the scientific method and the inevitability of historical process. Macdonald, however, made it clear that he was not giving up on socialism, at least a certain kind of socialism that could reaffirm fundamental values such as equality, honesty, and morality—knowing what is good and what is bad. In his shift from Marxist theory to democratic socialism, Macdonald was one of many former fellow-travelers and disillusioned radicals who had turned away from their past associations with political parties and sectarian organizations in an effort to move forward toward a "New Left" politics, nascent in the 1940s and 1950s (see Chapter 4). When Macdonald wrote in 1946 that "we must reduce political action to a modest, unpretentious, personal level—one that is real in the sense that it satisfies, here and now, the psychological needs, and the ethical values of the particular persons taking part in it," he was describing a way of life that Day and her Catholic Worker colleagues already had been promoting for a decade and a half. His call to "begin way at the bottom again, with small groups of individuals in various countries, grouped around certain principles and feelings they have in common," also echoed the appeals that Day and Maurin made in the early 1930s.[178]

During that decade, Macdonald had been radicalized, like many Americans, by the crisis of capitalism, and at first he "leaned toward the Communists because," as he put it, "they alone . . . seemed to be 'doing something.'" Accordingly, he quit his job writing for *Fortune* magazine and began working for magazines like the *Partisan Review*, a Communist periodical. After learning about the Moscow Trials, however, the "tepid Communist sympathizer" transformed quickly into an "ardent anti-Stalinist" and thereafter became involved in faction fights over the nature of the Soviet Union and the heroic role of intellectual revolutionaries like Trotsky. For a few years, Macdonald considered himself a Trotskyist, but not necessarily a Marxist. "I could never really make up my mind," he wrote. Though he appreciated the call for protest against economic injustice, the dogma, the "moral callousness," and the "undemocratic elements" of Marxist-Leninism bothered him to no end. He had embraced the revolutionary Left because he thought they were "doing something," but he slowly realized that they were doing little, if anything. "We were really engaged not in politics but in metapolitics," a kind of passionate, overly intellectualized debate club dissecting questions that had no meaning for exploited workers. "The masses," he concluded, "remained apathetic about socialism," at least that type of socialism, impersonal and abstract.[179]

As Macdonald soon discovered, however, the theory and practice of Catholic Worker made socialism more personal and, in his mind, more effective as a means and not just as an end. Analyzing her efforts to "make a better world" in a two-part piece for the *New Yorker* in 1952, Macdonald referred to Day as an "extremely successful evangelist," who acted as a model of moral behavior, doing the hard, prosaic social work that often fell by the wayside among political radicals.[180] Day was cultivating a Christian revolution instead of a Marxist or workers' revolution, but that did not make her radicalism any less potent. Macdonald, though nonreligious, recognized Day's contribution to the Left as part of an ongoing struggle to overcome the perennial problem of translating idealism into practical action. He listed her in a "Saints" section in his collection of essays, *Memoirs of a Revolutionist*, along with Gandhi. But he also placed her firmly in the pantheon of serious radicals.

Acknowledging the irony of his turn to religious figures as the best exemplars of socialism, Macdonald made it clear that he did not believe in God, though he did believe in religious values as a path to revolution. In an essay, "The Question of God," he identified his new political mentors, including Christ, Socrates, Tolstoy, Gandhi, and Simone Weil, who were not only asking the same questions as he, but also answering them in their "more modest and, so-to-speak, intimate approach" to social change. "Reform, reconstruction, even revolution must begin at a much more basic level than we imagined in the confident thirties," he stated. Rather than spin one's wheels on the metapolitical problems of history, Macdonald could appreciate the radicalism of confronting "the 'small' questions" such as "how do people really live and feel and think in their everyday lives?" Though often considered out of touch with reality in their focus on the metaphysical and transcendent, it was religious-minded people, Macdonald found, who were delving into the gritty but gratifying work of daily life and building the bridge between socialist means and ends.[181] The Good Samaritans, he concluded, made the best socialists, courageously approaching individuals as human beings and not as Party recruits, working-class heroes, or theoretical pawns in the great game of History.[182]

Back in the mid-1940s, Macdonald was still only writing about a new radicalism in his short-lived journal *politics* and in essays such as "The Root Is Man," in which he lauded the notion of community building. "These should probably not be physically isolated communities as was the case in the 19th century since this shuts one off from the common experience of one's fellowmen," he cautioned in 1946. "They should probably consist of individuals—*families*, rather—who love and make their living in the everyday world but who come together often enough to form a *psychological* (as against a geographical) community." But by 1952, Macdonald could point to a model of moral socialism in Day. "She has revived the linking of the serious and the trivial that saints and prophets once did so effectively but that long ago went out of fashion," he wrote approvingly. "The union of the everyday and the ultimate is the essence of the Catholic Worker movement."[183]

Labor activists such as Saul Alinsky would challenge the Left to develop more effective community organizing in the 1950s and 1960s, when he began approaching individuals holistically, getting to the heart of their everyday lives. But, unlike Day, he did not link quotidian concerns to "ultimate" or "transcendent" ends, thus missing the deep spiritual component of socialism that Day made central to her mission. According to Macdonald, Day was special, not as an antimodern anarchist as others had pegged her, but as a practical model of spiritual socialism, intent on counteracting the inhumane tendencies of modernity with fellowship and community. She was not rejecting the world, but working to improve it. She was not trying to turn back the clock; she was attempting to move forward toward the Kingdom of God.

Eddy's missionary experience and Day's hospitality houses were not just significant in terms of the liberal, modernizing shift in Protestant evangelism or social Catholicism, respectively. Their religious activism is also important in the history of the American Left. At a time when many radicals were becoming disillusioned with the amoral means of party politics and the corruption of bureaucratic leadership, they offered a non-Communist, post-Marxist alternative. They were kindred spirits in their devotion to building a completely new social order from the bottom up, through simple Christian acts in local communities. Eddy's project, the Delta Farm, folded after twenty years, while Day's newspaper and hospitality houses continued to serve the poor throughout Day's life (she died in 1980 at age eighty-three) and still exist today. "It is a permanent revolution, this Catholic Worker Movement," she prophesized, back in the early 1950s.[184]

Though her projection may have sounded overly optimistic or confident, Day meant it more as an expression of commitment and faith more than anything else. She knew the constant struggle required of spiritual socialists to keep cultivating the Kingdom of God, even in the face of intense disappointment, opposition, and failure. World War II, with its horrors of violence and social discord, had only ended five years earlier, and international peace did not seem imminent. On this issue, the issue of war, spiritual socialists did not always see eye to eye. Eddy supported U.S. intervention in the European and Pacific theaters as a necessary battle of good against evil. Day and Muste pleaded for pacifism, and they paid the price of public denunciation for their civil disobedience. Debating the merits of means and ends, spiritual socialists saw the war as an opportunity to advance, not suspend, their efforts for the Kingdom of God on earth.

CHAPTER 3

Spiritual Power and the Kingdom Abroad

On February 7, 1967, Dorothy Day of the Catholic Worker movement trudged through hip-high drifts of New York City snow to reach the courtroom where A. J. Muste and a group of pacifists awaited trial for protesting the U.S. bombing of civilians in Hanoi. Day was there to help exonerate the most recent actions of her friends, but Muste's mind was already making plans for his next radical demonstration. "[He] asked me again about going to Hanoi," Day wrote in her diary that night. As it turned out, the matron of the Mott Street Hospitality House did not have much time to consider the request. Four days later, she recorded that Muste had died, suddenly and without illness.[1] The news came as a shock, but Day soon reminded her readers to celebrate Muste's eighty-two-year legacy rather than mourn his loss. "His had been a long and happy life of work for brotherhood and peace," Day wrote in a *Commonweal* essay, memorializing her friend.[2]

Day and Muste were well-known comrades in the cause of "brotherhood and peace." For decades, the two had picketed together and spoken alongside each other on issues of fair labor, civil liberties, and nonviolence at places such as Lawrence, Massachusetts, and at Riverside Church, Union Square, and the United Nations headquarters in New York City. They had developed their pacifism during World War I and had become two of the most outspoken critics of World War II, the Korean War, nuclear arms, and the military escalations in Vietnam. Scholars still remember Day and Muste primarily on these terms, as passionate pacifists who channeled their religious beliefs into conscientious objection and civil disobedience.[3] However, Muste and Day not only shared a commitment to pacifism, but also were kindred spirits in their devotion to building a completely new social order from the bottom up, through simple Christian acts in local communities. Pacifism was certainly part of their program. In 1936, Muste had made his dramatic "return to pacifism," contending that it was the only way to keep the ethical high ground in the fight for social justice and the Kingdom of God on earth. Day, since the Great War, had persisted in her belief that violence, and, in fact, any unkindness, both contradicted Christ's commandments to love one another and undermined the advancement of God's plan for humanity. For Day as well as Muste, complicity in war helped sow the seeds of evil by breaking away from the Kingdom's proper teleological course. They insisted that to create peace, one had to act peacefully without exception or excuse; that was the only way to change culture and the world. "We look upon the striving toward perfection as a precept, a basic precept, an essential law of Christianity and for ourselves we must refuse to bear arms against our enemies," Day stated in a 1941 letter to a priest advocating the just cause of fighting in the global conflict.[4]

Depicting Day and Muste as solely pacifists, however, skews our understanding of their larger mission to remake the world into the Kingdom of God on earth. Their stance against violence and their discussion of nonviolence were much more practical than often thought. They were not debating the merits of pacifism as an abstract question about moral purity. They were trying to promote the best means toward a specific end: a socialist society wherein values and ideals are fully realized. Day and Muste insisted that the world would never get to that point unless people began adhering to those values as a matter of course, even during times of crisis. For them, nonviolence represented one part of a more complex religious value-system and worldview, which hinged on a revolution in social behavior. People certainly should not kill or do harm, but Day and Muste also believed that people should treat each individual with dignity, help the poor and needy, heal the sick, visit the lonely, and share and cooperate. Pacifism, then, stood as an important component of spiritual socialism. It did not stand alone. As Muste put it, "Pacifism must be, is, religious." Unpacking Muste's meaning here becomes easier when we consider such comments in light of his comprehensive eschatology.[5] He conflated pacifism and religion because they were means to the Kingdom of God, if and when carried out in good faith. Antiwar measures could be secular in nature, but pacifism as a way of life required religious devotion and religious vision—a long-term vision. Pacifism, for Muste as well as Day, served a higher, transcendent purpose. It was the dynamic that made spiritual socialism work, for to view each individual as an equal, to respect their dignity as a product of God, to treat them as a brother or neighbor in need, meant to act in a way that made violence unconscionable. Violence canceled out the Kingdom of God. It shattered the entire effort.

Muste and Day engaged in direct action against war, marching in peace parades and refusing to pay taxes to support the military. But they also practiced direct action through spiritual socialism, in general, by offering food, shelter, and fellowship at Catholic Worker houses or the community-building projects of Brookwood Labor College and the Labor Temple of New York City, a working-class outreach center affiliated with the Presbyterian church. They become too easily marginalized from scholarship on the left, and socialism in particular, if we catalog their resistance to war, but not their activism against the entire sociopolitical system.

Acts of individual protest, according to Day, were crucial levers of counterforce against state-sponsored violence. In fact, her assumption that the U.S. nation-state would never enact Christian values because it represented an inherently non-Christian entity paralleled the arguments that Reinhold Niebuhr and other Christian realists were making at this time, at least up to a point—a very important point of divergence. Day shared their cynicism about the moral potential of the state as such, but she refused to take a defeatist position regarding the possibilities of creating a peaceful, perfect world without evil. Until the state dissolved into a "community of communities," she believed it was up to ordinary citizens to bear moral witness and refuse to feed the federal government any of its war-making resources, whether in the form of taxes, patriotic fervor, or draftees. Christian realists might consider it folly to forgo violence in an inherently evil society, but Day argued that true Christians could never play politics on the world's terms. She remained faithful to the idea that performing works of mercy would eventually root out evil. War, however, reversed the course, allowing people to unleash their base behaviors instead of their best behaviors. As a journalist explained in 1971, Day's pacifism reflected her entire philosophy: "It is grounded in the fundamental perception that the poor and the powerless bear the brunt of every war and that contemporary warfare in particular entails modes of conduct that are the direct antithesis of the works of mercy, to which we are enjoined by the Gospel. Instead of feeding, clothing and sheltering our brothers, we bomb, starve and incinerate them to obtain their capitulation."[6]

Yet Day's was not the only voice on the religious left, and spiritual socialists, in particular, held a diverse set of opinions about World War II in the 1940s. Some, such as Muste and Day, were absolute pacifists, rejecting violence completely. Others such as Sherwood Eddy and Henry A. Wallace rationalized fighting the good fight on the grounds that, in an imperfect but perfectible world, Christians needed to root out the weeds of evil lest it interfere with the cultivation of the Kingdom of God on earth. The debate among spiritual socialists, then, did not pivot on issues of war and peace, violence and nonviolence, as ends in themselves. The debate was actually about which approach to war would yield the most effective results for the long-term project of building a socialist society. Day and Muste contended that the means must always match the ends, making violence counterproductive to God's will for the world. Eddy and Wallace, on the other hand, argued that the objective to protect the seeds of the Kingdom from being trampled underfoot by Fascist soldiers made a temporary resort to violence necessary and realistic.

Despite these differences, all spiritual socialists insisted that the United States had to project its "spiritual force" or "spiritual power," not just military and material power, into the world. By "spiritual power," they did not mean missionizing U.S. culture to other nations, but the missionizing of universal, moral values, including human dignity, equality, and freedom, that dovetailed with socialism. They condemned U.S. imperialism as a betrayal of these principles, arguing that a top-down authoritarian approach would never win the hearts and minds of people who needed to see the light of a better world ahead. True to their shared belief in decentralized decision making, spiritual socialists insisted that Americans must allow communities abroad to determine their own way forward, toward peace and cooperation.

The cause of pacifism, of course, was not always popular, especially during times of crisis and fear. After the bombing of Pearl Harbor on December 7, 1941, and Congress's declaration of war against Japan the following day, public demands for neutrality and nonintervention gave way to a surge of patriotism and support for U.S. involvement in a war that had finally made Americans feel vulnerable. Progressives and radicals, including Communists, formed temporary alliances with liberals against a common Fascist enemy. Religious leaders sermonized on the need to take up arms in a battle of good versus evil. And many advocates of nonviolence during peacetime changed their tune to join the chorus of wartime defenders.

Day, for one, did not. Instead of joining the Popular Front, she committed herself to the "unpopular front" held by pacifists and conscientious objectors during the 1940s. The uncompromising nature of her moral absolutism created considerable controversy for *Catholic Worker*, which lost a large portion of its readership and support during the war. The pressure to conform to the national consensus certainly took its toll on Day, even as she stuck to her convictions. "The more you see of the world the more it seems hopeless that Christianity will work, enforce order, brotherly love. The more obscure seems our mission!" she admitted in 1943, shortly before deciding to take a break from her mission in New York City. Tired of struggling through "thickets of misunderstanding" and "beating a path and not making much headway," the woman with seemingly boundless reserves of energy left Mott Street for about a year to engage in spiritual retreat and discern God's will for her future. Day, in short, was unsure about how to proceed in the face of such overwhelming reproach. In a rare expression of futility and despair, she wrote, "I feel sorry for anyone coming in on the CW now. How did it come about? What is it all for? And no matter how much you may try to talk, to explain, it seems impossible. People hear what they want to hear. . . . The world always will be in a mess."[7]

Some of her acquaintances, such as Muste and David Dellinger, did understand. There was also support from her distant admirer, Dwight Macdonald, who did not blame Day for failing to side with the mainstream, including most major labor unions. Several years after the cease-fire, Macdonald wrote that "the [Catholic] Workers did not desert the union man so much as the union man deserted them, partly because he no longer needed their help, partly because in a period of war and disillusionment their radical purity at best bored and at worst shocked them. Their pacifism, for example, was no embarrassment in the thirties, when liberals and Leftists thought in terms of 'merchants of death,' but in the decade after Pearl Harbor, when 'arsenals of democracy' became a more popular phrase, the *Catholic Worker*'s circulation declined slowly but steadily."[8]

During her leave of absence, Day did not cease reaching out to a larger audience. She continued to write for *Catholic Worker*. She also traveled around the nation, giving speeches, receiving honorary awards, and visiting the many Catholic Worker projects that her work in New York City had inspired. And, after about a year, she felt compelled to return to her local community. "No matter how much of a pilgrim I consider myself, and call myself, I am wedded to home, to the house of hospitality, to the parish where we live in New York. It is my vocation," she affirmed.[9] Catholic supporters remained confident that Day and her movement would endure despite ideological opposition and a decreased interest in social welfare in the wake of the war. "The Catholic Worker is a living and dynamic movement," a Catholic student magazine declared in 1948. "It may change some of its forms because it is alive and not ossified, but it is still one of the most potent lay Catholic influences in the world. The work of Dorothy Day is far from finished."[10] Macdonald agreed, referring to Catholic Worker as "a chimera perhaps, in Marxist taxonomy—but also a phoenix." The organization that Day started, in other words, was difficult to classify on the left, but this did not mean it lacked radical vitality. To the contrary, Macdonald praised Day's "longevity" and "consistency" with her values as a rare example of radical resolve to remain "relevant" despite the ups and downs of the political climate. "I welcome the viability of the Catholic Workers as one of those frequent, indeed chronic, irruptions of the unexpected that shows history is not a well-trained valet to any system of ideas but a chancy affair," he concluded.[11] Though Macdonald shared Day's pacifist worldview, it is clear that he did not admire her solely on these grounds. He considered her a model of spiritual socialism, the kind that could endure because of its commitment to practicing values day to day.

Others identified the Catholic Worker *network* as a lasting, dynamic force in American society. As one author noted, many social activists had been "quickened by [Day's] vision" "of human unification," and thus inspired to carry on the message and mission of Catholic Worker into various forms and fields of action.[12] Bruce Cook recognized this virtue in 1966. "Perhaps this is what makes the Catholic Worker truly important as it is," he reflected. "[It is in] the quality of people it graduates. For over three decades it has served as a sort of intellectual finishing school, offering courses in pacifism, Catholic radicalism, and works of mercy" to intellectuals and activists such as James O'Gara, John Cogley, Ed Marciniak, Michael Harrington, John Cort, J. F. Powers, Jim Forest, Tom Cornell, Jack English, Ammon Hennacy, and Eugene McCarthy.[13] Communities like Catholic Worker were few and far between, but Day knew they were connected, spiritually and historically, and working together to advance the Kingdom of God. As she told her former volunteer Robert Coles,

> We are communities in time and in a place, I know, but we are communities in faith as well—and sometimes time can stop shadowing us. Our lives are touched by those who lived centuries ago, and we hope that our lives will mean something to people who

won't be alive until centuries from now. It's a great "chain of being," someone once told me, and I think our job is to do the best we can to hold up our small segment of the chain. That's one kind of localism, I guess, and one kind of politics—doing your utmost to keep that chain connected, unbroken. Our arms are linked—we try to be neighbors of His, and to speak up for his [sic] principles. That's a lifetime's job.[14]

Day's "intense, persisting localism," however, did not deny the Kingdom of God its global reach.[15] Instead of encouraging isolationism, she looked forward to a time when the love of Christ would win the world over and unite all people together as spiritual brothers and sisters. In short, Christians would go global by first going local. Day's message about the importance of Christian internationalism was broadcast loud and clear in the *Catholic Worker*'s October 1934 front-page headline: "Christ the King Alone Can Reconstruct the World."[16] The article listed the corporal works of mercy as the most fundamental steps for social reconstruction, and it encouraged readers to begin implementing them in their communities. Christ could change the world, but He depended on loyal followers to put principles into practice and reveal God's immanence. As Day often said, "Pray as though all depended on God, and work as though all depended on yourself."[17]

Far from rejecting international goals, then, Day and the volunteers who devoted their time to Catholic Worker projects put their faith in an aspiration to transform the world into the Kingdom of God on earth. Again, the concept of cultivation is the key to understanding Day's thought process. Christian activists could only sow the seeds of cooperation at the local level, in their daily lives, because that is where the most basic behaviors are rooted and expressed. Over time, however, the results of that concentrated attention in small institutions would extrapolate, slowly but surely, into a global movement, just as Christianity began with only twelve disciples. As Coles wrote, Day called for "rock-bottom 'organization,'" yet she believed that if "more and more such communities were to form, a local politics would be at work and would affect the quality of more and more lives, and, she prayed, the nation as a whole."[18] With the faith of a gardener, Day encouraged her readers and coworkers to serve God by cultivating their own plot of soil, all the while trusting in God's unseen process to develop small acts into major, miraculous produce. "To aim at illuminating the universal through an examination of the particular," she wrote in her diary.[19]

Day conceived of the houses of hospitality in this context, exclaiming "What a universal appeal the CW has in its simplicity."[20] Instead of working to create legislative policy, lobbying proposals, or political blueprints, Catholic Workers put their energy into treating each other with love and kindness, as a family. Everyone knew how to do that, she felt, as long as one's selfishness could be kept at bay. It was simple, but transformative. As Coles explained in his interview biography of Day, the Catholic Worker mission "always focused on particular communities of men and women and children, their needs and concerns, and the possibilities of a certain neighborhood's extended family rather than national or international politics."[21]

Evaluating the state of human relations from a global perspective, and facing the seemingly endless pattern of violence and suffering, activists were more likely to become overwhelmed and disillusioned. Day, however, kept positive by focusing on the particular and by remembering the mantra of "the little way," which she imbibed from one of her favorite saints, Thérèse of Lisieux. Little by little, she believed, small acts of kindness could accumulate into an infrastructure of change, gradually and nonviolently, but still become radically permanent. "We must lay one brick at a time, take one step at a time," Day entreated. "But we can beg for an increase of love in our hearts that will vitalize and transform all our individual actions, and know that God will take them and multiply them, as Jesus multiplied the loaves and fishes."[22] In this way, Day challenged religious voices like Niebuhr, who claimed that interpersonal morality was irrelevant to international relations.

Eddy, using language very similar to Day, also regarded the Delta and Providence farms as vanguard communities in a much larger local-to-global movement to transform the world, though he had higher esteem for Niebuhr and his theories about forceful justice. "The possibilities of this constructive program are staggering," he stated. The cooperative spirit certainly seemed to be on the rise in the 1930s, as communes and urban settlement houses such as Catholic Worker sprang up across the nation and the world, giving his small, rather isolated initiative in Mississippi a broader sense of purpose. "Members feel they are now part of a world movement," Eddy wrote.[23] A writer for the *New Republic* reinforced Eddy's assumption in 1937. "The Delta Cooperative Farm is a social act of strict heroism," the reporter described. "Here are men and women—disease-ridden, illiterate, exploited—conducting one of the most daring, complex, highly civilized experiments in living that the Western hemisphere has known."[24] Upon the small gains of an "ever-imperfect but improving social order," Eddy prophesized, the Kingdom "shines as a beckoning possibility and imperative that is to be partially but growingly realized here and now."[25] The Mississippi Delta projects, he believed, had made a modest but significant contribution to that eschatological mission. Encouraged by their potential, Eddy continued to sponsor small, radical community projects such as the Highlander Folk School that his acquaintance Myles Horton founded in Tennessee in 1932 (see Chapter 4).[26] Eddy's old friend Reinhold Niebuhr, who had served as president of the Delta Cooperative trustees, also lent his support to Horton, a former student.

When it came to spiritual community building and, later, issues of war, Eddy and Niebuhr fostered a collaborative friendship and mutual respect, despite their differing perspective on the Kingdom of God. The two had first met in 1922 when Niebuhr helped found a Detroit affiliate of Eddy's organization, the Fellowship for a Christian Social Order (FCSO), a left-liberal Christian critique of industrial capitalism. It did not take long for Eddy and his colleague Kirby Page to recognize the young evangelist as a talented speaker. The following year, the three men traveled together as part of Eddy's annual American Seminar, which Niebuhr praised as an enlightening means of understanding U.S. power in a complex, violent world.[27] Upon their return, Eddy and Page offered the pastor high-ranking positions in the FCSO, though Niebuhr decided to stay at his home church in Detroit.

At this time, Niebuhr still subscribed to the liberal Christian belief in the coming Kingdom of God on earth, an optimistic outlook about the ever-increasing practice of love, peace, and fellowship in the world. Ten years later, in 1932, Niebuhr published *Moral Man and Immoral Society*, a blatant attack on the notion of perfectibility within human nature and social relations. As biographer Richard Wightman Fox noted, the polemic's "chief importance" rested on its author's "biting repudiation" of the "liberal Protestant quest for the Kingdom of God." "He dismissed with utter derision the deepest hope that animated thousands of radical and liberal Christians, including Sherwood Eddy," Fox wrote.[28] Violence, war, and evil would always exist in the world, Niebuhr now contended, and only the leverage of justice, applied through coercive power, could combat these natural forces, though never completely subdue them. "The dream of perpetual peace and brotherhood for human society is one which will never be fully realized," Niebuhr bluntly stated.[29]

Not prone to pessimism regarding God's plan for the world, Eddy refused to give up on that dream. "I never saw Sherwood discouraged," Sam Franklin said of his friend. "An inner strength sustained him."[30] Eddy never gave up on the Kingdom of God, but he never gave up on Niebuhr either.[31] In fact, he appreciated the Christian realist for exposing the flimsiness of the moderate, moralizing social gospel that had been promoted by early twentieth-century liberals like Walter Rauschenbusch. The Kingdom of God would emerge, Eddy maintained, but not without a deep engagement with economic and social sources of corruption. On these terms, *Moral Man*'s "piercing insights" into the persistence of sin captured Eddy's interest and met with his approval. He had long believed, in fact, that both moderate reformers and hard-line leftists failed to engage with the flaws of human nature. Niebuhr was merely exposing this truth, not as a "pessimist," he said, but as a "realist." "[He] is one of the most merciless critics of the futilities of modern liberalism," Eddy wrote in 1955, and "also a scathing critic of Marxism as a total interpretation of life."[32]

As for Niebuhr's argument about the impossibility of extrapolating interpersonal morality to the realm of national or international politics, Eddy did not say. His entire worldview and life's work concerning the Kingdom of God certainly seemed at odds with Niebuhr on this point. Small acts of care and kindness, practiced in small communities, would eventually change the world, he repeatedly stated. "If we are to save our world from atomic destruction we must do away with war. We must build up both world community and world organization, however long the task may take."[33] When one considers Eddy's emphasis on "eventual" progress, though, the affinity with Niebuhr becomes clearer, even if his consistency as a spiritual socialist becomes muddier. Eddy believed activists had to work with the imperfect world they inhabited, not the perfect world they *wished* they inhabited. For instance, the organizers of Delta and Providence farms had hoped to challenge racial inequality, but they were forced to live with the reality of prejudice predominant in American culture. Eddy also parted ways with many of his pacifist friends, including Page, on these grounds as well. In a perfect world, war would no longer exist. In the world of the mid-twentieth century, however, Christians had to contend with forces of evil that threatened to keep the Kingdom of God from developing at all.

During World War II, Eddy kept company with Niebuhr and his "realistic" rationalizations for "just war," supporting armed intervention against Fascism and imperialism as a worthy cause of Christian conscience. Hitler and his corrupting philosophies had to go by any means possible, lest he poison the wellsprings of the new world order. In this sense, Eddy advocated war measures as a means of defending the Kingdom of God on earth and keeping alive its opportunity to flourish. The hate and evil unleashed by Fascism roved the world as dangerous, destructive forces that could ruin, in a few days, what had taken decades for spiritual socialists to build.

Day would have noted the folly of engaging in acts of violence for the sake of peace, but Eddy's writings reveal that he also understood the inseparability of means and ends. "I believe that thought and action, theory and practice, must be one," he asserted in 1934's *Pilgrimage of Ideas*. "Faith helps to create fact."[34] In another book, written in 1941, he also seemed to echo the pacifists' devotion to fostering peace, stating that Christians must "strive to build the new world order on the basis of the Kingdom of God and the democratic dream even amid the hell of war."[35] Eddy, however, never considered himself an absolutist, one bound to rigid principles. He identified instead as a pragmatist or "idealistic realist," someone who could "cultivate the ideal possibilities of the actual."[36] This open worldview set him apart with an ideology at once more flexible and less consistent than many other spiritual socialists, especially on issues of human nature and the Kingdom of God. Hesitant to make any definitive statement of belief, Eddy often chose to hedge his bets. He believed, for instance, in the "*almost* indefinite improvability of human nature." The question of whether the Kingdom of God would emerge within or beyond history was also up for debate. He continually bounced back and forth on the subject, all the while conceding that "although the perfect ideal is unattainable I must seek nothing less than moral perfection." The Kingdom of God, in other words, was worth struggling toward, in spite of prophetic blind spots and human failings. "Because it is human, it will remain imperfect, but it will bring more good to humanity than in the past. And, it will surely come," he affirmed.[37]

Henry A. Wallace, a spiritual socialist at the height of national politics, also proclaimed his faith in the coming Kingdom of God, though he agreed with Eddy that compromises were sometimes necessary in an imperfect world. During the war, he served as vice president under Commander-in-Chief Franklin D. Roosevelt, who granted him insider access to strategic and diplomatic decision making, a behind-closed-doors inclusion rarely extended to vice presidents. Wallace was not keen on war, but he desperately wanted to defeat Fascism, believing that the modern world required a practical plan for peace, one that could forestall the narrow-minded interests that threatened to reel mankind into a constant state of violence and intrigue. Politicians and statesmen, not just ministers and missionaries, he insisted, had to project a "religious purpose" by embracing a "higher law of cooperation." As he declared prophetically in his 1934 book *Statesmanship and Religion*, national purpose and God's plan were best kept intertwined: "When cooperation becomes a living reality in the spiritual sense of the term, when we have defined certain broad objectives which we all want to attain, when we can feel the significance of the forces at work not merely in our own lives, not merely in our own class, not merely in our own nation, but in the world as a whole—then the vision of Isaiah and the insight of Christ will be on their way toward realization," he wrote. "This is the only safe kind of nationalism I know for the United States."[38] In other words, Wallace did not want to win the war for U.S. power and prestige, but for mankind to realize the spiritual power of the Kingdom of God.

When the Second World War broke out in Europe and Asia, Wallace's socioreligious message seemed most prescient and more urgent than ever. Roosevelt, while campaigning for an unprecedented third term in 1940, had named Wallace, then secretary of agriculture, as his running mate. Upon winning the election, Wallace took to his new post with gusto, earning a reputation as "the busiest" vice president in American history.[39] The vice president definitely wanted to be heard, especially on timely topics of war and foreign policy that were typically beyond the purview of the office. Wallace's image of himself as a spiritual statesman had a lot to do with it. As Andrew Preston has noted, the unofficial "hierarchy" of America's civil religion positioned the president as "de facto pope."[40] Roosevelt definitely assumed this role when conveying the moral purpose of the war to the American public; and Wallace respected his commander-in-chief's crusading vigor. However, Wallace believed that he, more than anyone else in high office, understood the religious implications of the global conflict. It was more than a matter of preserving liberties; it was a fight for the fate of humanity and the Kingdom of God on earth. The grave tone of Wallace's war rhetoric is revealing. While Roosevelt invoked images of God and Scripture in his speeches about the importance of defending freedom of religion, Wallace raised the stakes much higher, framing the war as a battle against evil forces of Armageddon, with the Kingdom of God held hostage.

Henry Agard Wallace, on October 7, 1888, was born into a family known for farming and religion. His paternal grandfather, Reverend "Uncle Henry" Wallace, a former Presbyterian minister, published the local newspaper and edited an influential farm journal, wherein he offered agricultural advice and spiritual guidance to the god-fearing farm families of Iowa. Joined in journalism by his son Harry (Wallace's father), the two men launched *Wallaces' Farmer* in 1895.[41] The weekly publication made the Wallace clan so well respected among Iowans and so well versed on issues of agriculture that when President William McKinley went looking for a suitable secretary of agriculture in 1897, he tapped the shoulder of loyal Republican Harry C. Wallace, though Wallace declined the post. He finally accepted the appointment from Warren G. Harding in 1921.

Leaving Iowa for Washington, D.C., that year, Harry imparted *Wallaces' Farmer* to the capable hands of his eldest son, Henry A. From an early age, the younger Wallace had followed in his family's footsteps by taking an active interest in agriculture. He began tending his own garden in Des Moines at age ten, and by age fourteen, he was demonstrating a precocious knowledge of crop cultivation, especially corn. As biographers John C. Culver and John Hyde wrote, "Corn became his passion, his cause, the medium of his genius."[42] Wallace experimented endlessly with cross-fertilization and kept meticulous statistics on his results. In 1906, he enrolled at the Iowa State College of Agriculture in Ames, where he majored in animal husbandry. Botany, however, remained a favorite past-time, and the freshman was often found volunteering in the school's experimental corn plots. The family business, ag-journalism, also became an extracurricular outlet for his academic interests. While in college, he edited the *Iowa Agriculturalist*, and in 1909, he accepted a three-month commission from his father and grandfather to travel throughout the American West and report his observations for *Wallaces' Farmer*. By 1914, the Wallace wunderkind had earned a position as assistant editor of his father's journal. By 1920, he had published many articles on agricultural science and one book about the plight of farmers during the postwar deflation in crop prices.[43]

Young Wallace, it seemed, had found his niche, even if it fell within the shadow of his father. He possessed all the skills and talents to make him heir of Harry C. Wallace's publishing enterprise. He displayed few of the characteristics, however, that would suggest he follow his father into politics. Studious, quiet, and introverted, Wallace had the disposition of a scientist or scholar, not the garrulous, gregarious zing of the typical politician.[44]

Wallace's introspection and sensitivity went hand in hand with his deeply spiritual nature, and it was in this realm that he charted his own path. The Wallace family had always been religious. They read and quoted the Bible regularly in the home and in their newspaper columns. They attended church on Sundays and lived a life of traditional Protestant piety. For much of his youth, Wallace followed suit, accepting a formal, doctrinaire, and institutional understanding of religion. In college, however, he began to broaden his view. The writings of Transcendentalist Ralph Waldo Emerson, the mystic Ralph Waldo Trine, and the spiritual scientist William James introduced Wallace to a much more extensive and inclusive religious outlook than he had known. God, he now believed, reigned immanently, not distantly, within nature and for all creation. Religious truth, therefore, existed everywhere, with multiple paths to it. Wallace, equipped with an experimental mind-set, embraced the ecumenical exploration of books such as *The Varieties of Religious Experience*, James's famous study of mystical diversity, excerpts from which he read to his Sunday school class. When the Presbyterian elders informed Wallace that such speculative philosophy had little relevance to the standard catechism, he left the church.[45]

Wallace soon left behind another of his family's esteemed institutions, the Republican Party. During and after the war, the Republicans had convinced many Americans, young Wallace included, that they cared more for profits than people, more about pandering to the interests of big business than the needs of small business, and more about urban finance than farming. Wallace did not think much of the Democrats in this regard either. They too, he felt, had lost touch with agrarian issues and their rural constituencies in the West and Midwest. The only "people who wanted farm relief legislation," he remembered, were regarded as "radicals and crack-pots."[46] In the fall of 1924, two weeks after the death of his father, Wallace cast his vote for the only candidate who seemed to care about farm relief: Robert La Follette, the Progressive Party alternative from Wisconsin.

Wallace's enthusiasm for political experimentation paralleled his quest for spiritual experimentation during the early 1930s. Despite his misgivings about the importance of organized, formal religion, the progressive farm journalist attended Liberal Catholic, Episcopal, and Unitarian services, consecutively, none of which completely satisfied his search for mystical experience. It was not until he started studying the tribal religions of Native Americans that Wallace found the kind of devout naturalism that he had felt when reading Emerson, Trine, or the case studies of James. He also discovered a kindred spirit in an eccentric composer and didactic medicine man named Charles Roos, whom he met near St. Paul, Minnesota, in the summer of 1931 while conducting research on the area's Indian religious culture. Wallace admired Roos's extensive knowledge about Native Americans, but more than that, he appreciated Roos's "esoteric tendencies," especially the search for a no-holds-barred mysticism, which Wallace had a hard time discussing within his Protestant circle of friends.[47] As the world seemed to be falling apart around them in the early 1930s, Wallace and Roos exchanged letters and religious materials regularly, referring to each other by their acquired tribal nicknames (Poo-Yaw or Chief Cornplanter for Wallace) and speaking in a code punctuated by Indian religious symbolism. They formed a friendship in which Wallace felt comfortable enough to discuss not only his deeply held religious beliefs but also his doubts and dilemmas about the future. Most pressing, Wallace's decision on whether to pursue politics by running for the U.S. Senate or to retreat into agrarian solitude became a frequent topic in their correspondence.

On the one hand, Wallace relished the thought of living like a farmer-intellectual, spending his days tending crops on a hobby farm or perusing his library of books on agricultural science and spiritualism. As he told Roos, "I would much rather talk with you about things of the next world than of this [world]."[48] Yet the call of politics, and particularly the practical application of religious truth, rang loudly within Wallace's conscience. The financial crisis had quickly devolved into a crisis of faith as ordinary men and women struggled to grasp at some hope for relief and recovery. He regarded the Depression as a tragedy, certainly; but he also recognized it as an opportunity to build a new social infrastructure and find "the religious key note" of the next spiritual dispensation.[49]

As early as November 1931, Wallace was reminding Roos that "these are transition days and it is hard to find the right kind of a foothold in the new era."[50] Positive changes seemed imminent, but he knew that the fate of humanity remained uncertain. "Love and wisdom are gaining strength from the conflict," Wallace wrote, "altho [sic] for some years yet the issue will be in doubt."[51] Wallace believed he had something to offer, a role to play in helping accelerate the momentum of social change toward the "Promised Land," or the Kingdom of God on earth. His dream of making a "peaceful exit" to bask in the "Inner Life under the golden maple," then, would have to wait, at least until he decided how best to devote his time and energy. Politics still filled him with many misgivings, to the point of psychological paralysis. "Fate may decide that I run," Wallace resigned to say, "but it will not be my decision."[52]

On February 6, 1933, Wallace received Roosevelt's invitation to become secretary of agriculture, the same office his father Harry Wallace had held for Republican administrations in the 1920s. Wallace waited a week before accepting the cabinet post. A few days later, he penned a farewell to the readership of *Wallaces' Farmer*, recalling the legacy of his father. The senior Wallace had gone to Washington to "restore the agricultural values smashed in the decline of 1920–21," he wrote. That decline had steepened in recent years, but, Wallace acknowledged, "I have an advantage he did not have—a chief who is definitely progressive, entirely sympathetic toward agriculture, and completely determined to use every means at his command to restore farm buying power."[53] Roosevelt had made a convincing case to the native Iowan that agricultural interests were high on his agenda, and Wallace had done grassroots campaigning for him in the Midwest. Now, Wallace stood ready to help his chief executive execute a New Deal for farm relief in the most expedient way possible. "For the first time," wrote biographers Culver and Hyde, "Wallace had committed himself to the success of a politician rather than to a cause."[54]

Not quite. Wallace appreciated Roosevelt's energetic activism and commitment to the general welfare, but he ultimately considered the president-elect and the New Deal as "temporary" projections of a much deeper movement, unfolding into a new era in human history that Wallace referred to as "the Kingdom of Heaven."[55] The policies passed under the New Deal were not unimportant for Wallace in the short term, but they were unsubstantiated in the long term if unaccompanied by Americans' commitments to fundamental social change and spiritual renewal. The emergency measures of the New Deal, revolutionary as they were, could not last indefinitely, Wallace contended, if they were intended as mere political balm on the nation's gaping social wounds. Similar to Eddy, Day, and Muste, Wallace was calling for the creation of a completely new society that he hoped would "carry out the Sermon on the Mount as well as the present social machinery carries out and intensifies the law of the jungle."[56]

With his explicit references to Scripture and eschatology, Wallace did not sound like a typical politician, peppering speeches with rhetoric to appeal to religious Americans. A closer reading of his written and oral record reveals that he intended to contribute to the coming Kingdom of God in national and international politics, not merely as a New Deal liberal, offering piecemeal reform, but as a spiritual socialist envisioning a long-term revolution. He criticized the effects of capitalism but did not believe that the economic system should be immediately replaced via Marxist insurrection. Instead, he contended that economic hardships would eventually dissolve after a social revolution heralded the Kingdom of God. Wallace was willing to accept the New Deal and reformed capitalism as temporary measures to lay the groundwork for the Kingdom, just as he was willing to accept war against Fascism as a temporary fix for protecting that groundwork. The self-proclaimed spiritual statesman, however, had a hard time translating his spiritual socialist message into a viable political program that could appeal to the American masses, as detailed in Chapter 4. The obstacles did not stop him from trying to build a Gideon's Army of underdogs to undertake the task.

In January 1934, when Wallace addressed an audience at the Chicago Theological Seminary, the United States was still grappling with the most devastating economic depression it had ever experienced. Wallace knew that the stakes were high and confidence was low, especially among the millions of farmers he had tried to help stave off bankruptcy, foreclosure, and starvation during his first two years as Franklin D. Roosevelt's secretary of agriculture. The New Deal had established some makeshift "social machinery" to aid the less fortunate and correct a troubled course in times of financial crisis; but Wallace worried that without an accompanying spiritual revolution across the nation, the New Deal's sheen would soon corrode into bureaucratic dowdiness. "I know that the social machines set up by the present administration will break down unless they are inspired by men who in their hearts catch a larger vision than the hard driving profit motives of the past," he stated, in reference to the conditions of capitalism.[57] Wallace wanted to push the New Deal to its most radical potential, setting the stage for a complete change in society. He did not see it as a safety net for existing institutions and economic systems, but as a framework for the coming Kingdom of God.

The grasping greed of capitalism had caused the crash, according to Wallace; but to fix it for good, the nation needed spiritual statesmen, even prophets, to rouse Americans to build a better economic, social, and political way of life. Roosevelt had his "brain trust" of intellectuals and technocrats. Wallace, however, wanted a "heart trust," comprising policymakers who could bring economic activity under a religious consciousness and shepherd the United States away from self-interest and toward spiritual socialism.[58] Instead of sounding the despair of financial ruin, then, Wallace told the theologians in Chicago that they were on the cusp of a worldwide spiritual awakening: "The Century of Progress has turned to ashes in our mouths. Is it possible that the world is finally ready for the realization of the teachings of Jesus, the appreciation of the Sermon on the Mount, the bringing of the kingdom of heaven to earth?"[59]

The Kingdom, Wallace warned, would not come easy. "To enter the kingdom of heaven brought to earth . . . it will be necessary to have a reformation even greater than that of Luther and Calvin," he predicted. Incremental reformism, such as the New Deal offered, would not do it. Neither would legislation or superficial rhetoric. Wallace's envisioned spiritual statesmen playing important roles as stewards of national longing and facilitators of nationwide cooperation. But he also spoke for the kind of fundamental change that spiritual socialists championed, a revolution of values in the hearts of ordinary people and to the roots of human nature. "More than [administrative reformers], the men in the street must change their attitude concerning the nature of man and the nature of human society," he affirmed in the same vein as spiritual socialists such as Day, Muste, and Eddy. "They must develop the capacity to envision a cooperative objective and be willing to pay the price to attain it. They must have the intelligence and the will power to turn down simple solutions appealing to the short-time motives of a particular class."[60]

Wallace's disdain for narrow-minded politics also applied to Marxists, whom he faulted for ignoring the spiritual needs of mankind. However, he was not opposed to socialism per se. His concern for cooperation, coordination, and wealth redistribution made it clear that he shared some goals with left-wing radicals, a tendency that both colleagues and critics observed. Writing an introduction to the essay collection *Democracy Reborn* in 1944, Wallace's friend Russell Lord admitted, "I would sometimes think, hearing him talk objectives, that he was inclining toward Socialism . . . manned by intelligence, not wealth."[61] In other words, Wallace approached socialism as a spiritual process rather than a material panacea. A political cartoon published in September 1940 reflected the anxiety of conservatives who resented Wallace's seeming influence on left-of-center policy. In the sketch, the vice presidential candidate leers over Roosevelt's shoulder, discussing topics such as "Antibusiness Policy," "Unemployment," "Growing Bureaucracy," and "Dictatorship."[62] Westbrook Pegler, a journalist who would plague Wallace throughout his political career, also wrote disparagingly of this "mysterious stranger" trying to convince Americans that they had something to learn about democracy from the Soviet Union.[63] These detractors definitely did not want Wallace developing the vice presidency into an active and dynamic leverage point for the Left.

Wallace was more to the left than many of his colleagues in Roosevelt's administration. In fact, his association with the Democratic Party depended on its degree of radicalism. Wallace did not support the Democrats in the 1920s or the late 1940s, when he believed the platform too moderate. It was only in the 1930s, when the party took a left turn and, in many ways, co-opted the radicalism of socialists, that he embraced its potential and accepted a high-ranking position when offered. Perhaps thinking from a farmer's point of view, Wallace refused to reject capitalist enterprise completely. He did not see the harm in selling one's wares or produce as a small business owner for profit, though he did criticize big business for its exploitation of the common man. At a time when even the Communist Party USA leader, Earl Browder, accepted capitalism to a certain degree, Wallace's wishy-washy opinions about economic reform did not disqualify him as a man of the Left.[64]

Ultimately, however, Wallace offered an alternative to the traditional Left in both substance and method. As a national administrator and statesman, he wanted "national coordination," but not necessarily national planning, centralized and exclusive.[65] He supported the "radical" tendencies of New Deal programs that allowed "government [to] buy from those who had too much, in order to give to those who had too little," all the while cautioning against a command economy. "I see no reason as yet why we in the United States should go into precise detailed planning except, perhaps, with respect to natural resources and to certain rather small segments of our national life on an emergency basis," he stated.[66] Instead of top-down strictures and structures, Wallace envisioned a combination of federal planning and decentralized, local control to bring about the new era of national cooperation. His experience administering New Deal programs through the Department of Agriculture in the 1930s convinced him that such an arrangement could prove practical. Across the country, farmers formed committees and partnered with federal representatives to implement solutions for land conservation, price controls, and surplus management. As Wallace described, "The task of adjusting these allotments out in the counties could not have been done by Government agents. Yet the plan as a whole could not have been inaugurated without the use of the centralizing power of the Federal government."[67]

This process of shared policymaking, Wallace assured, would preserve the nation's essentially democratic character, a concern he found missing in the manifestos of Marxists. "They display a gross ignorance of the American people. They make very little appeal to our characteristic attitudes and customs; they scorn our tradition of tolerance and liberty; and they overlook our resources of ingenuity," he admonished. Rejecting a top-heavy revolution predestined for despotism, Wallace maintained his faith that local reforms could generate revolutionary change in the long run. Marxists might claim to possess the playbook of modern economic man and the inevitability of centralization, but Wallace did not subscribe to it. "The future seems more and more to favor decentralization," he concluded.[68] In his ideal economy, industrial democracies and family farms would develop and cooperate along regional lines, while the federal government would facilitate, but not tightly control, their productive activities (a federation, not Fascism or Communism). In a letter to a fellow-traveling friend, he made the distinction, protesting that the general "spirit" of socialists seemed mired in "mere opposition to the existing order." "I would like to see a sweeter spirit on the parts of the socialists," he concluded.[69] By this, Wallace meant *Christian* substance and also *democratic* method, twin instruments in the process of building the foundations of community and economic justice.

Like many spiritual socialists, Wallace walked a middle ground between traditional Marxism and a fair market. The former owner of a thriving plant-seed business saw no need to completely dismantle the prevailing economy. Instead, he championed his concept of "progressive capitalism" in articles such as "We Must Save Free Enterprise," which appeared in the *Saturday Evening Post* in 1943. Capitalism, he claimed, did not possess "inherent faults" but operational faults in its current state of control by "small, powerful, privileged groups." If the system were redirected away from its cutthroat tendencies, Wallace argued, capitalism could function as "the most efficient system of organizing production and distribution on principles of freedom and equal opportunity yet devised by man." "It should not, as many radical reformers have suggested, be uprooted," Wallace made clear. "It should be modernized and made to work," made to work for "the little man with a big idea"—small-business entrepreneurs who wanted a stake in the world of economic opportunity as well as ordinary workers who wanted their fair share of economic prosperity.[70] If private business owners refused to even the playing field, he warned, the federal government would do it for them.

Wallace's defense of free trade, in fact, had more to do with spiritual than material concerns, as he made clear in his critique of Marxists. In a 1934 article for the nondenominational *Christian Herald*, for example, he derided the revolutionaries' reckless methods, their "emotional dryness" and the "dogmatic thinness" of an economic theory that overlooked "the flesh, the blood and the spirit of the religious and artistic man." People amounted to more than just the "dry bones" of economic ecology, he reminded.[71] They aspired to live in peace and harmony, to make constructive contributions to society, and to fulfill their potential as creative and spiritual human beings. The free enterprise of capitalism, he believed, could channel those energies into something constructive and productive, with spiritual values keeping the profit motive in check. Ever the idealist, Wallace faulted both capitalists and Marxists for appealing to the basest instincts of economic self-interest, and thus perpetuating social conflict and class division. "It is a precarious business," he wrote in *Scribner's*, "to stake a whole civilization upon so simple and so fragmentary a view of human nature and human aspirations."[72]

While many critics misunderstood Wallace's economic ambiguity, some observers seemed to understand his spiritual socialism as a creative endeavor in a new direction. Writing a cover story for the *Saturday Evening Post* in July 1937, Stanley High reported that the secretary of agriculture might be on to something big. "The New Deal's premier crusader," as High described, "dreams dreams and sees visions" and projects "plenty of mysticism." Yet he also displayed a practical side, executing policy "of almost presidential proportions. No other department of the Government is so deeply indoctrinated with New Deal ideas or has so faithfully sought to make those ideas work," High wrote. "No previous Secretary of Agriculture has been able to devise a farm program substantial enough to constitute the first planks in a presidential platform." Citing Wallace's appearances on local news programs such as NBC's *Farm and Home Hour*, High told the tale of the all-accessible administrator preaching the gospel of farmer solidarity around the altar of the New Deal. The effect, other than a "major selling job for the Administration's farm policy," amounted to a nearly miraculous feat of "evangelism" that succeeding in cultivating the support and "rank-and-file participation" of 70 percent of the nation's farming constituents. "If Henry Wallace could not bring all the farmers to Washington, he did the next best thing. He brought Washington—its policies and its visions—to the farms," High reported.[73]

Moreover, the Wallace way, which High described as a combination of central planning and local control, seemed to be working. Farmers enlisted in federal programs on a "voluntary" basis and were never asked to "swallow" federal policy, but to vote for it, invest in it, and implement it on their own. According to High, "There was . . . practically no Federal policing. Instead, the job was turned over to the farmers. The farmers, with blueprints supplied by the Department of Agriculture, built their own administrative mechanism." This so-called mechanism consisted of committees and associations created in townships, each with its own board of directors and representatives sent to county-level committees, which then conferred with the home-state committees and so forth up to Capitol Hill. High called it "a hierarchy, built from the ground up." He also considered it an act of political genius. In less than a decade, Wallace has roused farmers into a powerful political bloc more united in their interests than at any time since the 1890s Populist movement. "No politician ever subjected his constituents to more intensive cultivation," the journalist claimed, using the language of grassroots activism akin to spiritual socialists.[74]

After 1941, Wallace turned his talents to organizing another major endeavor: inspiring the American people to support mobilization and the cause of the war, a cause, as he saw it, to protect the vulnerable cultivation efforts of the Kingdom of God. In his most forceful and famous speech of the era, "The Price of Free World Victory," Wallace distilled the significance of the war down to its metaphysical essence in a language more prophetic and embellished than any of his public discourses to date. At the beginning of the talk, given to the Free World Association in New York City on May 8, 1942, and broadcasted nationally by CBS Radio, Wallace defended the dignity of democracy and framed the war as a fight between slavery and freedom. Very quickly, however, the vice president carried his thoughts well beyond a rehashing of Wilsonian rhetoric to a serious summons for spiritual warfare. The notion of freedom, he reminded, was spiritual in origin, "derived from the Bible," and only expressed superficially in political terms. Hitler's move to topple political regimes and seize states, therefore, was bound to fail as long as religion reigned in the hearts of men and women around the world. "No compromise with Satan is possible," Wallace wrote.

"Strong in the strength of the Lord, we who fight in the people's cause will never stop until that cause is won."[75]

Wallace's portrayal of the enemy as "Satan" may seem bizarre and melodramatic, but his words were not hyperbolic in his mind.[76] Beneath the speechifying sound bites and biblical passages, in fact, lay a concrete understanding of leveraging morale. This was a people's fight for dignity more than a war among nations or even military machines. It was also a fight for democracy, yes, but not the kind of abstract concept that Wilson or Roosevelt had pitched. Such generalizations meant little to Wallace, who had once quipped that he hoped "to make the world safe for corn breeders."[77] Phrased another way, Wallace wanted to make the world safe for ordinary people or "the common man" (his watchword) to *develop* democracy, economically, politically, and socially, into a dynamic, daily practice. Wallace lingered on specifics: "When the farmers have an opportunity to buy land at reasonable prices and to sell the produce of their land through their own organizations, when workers have the opportunity to form unions and bargain through them collectively, and when the children of all the people have an opportunity to attend schools which teach them truths of the real world in which they live—when these opportunities are open to everyone, then the world moves straight ahead."[78]

Wallace spoke of the war in terms of people and their personal and collective security, not in terms of nations and national security. The people of the world were rising in revolution for the sake of independence and self-determination, meaning that victory against political and spiritual oppression would ultimately rise up, from those whose quest for freedom exceeded physical bounds. These grassroots revolutions, Wallace insisted, needed to be nurtured. "Everywhere the soul of man is letting the tyrant know that slavery of the body does not end resistance," Wallace wrote.[79]

Wallace hoped that victory would usher in his postwar vision of global peace and cooperation, prefiguring the Kingdom of God on earth. Peace, to be clear, did not denote pacifism. Even before the attack on Pearl Harbor, Wallace supported the drive against the German Reich. His passion for the war effort only intensified after December 1941. In an address to newly minted Army officers at the Aberdeen Proving Grounds in April 1942, the vice president encouraged the men to fight "wholeheartedly" against "the Germans or the Japs" and to "beat them at their own game." The objectives, though, transcended geopolitics. For Wallace, the war was about spiritual socialist ideas and the opportunity to implement those ideas in the postwar order. The Axis powers had their "dark philosoph[ies]," which the Allies needed to "destroy" "root and branch," he said. Achieving ultimate victory, however, meant building something new to replace it, "a decent philosophy of our own." U.S. soldiers had hardly touched boots to the ground in Europe when their vice president began composing his plans for the aftermath. He conferred a broad commission on the assembled "men at arms," calling on them to act as "captains in the peace effort . . . when the war comes to an end."[80] Like Eddy, who also supported the war effort for similar reasons, Wallace wanted to keep the momentum of the Kingdom of God moving in the right direction. Hitler and Fascism, as forces of oppression, threatened to impede that progress by replacing God with the nation-state and religious harmony with racial discord. Spiritual socialism could not long survive if communities were smothered under the bureaucratic weight of a state-centered society and democracy destroyed.

For all his concern about New Deal programs to promote the domestic welfare, Wallace rejected the isolationist positions that were popular among other progressive politicians such as Robert La Follette of Wisconsin and Burton Wheeler of Montana.[81] Neither did he seize the opportunity to enhance the anticapitalist and anti-interventionist arguments of the Nye Committee. Wallace, like all spiritual socialists, asserted a religious worldview international in its scope. Even someone like Day, who abhorred top-down solutions to interpersonal problems, encouraged international aid. "I do not believe in being isolationist," she declared in 1940. "I believe that we must hold ourselves in readiness to help with all our resources exhausted nations."[82] Day rejected any military means of assistance, but she believed that Americans had a Christian duty to alleviate the suffering of those in need, regardless of racial, religious, or national differences. Wallace, though he differed with Day's pacifism, agreed that an allegiance to transnational human values and the notion of world brotherhood compelled a commitment to help the underprivileged everywhere. His support for Allied liberators during the war and international institutions such as the United Nations afterward extended from this basic belief, as did his defense of indigenous revolutions.

Appealing to ordinary men and women around the globe, Wallace's war rhetoric did not champion the priorities of any single nation or sound the trumpet of American triumphalism that one found laced in war propaganda or in the pages of popular magazines. A February 1941 *Life* article by owner-editor Henry R. Luce, the son of a Young Men's Christian Association missionary who had worked with Eddy in Asia, had called for an

"American Century," marked by "American leadership of the world" through U.S.-directed internationalism. The European conflict, Luce argued, was not an avoidable foreign catastrophe but an irresistible opportunity to finally "bring forth a vision . . . which is authentically American." In the vein of Wilson and even Wallace, Luce clarified the principles at play. Americans would not wage war to defend U.S. territory, but "to promote, encourage and incite so-called democratic principles throughout the world." They would take to the fight on behalf of mankind, to ensure future peace and freedom from want. Unlike Wallace's vision of spiritual socialism, however, Luce projected a singularly nationalistic perspective. "America and only America can effectively state the war aims," he frankly stated.[83]

Wallace, in contrast, spoke of the United States as a nation of privilege, not entitlement. Blessed with a wealth of material and educational advantages, Americans had a responsibility to share their resources with the rest of the world. Yet Americans still had as much to learn as they had to teach. "Down the years, the people of the United States have moved steadily forward in the practice of democracy," he wrote, but "they are still learning the art of self-government." Americans, in Wallace's opinion, had not fully developed a social democracy of racial and economic equality and, therefore, did not possess a perfect political or social model for others to emulate. In direct response to the *Life* magazine article, Wallace made his objections to Luce plain. "Some have spoken of the 'American Century,'" he wrote. "I say that the century on which we are entering . . . can and must be the century of the common man."[84] Freedom-loving people in foreign lands would not accept an American system imposed on them from above, Wallace warned. Instead, they were likely to resent and reject such impertinence as another form of imperial oppression. Wallace envisioned an international form of the New Deal, providing relief and recovery to ailing nations, but not at the expense of America's spiritual standing. The United States had to practice Christian values of compassion and cooperation, he insisted, in order to earn its reputation of benevolence throughout the world.

Not everyone discerned the differences between the worldviews of Wallace and Luce. Leftist-critic Dwight Macdonald, referring to the dueling essays in his 1948 harangue against Wallace as a presidential candidate, concluded that both men condoned U.S. imperialism in developing nations, though Luce did so more "bluntly" and "without the doubletalk to which liberals are accustomed." Wallace's "passionate rhetoric" may have masked the particulars of his imperialist intentions, Macdonald explained, but his call for conquest and democratic reconstruction made him "the Woodrow Wilson of World War II."[85] An April 1941 editorial in *Christian Century* also detected a paternalistic strain in the vice president's triumphal language. Noting his rigid religious interpretation of the war as a battle between angels and demons, the author dubbed Wallace "the high priest of a new religion of nationalism" "primarily concerned with the survival of the State." Wallace's seemingly virtuous verbiage about future peace and democracy, according to the article, actually concealed a coercive edge, designed to shape the world to American specifications. In the breach between idealism and realism, the article concluded, Wallace's international "messianism becomes imperialism."[86]

Wallace sometimes did call for an outright American "missionary crusade" throughout the world, an unfortunate phrasing that both muddied his concept of democratic cooperation and caused confusion in the press.[87] During a speech entitled "Why Did God Make America?" in June 1942, for example, he described the United States as a repository of the best ideas and best intentions, chosen to advance God's plan "for the sake of all the world."[88] The next day, the *Washington Star* headlined its review of the address as "Wallace Declares U.S. 'Chosen of the Lord' to Lead World Peace."[89] The vice president certainly had "the reputation of being the most religiously-minded man in Washington." Alas, few people understood what his notion of religion entailed. Wallace did little to help matters by claiming that his credo encompassed "everything" and applied to "*all* men, all over the earth, whatever their habits of life." In an interview for the *Christian Herald* in 1943, Wallace inadvertently added to his imperialist image by saying that "religion must expand and take in a lot more territory" and project "new, broad knowledge of scientific, economic and political forces" in places such as China and India.[90] To be fair, Wallace did not charge this task to any particular faith, denomination, or institution. In fact, he did his best to dissolve doctrinal differences in a crucible of ecumenical fusion. Protestants, Catholics, Muslims, Jews, Hindus, and Buddhists, he argued, had much in common, because they all believed in the dignity of the individual soul, the value of fellowship, and the "essential unity of the entire world."[91] Wallace wanted this religious spirit to expand, not to capture *physical* territory, as his words seemed to indicate, but *social* territory in the everyday lives of ordinary people. Professing that "every minute of the day is a religious experience," the vice president encouraged his listeners to pack their time on earth with spiritual substance by practicing brotherhood and cooperation in all social activities.[92]

In this respect, Wallace was echoing spiritual socialists such as Day and Muste, though they differed markedly on the issue of violence.[93] For Muste, the way of war reflected a particular way of life—an accumulation of bad habits built into the conduct and culture of mankind. If violence, conflict, and competition in routine social relationships stoked the fires of international strife and military arsenals, then the revolution in values must begin at this source, at the interpersonal level in one's local community. "Daily, in humility and love, we must show forth toward all men and in all relationships the power of that life which 'taketh away the occasion of all war' . . . in those 'little fellowships of the holy imagination, that keep alive in men sensitivity to moral issues,'" Muste wrote. Wallace and Eddy believed this too, but they were willing to defend these "little fellowships" with violence when necessary. Muste insisted that the means must match the ends. "Only religious pacifism," he argued, could foster a socialist society by "build[ing] a movement which goes to the root of evil in man and in society, a movement which men will trust and which can take over when the war is ended or has run its course."[94] Though he sounded overly idealistic, even naïve, Muste believed he grasped the situation more realistically than most. Any national or international renunciation of war would amount to a "miracle," he acknowledged. That is, unless the system underwent complete reprogramming.[95] He had tried the shortcuts, and he had found them wanting and wasteful. "There is no cheap and easy way out," he avowed in 1941.[96] Victories on the battlefield did not translate, for him, into victories of spiritual warfare, because those battles had to be fought at the grassroots level, in daily social relations. "Fighting back does not change things essentially," he warned. "At most it may reverse the role of the top dogs and the underdogs."[97]

Unlike the practitioners of Realpolitik, Muste did not dismiss spiritual faculties as a form of soft power. He considered it, instead, as the most potent form of strength and authority that the nation could wield. "Spiritual forces are as real as physical or military," he stated.[98] This projection of spiritual power, however, had to have substance, not just superficial rhetoric at the national and international levels. It needed to be cultivated carefully everyday, so that it could eventually percolate to the top echelons of policymaking. On these terms, Muste challenged the so-called realism of religious thinkers such as Niebuhr, who argued against the moral accountability of nation-states.

In an open letter to Niebuhr in 1948, Muste blamed the Christian realist's 1932 polemic *Christianity and Crisis* for conceiving a "theology of despair" that had duped would-be moralists into rationalizations of violence and war throughout the 1940s.[99] Muste had a hard time believing that "America's foremost theologian" could interpret the gospels so inaccurately and offer "counsel which is no whit different from that which we may hear from enlightened secular sources." Both Marxists and Christian realists, he noted, shared a misconception about human nature as fixed, fated, and incapable of creating good in the world. Both suffered from the same fatalistic mind-set about inevitable, immovable forces of nature and history. Both also advocated violent means to enforce a small measure of justice in the meantime, before the respective, doctrinal, world-ending "catastrophe" would take place.[100] This sort of thinking Muste recognized as remnants from nineteenth-century theories about mechanical ontology or social engineering, paradigms of "the system," and the search for external solutions to existential problems. Muste had come to expect such dated and detrimental messages from atheist radicals, but he demanded more from Christian voices who marshaled their evidence from living Scripture. To him, neo-orthodox theology and its cousin, Christian realism, were "in essential respects" "un-Scriptural" and "not fully Christian." He could appreciate Niebuhr's disdain for self-righteous postulations about mankind's ability to reform the world without God. Given its extremely "negative" assessment of human potential for moral progress, however, Christian realism represented "a source of the gravest danger to the Church and to mankind today," Muste wrote.[101] Like the Communists he deplored, Niebuhr, in his "defeatism," failed to recognize the religious context for social change.[102] Muste's theories of projecting "spiritual power," however, offered an alternative perspective about the potential for nations to act morally in the world.

During the 1940s, Muste's public expressions of pacifist thought seemed standard enough, given that the nation and the world were at war. Yet the deeper meaning of pacifism, in its communal context, was always on his mind. Hitler and his German army had broken faith within the international community by committing acts of evil. Muste did not disguise his disgust for the Fuhrer's regime. "I want to blot out fascism and Nazism from the face of the earth," he baldly declared in a speech in 1940.[103] He did not believe, however, that violence would restore the spirit of community or overcome evil. A military approach might destroy Hitler as an individual, in the most immediate physical and material sense, but it would not solve the deeper spiritual problems that made a dictatorship like his possible. "Killing Hitler and his associates is not going to rid the world of Hitlerism," he avowed. "To think that any fundamental change in international relations is going to be accomplished by executing people is a childish idea. You don't get rid of an idea by killing the people who propound it."[104]

Christians and Christian nations, Muste argued, would not gain much traction in the battle of ideas by meeting Hitler on his own terms, in a showdown of martial force. Instead, Christians needed to claim the moral high ground and undermine the dictator's appeal to a people desperate for collective belonging. If Hitler offered the German masses a sense of national pride and military strength, Muste wanted to offer them a universal alternative, a sense of unity with the entire human race and not just with the Aryan race. A brotherhood of man should be beholden to God the Father, not the Führer. "What the world needs today is to take the spiritual initiative away from Hitler. And that cannot be done by copying him and his methods, but by opposing to him an utterly different ideal, an opposite dynamics and method," Muste exhorted.[105] Succinctly put, Muste wanted to replace military and political power with *spiritual power*, a concept he began to develop during World War II but would express more explicitly in the postwar era. In the early 1940s, he could only decry the lack of spiritual values on the international agenda. "The trouble with the world today is precisely that men have come to believe that 'the only means which work are material ones, and the only goal attainable is material,'" he lamented in 1942.[106]

Unfortunately for Muste's purposes (and later for Wallace's presidential hopes), spiritual socialists could not count on many Christians to reject immediate, material solutions in the midst of an international crisis. The mainstream ministry had always tended to reinforce the nation's military mentality with combat-mode homilies during wartime (or they had been pressured to resign their positions as dissenters). World War II was no exception. The fight for justice against evil empires threatening to encompass the globe became a ready justification for American military response, especially after the Pearl Harbor attack. As Muste wrote about abolishing war in 1942, he conceded, "It may well be that now . . . this cannot be done save through small groups of men and women who austerely renounce outward things, strip down to the bare essentials, and [give] themselves to the task of 'purifying the springs of history which are within ourselves,' and to 'that secret labor by which those of little faith rise, first of all in themselves, the level of mankind's spiritual energy.'"[107]

This focus on the primacy of inner transformation does reveal a point of distinction between Muste's means to the Kingdom and that of Wallace and Eddy. Eddy, as shown above, believed that institutional or structural change had to occur before men and women could express, fully, their selfless virtues. Muste, on the other hand, argued that individuals needed to foster a moral sensibility first in order to revolutionize society at large. Spiritual socialists never reconciled this "chicken or the egg" debate, which amounted to a subtle inconsistency rather than any rigid variance. At the very least, they agreed that these radical changes should start at the most primitive source of interpersonal relations, the local community, and culminate in the Kingdom of God on earth.

The moral makeup of the world in general, according to Muste, depended on what people chose to cultivate in the particular. "We will not get another kind of harvest unless we sow another kind of seed," he said succinctly. This meant that the motives of individual men and women in their daily behavior toward neighbors, coworkers, and employees mattered in the grand scheme of things. "Men who are autocrats and lovers of power in their own souls will not build a democratic world; men who are essentially self-seekers will not build a cooperative commonwealth," Muste explained. Unlike Niebuhr, however, Muste recognized the potential for growth in another direction. "It equally follows that men who have entered into the spirit of community will inevitably be driven to seek to give expression at once to their inner spirit in economic relationships."[108] Society, in short, reaped what it sowed. With this simple principle, Muste challenged Niebuhr's basic belief in moral action for particular cases, but not in general. "I don't see myself how we can believe it in the realm of personal relationships and not believe in it in the larger social relationships," Muste concluded.[109] Stated reversely, he also did not believe that war internationally could result in peace at home.

Surely, the agriculturalist Wallace would have understood the principles of cultivation that Muste used to express his pacifism. At times, Wallace even sounded similar notes of concern about achieving peace through force. "I am sure that, unless continuous, strenuous, and united efforts are made to attain economic justice, it will be impossible to prevent military war by any type of force. Force is important—but it is not enough," he acknowledged in a 1943 interview with the *Christian Herald*. The vice president of a warring nation, the crusader against the evils of Fascism, believed with Muste that Americans must recognize and cultivate spiritual power in order to reap the rewards of the Kingdom of God on earth. "When you speak of the dirt of the earth you speak of a holy thing; the ground whereon thou standest is holy ground, for God is there. When you hold a kernel of wheat in the hollow of your hand you hold the very handiwork of God. Be most careful with it," Wallace advised. "We must learn to use the heavenly powers that are about us to serve the cause of practical, useful living here on earth."[110]

Timing mattered differently to each man, though each acknowledged the long-term struggle toward a perfect society. In the 1930s, as New Deal programs made piecemeal progress toward relief and recovery, Wallace reminded Americans that the Kingdom of God would not come easily. Rejecting all "short-cuts to the Promised Land," he asserted that "it is simply impossible for us to let go overnight of the habits and beliefs of a lifetime."[111] Habits and beliefs were the pivot point of Wallace's entire worldview, just as they were for spiritual socialists such as Muste, Eddy, and Day. Change hearts, change habits, change national culture, and thus change the world—that is what Wallace envisioned. And, like his fellow spiritual socialists, he believed that only religious values could work as a transformative agent, prompting people to do good in their daily lives and local communities. "Religion to my mind is the most practical thing in the world," explained Wallace. "In so saying I am not talking about churchgoing, or charity, or any of the other outward manifestations of what is popularly called religion. By religion I mean the force which governs the attitude of men in their inmost hearts toward God and toward their fellow men."[112]

A change of heart, therefore, needed to accompany a change of economic condition lest the flaws of human selfishness persist in the new order. "Enduring social transformation is impossible of realization without changed human hearts," reminded Wallace. Yet if people took to the "daily discipline" of practicing religious and democratic values, the very means of social cooperation would engender the equivalent ends.[113] "So enlisted, men may rightfully feel that they are serving a function as high as that of any minister of the Gospel," Wallace explained in 1934. "They will not be

Socialists, Communists or Fascists, but plain men trying to gain by democratic methods the professed objectives of the Communists, Socialists and Fascists: security, peace, and the good life for all." Any attempted shortcuts were ultimately dead-ends of wasted time and energy. Better to build a lasting foundation able to stand the test of time. "The experimental method of democracy may be slow, but it has the advantage of being sure," wrote Wallace. "When you change people's minds you change the course of a nation."[114]

President Franklin D. Roosevelt, it should be noted, spoke a similar language. In his 1939 State of the Union address, for example, the president identified religion as the primary foundation for democracy throughout the world. "Religion, by teaching man his relationship to God, gives the individual a sense of his own dignity and teaches him to respect himself by respecting his neighbors," he explained. This concern for others, in turn, facilitated the practice of democracy, which Roosevelt described as a "covenant among free men" at both the national and international levels. Roosevelt and his second-in-command may have shared a similar "faith-based vision of politics and [world] peace," but the Episcopalian president never expressed his hope for the coming Kingdom of God on earth as explicitly as Wallace.[115] Perhaps his acute political sensibilities made him hesitant to speak in terms that might seem impractical or even delusional. For many, of course, the idea of a perfected society seemed preposterous. Wallace disagreed, claiming that such an ambitious course had never been tried. "No truly fruitful effort has been made to bring the kingdom of heaven to earth in terms of social justice," Wallace lamented in 1934.[116]

By saying this, Wallace was criticizing the halfway measures of the New Deal, which he believed scratched only the surface of America's social problems. While Wallace recognized "the religious fervor with which the New Deal has been launched" and the "potentialities" of its programs, he insisted that "it will take a more definite recognition of the Grand Architect of the Universe before the apex stone is finally fitted."[117] New Deal policies represented the letter of a new law, but not the spirit of a new age, and thus fell far short of Wallace's ultimate aims. Even *Saturday Evening Post* reporter High, who focused primarily on the secretary of agriculture's political genius, caught the drift of Wallace's spiritual direction: "He is a great believer, not only in the ordinary religious sense but, more particularly, in regard to the destiny of society. The New Order is a major article of faith with him."[118] Wallace, in other words, wanted more than a New Deal; he wanted an entirely New World Order. Roosevelt, gifted in the art of the possible, never went quite so far. He remained content to promote a civil religion geared toward political harmony, while Wallace prophesized the effects that social religion could have on altering the course of human nature and human history.

To get there, Wallace argued, reformers and revolutionaries would need to address the spiritual needs of their fellow man and confront the roots of social behavior in small, interpersonal communities, where people lived in mutual support and for shared benefits. Such was the site of Jesus' ministry. He had preached and practiced values of fellowship and cooperation in the context of community, not in formal religious institutions, but out in the fields, streets, and public commons. Wallace meant to bring this primitive spiritual socialist consciousness into the modern age. As he wrote in a 1936 article for *Christian Century*, "Jesus did not concern himself with social action in the modern sense of the term. In the first place he lived in a society in which the local community was almost entirely self-supporting . . . which means that most social action was chiefly local, neighborly decency."[119] At the community level, one could care for the sick, visit the lonely, and help those in need of help without the barriers and abstractions of bureaucracy. Community action also offered an outlet for human energy, creative expression, and the universal need to feel needed. "Many of the most lively, intimate expressions of spirit spring from the joyous, continuous contact of human beings with a particular locality," Wallace professed. He encouraged his readers to "think of cooperative communities not merely in a competent commercial sense but also from the standpoint of people who are helping unfold each other's lives in terms of the physical locality and tradition of which they are a part."[120]

The Christian message and the practice of Christian values in communities seemed particularly suited for times of economic and social crisis. New Dealers worked hard to refashion economic policy and administer material relief in the 1930s, but the spiritual needs of the nation, Wallace claimed, remained unmet. Only a "powerful religious attitude concerning the entire social structure" could help bind people together in common cause and shared interests, thus thwarting the tendency toward desperate measures of crime and violence.[121] "Perhaps Jesus Christ did have a more significant message on the remedy for [economic] depression than Adam Smith," Wallace speculated.[122] True democracy, whether economic, social, or political, paralleled Christian tenets in a number of ways. Both practices required cooperation and concern for the general welfare, placing community interests above self-interest. Wallace knew it would not be easy. In fact, he frequently referred to the serious obstacles on the "long tortuous" course of personal and social transformation.[123] "Humanity in a small community is not always lovely," Wallace observed. "Many petty meannesses will develop" and "all too often the emphasis is on the things which divide rather than on those which unite."[124] In a culture of social welfare, however, he believed these difficulties were bound to dissolve. "The pettiness of small communities will disappear as their economic disadvantages disappear," he assured.[125]

For the hard task of making economic disadvantages disappear, Wallace assigned the government and its leaders an important role. "It is the job of the government, as I see it, to devise and develop the social machinery which will work out the implications of the social message of the old prophets and of the Sermon on the Mount," he wrote.[126] In other words, there was a ghost in the political machine, and for Wallace, it was the Holy Ghost. The government had to enforce equality and fair play from the top down while awaiting the development of the Kingdom of God from the bottom up. For if the system were fair, if policies of social justice could root out the "bitterness, prejudice, hatred, greed and fear" that governed the actions of mankind, then that "tiny spark of divine spirit found in each individual could be fanned into an all-consuming flame."[127] As such, Wallace based his faith in the coming Kingdom not on changes in human nature per se, but on the cultivation of innate capabilities kept dormant by the current social, economic, and political climate. The most important job of a spiritual statesman, the image he had of himself, was to maintain social justice in an imperfect world until the Kingdom of God had time to catch up.

A similar line of thinking guided Wallace's assessment of the war and the need for U.S. intervention against Fascist aggression. If good men and women stood by and did nothing, then evil and corruption would poison the social well beyond repair, making it nearly impossible to set society on course for the Kingdom of God again. A show of force at the international level, in other words, would save the grassroots efforts from getting trampled underfoot. As a lifelong corn cultivator and farmers' friend, Wallace understood that a productive harvest relied on work at the ground, at the level of soil, as well as a favorable climate, those highest elements that could make or break the yield. Day, in her aversion to the state, left such chancy matters up to God. Wallace, however, put more faith in national and international governments to act in good faith for the many, not the few.

Wallace was willing to wait until after the war to get back to cultivating the Kingdom, telling reporters of his postwar plans "to start expanding religion and to get down to earth with it." "What we will need then will be men to whom religious faith is a matter of this world as well as the next," he said in an interview with the *Christian Herald* in 1943.[128] Muste and Day, however, thought the world needed that kind of commitment now, not later. "It seems to me," Muste wrote in 1936, "that one must be a romanticist capable of flying in the face of all the evidence to believe that such a war, under modern conditions, will be the portal to socialism or higher civilization or whatever one may prefer to call it. Rather must it set back the clock for generations, if, indeed, it does not involve the total eclipse of Western civilization."[129] Once again, Muste recognized the futility of shortcuts or the postponement of practicing Christian principles. "We must indeed resolutely refuse to be tempted to violence," Muste wrote in 1941, "[for] that is the short cut which invariably turns out to be the blind alley."[130]

While Wallace feared that the triumph of Fascism would force the Kingdom workers to start over, Muste claimed that a resort to violence had already done so. "Unless the world experiences a spiritual rebirth," Muste warned in 1942, "there can be no good peace after this greatest and most destructive of all wars."[131] Whether he realized it or not, Muste was speaking to Wallace, and he was prophesizing the political missteps that Wallace would make in his assumed postwar role as peacemaker. World War II, according to Muste, had set humanity to the march of war, and it would take more than pronouncements about amity and goodwill from politicians to alter its momentum. Back in the mid-1930s, Wallace had seemed to agree. Writing in *New Frontiers*, he stated that "this vague new world has thus far been approached chiefly by restless, romantic men who feel that the vast riches of a cooperative good life can be attained suddenly by making a speech on the New Deal, by electing some one [sic] to Congress, by writing a book, or by passing a law. All these things may be part of the necessary pioneering but the work that finally counts will be slower, less romantic and infinitely more difficult."[132]

These were the words of a spiritual socialist resigned to the reality of constructing a new world order from the bottom up, no matter how long it might take. But, for Muste, that meant standing firm in the discipline of matching means with ends. The war's Christian supporters, he judged, had dropped the ball, making the shift to a Cold War mentality all but inevitable, because Americans had been primed for half a decade to salve fears with violent solutions. Progressives like Wallace might talk about harmonious postwar relations, but Muste predicted that such lofty orations were bound to fall on ears deaf to notions of strength through diplomacy, security through cooperation, and peace at all costs, in the same way that Wallace had been deaf to those ideas for the duration of the war. In the late 1940s, Wallace would make his bid as a spiritual statesman for the highest office in the U.S. government; but he ultimately could not preserve the Popular Front, let alone promote the brotherhood of man in a time of international crisis.

CHAPTER 4

The Religious Left and the Red Scare

Despite the end of World War II, tense international relations continued to occupy the thoughts of spiritual socialists in the early Cold War era. Henry A. Wallace, who was replaced as vice president by Harry S. Truman just before Roosevelt's fourth inaugural and April 1945 death, peppered his 1948 presidential campaign with religious rhetoric and a call for mutual understanding and cooperation among the United States, the Soviets, and decolonizing nations. The Progressive Party platform that Wallace ran on also condemned free-market capitalism, racism, and the American aversion to social welfare, all within the candidate's particular religious context. Throughout his Progressive Party campaign, Wallace continued to measure policy by the ethics of the Kingdom of God, even as many of his Communist followers did not believe in God or moral, democratic politics. While an increasingly anti-Communist political climate in the late 1940s and the 1950s branded Communism, socialism, or any "ism" of the Left as a threat to the American way of life, Wallace did not change course, a complexity that disrupts the Communism versus anti-Communism dualism that historians have relied on to understand the 1940s and 1950s. For better or worse, Wallace welcomed anyone into his fold who professed at least a nominal interest in social revolution.

And Wallace *was* speaking of revolution—not an insurrection triggered by a violent or hasty contingent from the top down, but a long-term vision of social cooperation and equality, cultivated from the bottom up. Spiritual statesmen, he realized, could never coerce the populace to enact values of Christian love and fellowship. To the contrary, the Kingdom of God had to be made practical, springing from a source of basic need for "local welfare," and built on a "voluntary social discipline" among Americans who would carry out a revolution in values as "living reality." In other words, he wanted democratic socialism practiced as a way of life and as a religion. "I suppose the thing which I am arguing for fundamentally and eventually is a continuous, fluid, open-minded approach to reality, which at the same time is deadly in earnest," Wallace summarized.[1]

Whether he knew it at the time or not, Wallace had pinpointed, in that statement, the crux of a problem that would plague him for the rest of his political career. How could he, as a spiritual statesman, maintain a hard-nosed but liberalizing agenda and persuade people to stay the long-term course toward the Kingdom of God during short-term crises? Roosevelt was not much of a model. During the Depression, he had closed the gates on international cooperation for the sake of national recovery. During the 1940s, he traded his New Dealer hat for Dr. Win-the-War's helmet, much to Wallace's initial dismay. The emerging Cold War was also cold comfort for Wallace, whose pleas for "one world" of brotherhood and peace amounted to little more than a faint moralizing echo across the bipolar vacuum that he accused Harry S. Truman of steadily filling with tough talk and military buildup.

Running for president in 1948 as a left-liberal alternative to Truman, Wallace had a hard time translating what he called the "cloudy and vague" language of Kingdom idealism into practical policy, especially when national security seemed at stake.[2] Like Pope Celestine V in *Story of a Humble Christian*, a novel by former Communist Ignazio Silone, Wallace discovered that moral absolutism did not dovetail with presidential pragmatism. Truman won the campaign because he ran on a platform fitted for his time; Wallace lost because he ran on a platform projected for *all* time. The lifelong farmer's friend and corn-growing expert was not in it for quick fixes of national interest or incremental reform. He wanted to cultivate a spiritual revolution across the world.[3] For many American voters, however, the Red influence surrounding the former vice president represented a serious threat to democracy and civil liberties. Communists, in the American mind-set, would never foster community building. They would impose Soviet-style autocracy and, most likely, the agenda of the Kremlin. Wallace did not adequately address the Communist presence within his campaign, a failing that made him appear at best naïve and at worst insincere. He strongly believed that he could convert hard-core Communists into a "Gideon's Army" of religious Democrats once he revealed to them the spiritual roots of their socialist values.

He was mistaken. The positive changes in human nature that he and his spiritual socialist supporters insisted were possible had not yet come to fruition, especially among secular, power-oriented radicals. He could not convince Americans to embrace his vision of the coming Kingdom of God while associating with atheists, just as he could not dissuade fears of Soviet infiltration while sympathizing with the Soviets. Given the Cold War climate, it was much easier for national candidates like Truman to convince voters to contain the world rather than liberate it, to arrest fundamental change rather than embrace it, and to accept a divisive political philosophy rather than a unifying one. Americans could not or would not take Wallace seriously as a practical politician once his associations with Communists became known. However, Wallace's failure to appeal to a wide electorate also stems from his inability to project a concrete religious framework as national policy. His abstract language sounded rhetorical when many voters wanted realism. His elite position at the top echelons of traditional political institutions, moreover, did not model a down-to-earth model of grassroots, moral reform. In short, he talked the talk but did not walk the walk.

Wallace's career helps illustrate the viability of spiritual socialism in national politics; but it also tells us something about the American Left and the limits of its religious rhetoric in the realm of foreign policy. In policy debates on domestic issues, such as welfare, labor, and civil rights, spiritual socialists gained some traction by appealing to the moral and religious sensibilities of the American public. The role of religion as jeremiad and leverage in the civil rights movement at midcentury, for example, has been noted by many scholars. Activists such as Robert Moses, Bayard Rustin, and Martin Luther King Jr. demanded fundamental change as a logical necessity of Christianity and democracy, utilizing concepts of religious radicalism that they had learned in black churches and in organizations such as the Highlander Folk School, founded by spiritual socialist Myles Horton. The civil rights movement, in fact, became a new, dynamic outlet for spiritual socialist expression that had been hindered by anti-Communism since Wallace's 1948 campaign. But it too had its limits, especially when it came to criticizing foreign affairs or trying to radicalize international organizations such as the United Nations. Civil rights activists had much more success leveraging the Cold War contest toward reforming domestic issues of race and class than it did projecting spiritual values onto foreign policy.[4]

The road became much rougher, indeed, when attempting to convince Americans that peace, love, cooperation, and democracy should extend to international relations, especially toward perceived enemies like the Soviet Union and other Communist nations. To be effective after 1948, American leftists had to shed any semblance of Communist affiliation. Religious rhetoric helped. Spiritual socialists, who had always placed religious values above Marxist dogma, set the moral tone of the postwar Left, as it struggled to survive the Red Scare and the Cold War. What emerged in the 1950s was a "New Left" that focused more on local action, human values, and the spiritual needs of mankind.[5]

This New Left, of course, did not consist solely of religious radicals, but also included independent radicals such as Dwight Macdonald and Irving Howe, who had become disillusioned by the corrupt and amoral operations of Stalin's regime. They founded fresh journals of leftist thought, *politics* and *Dissent*, respectively, which focused on resetting the moral foundations of socialist values. Though they did not employ explicit religious language in their writings, Macdonald and Howe found common cause with spiritual socialists, such as Dorothy Day and Silone, who were intent on providing a moral and humane alternative to Communist doctrines. Despite the intensity of the Red Scare, spiritual socialists continued to make radical change on domestic issues more amenable to Americans without compromising their socialist ideals. They had been doing it for decades, before the non-Communist Left coalesced in the 1950s, and, consequently, they were often recognized as forerunners of a New Left politics.

Wallace, for one, was willing to build a Gideon's Army of religious radicals, though his support of intervention and unconditional surrender in the early 1940s made his sudden peacemaking agenda in the late 1940s suspect to many who feared Soviet aggression. During World War II, Wallace had relished his role as spiritual statesman, a role the vice presidency enhanced in terms of audience and impact. His tenure in that office, however, came to an abrupt end in 1944, when Roosevelt allowed the Democratic convention to nominate a new running mate and would-be vice president, Harry S. Truman. Historians can only speculate as to the reasons why Roosevelt decided to accept his party's preferences without a fight. Wallace's well-publicized disputes with cabinet members such as Secretary of Commerce Jesse Jones on issues of war production, many claim, contributed to his demotion.[6] Religion also may have played a part. Wallace's penchant for mysticism and unorthodox piety was well known; but a series of bizarre letters he allegedly wrote to Theosophy luminary Nicholas Roerich during his spiritual experimentation in the late 1920s and early 1930s threatened to expose him as a crank.

The so-called guru letters in which Wallace addressed Roerich in reverent, if peculiar, mystical code fell into the hands of Republicans during the 1944 campaign and soon hit the press circuit, where reporters such as Westbrook Pegler and Walter Lippmann pressured the vice president to admit or deny their authenticity. Wallace successfully dodged the questions, but the episode tarnished his image as a national politician.[7] Mainstream Christians could not relate to his broad and numinous sense of religion, even if it reflected his commitment to democracy and diversity. Yet Wallace's willingness to accept a variety of religious viewpoints, no matter how atypical, revealed a level of tolerance rare among politicians. Roosevelt had defended Wallace's spiritualism on these terms against critics in the past. But in 1944, it seemed, Wallace's mystical indiscretions had finally made the president nervous. Whatever the reasons, Wallace was out. As Gardner Jackson later recalled, "The machine politicians of the Democratic Party, who gagged when Roosevelt forced Wallace down their throats as Vice-Presidential candidate in the 1940 convention, had by this time determined he was a political liability. With the approach of the 1944 convention it was clear they had persuaded the President of this also."[8]

Given his choice of cabinet posts after Roosevelt's reelection, Wallace picked the Department of Commerce where he could bump out his rival Jesse Jones and exert more power on his bête noire, big business. Wallace's reputation as a left-wing anticapitalist immediately rankled conservatives and complicated congressional approval of his appointment. Only a year earlier, for instance, the vice president had "drawn blood" in the business community when he publicly depicted Washington, D.C., as a "subsidiary" or "way-station" "of Wall Street," an explicit censure of money interests and their propensity to wag the dog of American democracy.[9] Wallace maintained his intentions to "save free enterprise" by reforming it into a kinder, gentler institution of fair wages, fair prices, and fair trade. However, this plan for "progressive capitalism," as Wallace called it, did little to placate investors and CEOs who feared interference from a socialist-leaning secretary.[10]

As it turned out, Wallace did not make any major changes to economic culture or the Department of Commerce, especially because his time in the cabinet was foreshortened by a series of unfortunate events, beginning with the death of President Roosevelt in April 1945. Wallace now answered to a new executive and commander-in-chief, Harry S. Truman, who occupied the position that Wallace would have inherited had he continued to serve as vice president. Despite his rather discourteous demotion in 1944, Wallace had remained loyal to Roosevelt, whom he credited with the creation of a new era and a New Deal, for not only the United States, but for the entire world.[11] The Atlantic Charter and Four Freedoms did not strike Wallace as convenient wartime rhetoric; they represented to him an international extension of the New Deal for the common man, and the next stage of spiritual dispensation. Wallace's concept of the New Deal remained complicated, of course, going beyond liberal reformism. He considered it the conditioning for the Kingdom of God, not its culmination. But it was better, he believed, to build New Deal institutions as a stopgap than to abandon the world to the whims of amoral leaders and their power politics.

Addressing the Democratic National Committee in early 1944, Wallace insisted that "Roosevelt has never denied the principles of the New Deal and he never will. They are a part of his very being."[12] They seemed to remain part of the president's spirit even after death, at least according to Wallace, who continuously eulogized Roosevelt's legacy in tandem with his own social and political vision. Wallace, in short, saw himself as the true heir and spokesman of the New Deal, not Truman, a machine-dispensed politician who could execute the New Deal's liberal-reform policies, but never understand their true spiritual socialist potential. Wallace had been afforded access to domestic and foreign policymaking to a greater degree than most vice presidents in U.S. history. He had been privy to inner-circle conversations about war, peace, and postwar priorities. Truman, in contrast, was a newcomer to the executive office. Some high-profile observers agreed. At a memorial service for Roosevelt in 1946, Treasury Secretary Henry Morgenthau Jr., for one, introduced Wallace as "the one who more than anyone else is carrying on the spirit of the late President."[13]

Truman's limitations were nowhere more obvious to Wallace than in the realm of foreign relations. Indeed, the new president's blunt posturing at the Potsdam Conference and his increasingly militant threats to curb seeming Soviet aggression in Eastern Europe alarmed Wallace considerably, especially because he still regarded the Russians as wartime allies. He hoped to make them peacetime allies as well, arguing that cooperation was crucial to the development of any enduring postwar peace plan. As Wallace proclaimed in 1942, "In order that the United Nations may effectively serve the world, it is vital that the United States and Russia be in accord as to the fundamentals of an enduring peace based on the aspirations of the common man."[14] With Soviet tanks occupying Poland, it was difficult for many

Americans to see how the Russians were maintaining their end of that equation. Wallace pleaded for patience—patience to allow diplomacy and dialogue to smooth over differences, and patience to empower the United Nations to resolve territorial disputes. Otherwise, he feared, war would erupt between the United States and the USSR, and the world would plunge back into chaos. Truman, Wallace believed, was threatening the postwar peace plan before it had been tried.

In 1946 and 1947, Wallace was not alone in this belief, as progressives and liberals from around the nation criticized Truman's policies. Sidney Hillman, Henry Morgenthau, Max Lerner, Michael Straight, Claude Pepper, Robert F. Wagner, Frank Kingdon, and even Eleanor Roosevelt were initially part of the pack that put pressure on the new administration for an amiable approach to postwar problems. Many even mentioned Wallace as the most obvious political alternative to Truman in the 1948 Democratic nominating convention or, if need be, as a third-party candidate. At this point, Wallace was not ready to consider such drastic measures. He was still a cabinet member, an inside man, who could exert influence on the peace from within the ranks, just as he did while he was vice president during the war. Such was the impetus for Wallace's controversial address at Madison Square Garden on September 12, 1946.

Taking the stage to "talk about peace," the secretary of commerce spoke more about the dangers of war, particularly the dire consequences that new developments in airpower and atomic bombs could cause for the world. "Another war would hurt the United States many times as much as the last war," he warned. From there, Wallace went on to assess America's shameful race prejudice as a precondition for international violence. "Hatred breeds hatred," he stated. "If we are to work for peace in the rest of the world, we here in the United States must eliminate racism from our unions, our business organizations, our educational institutions, and our employment practices." In other words, Wallace was arguing, once again, that social behavior at the international level reflects social behavior at the local level. There was, however, a middle stratum, a national altitude where statesmen had the opportunity to transcend the people's petty prejudices and project moral principles into the world. Without referring to Truman by name, Wallace made it clear that he considered the president a failure in this regard. "We are reckoning with a force which cannot be handled successfully by a 'get tough with Russia' policy. 'Getting tough' never bought anything real and lasting—whether for schoolyard bullies or businessmen or world powers. The tougher we get, the tougher the Russians will get."[15]

Whether or not Wallace knew he was undermining the president remains open to speculation. Earlier that morning, he had at least attempted to review the content of the speech with Truman, who apparently gave his blessing. The president may have been too preoccupied with other matters to realize that Wallace's words contradicted the policy tone of the Department of State. Those who heard the speech, however, did not miss its implications of dissent. The next day, the *New York Times* felt the need to reiterate throughout its article outlining Wallace's argument that he had the approval of the president, as if to remind its readership that the secretary of commerce was not as defiant as he sounded.[16] The *New York Herald-Tribune* also expressed confusion about the nature of Truman's consent in a press conference the next day. Though reporters confirmed with Truman that he did not consider the speech a departure from official State Department policy, the *Herald-Tribune* added that "diplomatic quarters in Washington were startled by the President's indorsement [*sic*]." Secretary of State James Byrnes, they speculated, "might take it amiss."[17]

Earlier in the year, Joseph Alsop and Stewart Alsop of *Life* magazine had editorialized that Wallace, though well meaning, should stop stirring the confusion, "which now afflicts American liberalism" with his "irresponsible intervention[s]" in U.S. foreign relations. They concluded that Wallace had only two options: "to resign or to remain silent."[18] After the controversial and divisive Madison Square Garden speech, Truman presented Wallace with the same ultimatum. A week later, Wallace resigned from his post in the cabinet, his anger evident. The president had rejected his expert advice in foreign relations, even while Wallace believed he had a moral alternative to offer the American people. Before long, he would seize the chance to become a spiritual statesman, preaching and implementing his radical vision from the Oval Office, instead of administering piecemeal reforms from the executive cabinet.

Even as secretary of agriculture in the 1930s, Wallace had claimed a "bias" toward global issues and, ultimately, the creation of the Kingdom of God *on earth*, not just in rural Iowa.[19] He respected local activism, but believed firmly that cooperative communities also possessed world-changing potential, a point that Wallace made repeatedly in his plea for international peace. Wallace as a postwar planner did not intend to choose between local, national, or global politics, because he envisioned them tied together as interrelated links in a great chain of cooperative development. Small communities were part of a larger context, Wallace reminded his constituents. Consequently, they should make decisions "with reference to the national and world community." Spiritual values were bound to broaden the local lens. Instead of thinking in terms of personal welfare and narrow regional interests, the citizens of cooperative communities, he hoped, would view themselves as contributors to the general welfare and benefactors for the well-being of their fellow-man abroad as much as their next-door neighbor. "Out of these communities gradually developed will slowly emerge many cooperative ideas of profound significance to the New World," Wallace prophesized in the mid-1930s. "Such communities will be strung like many-colored beads on the thread of the nation and the varied strings of the beads will be the glory of the world."[20]

In short, Wallace believed in going global by going local, a prescription he also applied to national policies. "Our nation must serve itself by serving the world," engaging in those "ageless operations that bind all humanity together," insisted Wallace. Those "ageless operations" amounted to a spiritual quest for unity and cooperation in global terms as well as a political process that transcended the traditional claims of patriotic duty.[21] Wallace's "war against [the] barriers that divide mankind," as Russell Lord phrased it, was one waged for God and his Kingdom of God on earth.[22] On this theme, Wallace stayed very clear and consistent. Calling for an ecumenical approach to economic and political matters, he denounced "any religion" that does not "of necessity have grave questionings concerning those national enterprises where the deepest spiritual fervor is evoked for purely nationalistic, race or class ends."[23] If Christ did not recognize the man-made divisions that kept people from caring for one another, Wallace insisted, then neither should his followers.

Wallace wanted people to be involved in others' lives in a process of sharing and mutual support. However, he did not advocate paternalism or imperialism, two foreign policy positions he went to great lengths to oppose. "No nation has the God-given right to exploit other nations," he insisted. "Older nations will have the privilege to help younger nations get started on the path to industrialization, but there must be neither military nor economic imperialism. The methods of the nineteenth century will not work in the people's century."[24] It was up to the citizenry of each developing nation to decide whether it wanted industrial materials. If so, Wallace held, the United States should do its duty to assist them. If not, the United

States should stay out and allow other nations to pursue other methods of production. "Exploitation and discrimination, like the old dollar diplomacy, are things of the past," he stated.[25] Wallace admired the primitive agricultural know-how of the world's pastoral people, a way of life he witnessed firsthand during his travels throughout Latin America promoting Roosevelt's Good Neighbor Policy and while visiting Siberia and China in 1944. In fact, Wallace recommended improved, nonmechanized farming techniques as a path to progress as much as he did industrialization. "I think it is necessary for some of us at least to get a little closer to the farm," he told soil conservationists in 1942. Billions of people in China, India, and Latin America, he continued, "have the direct first-hand contact with the soil in the way that we have not. They have many things to teach us. We have some things to teach them."[26]

Wallace's "people's revolution," as he described it, would take the form of a gradual change in international relations, toward a world in which powerful nations no longer played power politics with the less fortunate. He did not promote an immediate uprising in the vein of Lenin. Neither did he favor the protectorate system of Woodrow Wilson. Modernity had made the world an interdependent "neighborhood" or "human family," and only cooperation among equal partners for the general welfare could secure peace. It seemed pointless to fight and win the war, he argued, if the resulting armistice allowed "an international jungle of gangster governments" and "money-mad imperialists" to continue their "old tyranny." Wallace included the United States among them. He urged his countrymen to seize the opportunity to set a moral example for the world in terms of race and class relations, education, and economics. "We cannot assist in binding the wounds of a war-stricken world and fail to safeguard the health of our own people," he stated in his speech "America Tomorrow."[27] In other words, the Kingdom of God or the practice of spiritual socialism must begin at home before it could make a global impact.

To some critics, such as Dwight Macdonald, Wallace's vision "combined provincialism and internationalism in a bewildering way."[28] They did not understand Wallace's intention of cultivating changes in social behavior and values from the local level to the international arena, or they simply chose to dismiss such plans as naïve. One journalist, however, did recognize the deeper substance in the vice president's message. Writing for Wallace's future employer the *New Republic*, the author agreed with many liberals that "internationalism cannot be had without binding commitments on the part of America to a world community." Yet Wallace, he said, went further on this point than his colleagues in the administration. "It is hardest of all to see what Wallace sees—that even binding political agreements and legal commitments cannot hold together the structure of world peace unless the *underpinning* is there, in the form of economic health both in America and in the world as a whole."[29] The "underpinning" or social fabric, stitched together by spiritual cooperation in hundreds of communities and nations, was crucial to the success of any lasting postwar peace. That's precisely what Wallace wanted to get across, and it echoed his opinion about the New Deal as mere "social machinery" unless accompanied by grassroots change.

Not that Wallace rejected international institutions of regulatory power. In fact, he threw his full support behind the newly forming United Nations as a forum for democratic participation and as a legal instrument for enforcing international law. Cooperation between the United Nations and its diverse delegates, he assumed, would operate much like it had between the Department of Agriculture and local farm committees, each contributing to the process of planning and implementation in a "graded hierarchy of New England town meetings."[30] As a result, a new manifestation of democracy would replace tyranny in the postwar order. "The new democracy by definition abhors imperialism," Wallace stated unequivocally. That did not mean it would reject the use of force. The United Nations, Wallace knew, needed teeth, a method of dispensing hard power in cases where treaties and entreaties failed to curb aggression. "Willingness to support world organization to maintain world peace by justice implemented by force is fundamental to the democracy of the common man," he explained.[31]

This new international body, Wallace seemed to say, would burn the candle at both ends, maintaining peace and justice from the top down, while also fostering a spirit of cooperative social behavior from the bottom up. The first mission required the use of coercion. The latter precluded it. "You can't put Christianity into power by force," Wallace warned in the late 1940s. "If you do try to put it into a supreme position by force, the result is not Christianity but something else."[32] Clearly, the United Nations represented more than just a political organization to Wallace; he considered it a temporary facilitator of the coming Kingdom of God on earth. "This world was meant to be one world, and while it is proper that there should be the greatest diversity in unity yet there is a spiritual fellowship which means something so definite in terms of the brotherhood of man that it must of necessity be expressed to some extent in outward form."[33] The United Nations, he hoped, would give the Kingdom of God space to grow by promoting peace and harmony among nations. Once people learned to practice peace and harmony in all social relations, however, the United Nations' police enforcement functions would dissolve, no longer necessary.

It took over a year for Wallace to declare his candidacy as a progressive third-party alternative to Truman, and by the time he did so, the rising anti-Communist vehemence in the United States had reached the point where it was difficult for a politician to say anything conciliatory about the Soviet Union. Wallace's alliance-building overtures during the war had earned him a reputation as being pro-Russian. Now, in late 1947 and early 1948, he was denounced by many Americans as a puppet of the Soviet regime. Wallace *was* sympathetic to the Soviet experiment and often stated, like Sherwood Eddy, that Americans had as much to learn about economic planning from the Russians as the Russians had to learn about political democracy from the United States. The two nations, he suggested, were imperfect halves of a larger project to bring justice to the world.[34] The Soviets were not evil, Wallace insisted, and certainly did not deserve harsher treatment than did the imperialist Brits; they were just misunderstood and mistrusted. Thus, where many Americans saw Soviet aggression, Wallace saw insecurity. Where Wallace saw strength in cooperation, many critics saw weakness in appeasement.

As Communists began filling the ranks of Wallace's Progressive Party campaign, many left and liberal observers became increasingly concerned about the candidate's fitness for the presidency. The left-of-center but fiercely anti-Communist intellectual Dwight Macdonald, for one, referred to Wallace as an "apologist for Stalinism" whose "Stalinoid ghost writers" tailored his speeches to the party line.[35] Contemporary observer Gardner Jackson, however, disagreed. In August 1948, he clarified that "it is not a Communist Party campaign. [It] is a Wallace-seeking-his-destiny campaign."[36] More accurate still, it was a campaign that Wallace considered a God-given destiny, not for himself per se, but for American society and the world.

Wallace's role in this divine plan, as he saw it, was to act as a spiritual statesman, arousing the masses to vote their hope, not their hate (as liberal Hubert Humphrey would later quip in his own bid for the presidency twenty years later). The campaign promoted the cause of postwar peace, but Wallace had a much more ambitious mission than aversion to war. He wanted to advance the Kingdom of God from the smallest communities to the most complex international networks. Reminding readers in his column in the *New Republic* that "the essence of Christ's teachings is Peace and the bringing of the Kingdom of God on earth," Wallace reproached organized religion for failing to apply these principles in daily life, "in their dealings with all the peoples of the world," even those with whom one disagrees. "I very much question whether a person can be a true Christian or a real democrat if he belongs to a church—or to any other group—which excludes people from membership on any arbitrary ground," he declared, no doubt referring to demands that he prohibit Communists from contributing to his campaign.[37]

Wallace considered it a severe violation of civil liberties and Christian fellowship to deny someone the freedom of political expression. He might not subscribe to the "hard, bony" tenets of the "Communist religion," which he dismissed as a violent and misdirected surrogate of religion.[38] But he believed these activists had a right to be heard, especially since they demonstrated a passion for real social change. Civil liberties aside, Wallace also needed a strong showing of public support to challenge Truman, even if it came from the far Left. He did not consider himself a Communist fellow-traveler, but a Christian pilgrim who would eventually convince hard-line radicals to soften their socialist agendas with spiritual substance. Even Stalin, he assumed, was susceptible to the power of moral suasion. Wallace, therefore, did not mind Communists in his campaign. If anything, he believed they were fellow-travelers of *his* political philosophy, not the other way around.

In fact, winning the election, for Wallace, meant more than voting polls; instead he wanted to win the hearts and minds of the American people toward his particular vision. He seemed to care little for the strategizing usually involved in winning high-profile political elections. Campaign aides complained that their candidate fell asleep during discussions of political strategy and knew nothing about left-wing tactics.[39] Wallace's lackluster approach, however, did not emerge from a sense of political defeatism in this ill-fated run for the presidency. He had always valued the long-term process of social and spiritual change over short-term political gains. His moral message would survive, he presumed, whether he won this particular election or not. The important thing was to spread the gospel as far and wide as possible, a reminder to Americans that they could choose the Kingdom of God rather than the Cold War.

Understanding Wallace in these terms also complicates claims that the Progressive candidate represented an ill-fated attempt to maintain Popular Front liberalism in the early Cold War era.[40] Wallace displayed a Popular Front mentality in some ways, especially in his admiration for economic democracy, his disdain for Fascism and unregulated capitalism, and his interest in dissolving doctrinal differences. However, he preferred the term "progressive" over "liberal" and advocated a radical transformation of society, not mere reformism. As he distinguished in a 1943 interview: "It is good religious practice to feed the hungry and give drink to the thirsty and clothes to the naked. It is still better religion when men cooperate together to create an order of life in which nakedness, hunger and thirst become more and more impossible."[41] Wallace's issue with the New Deal pivoted on this very point; he witnessed the programs provide temporary relief, but not a fundamental change in social relations.

Seen from certain angles, then, Wallace resembled a man of the Left, but not necessarily the "Old Left" of the 1930s, which focused mostly on matters of class, labor, and secular struggles for political power. Wallace, in contrast, preached his gospel of God's kingdom to *everyone*, from the housewife, to the banker, to the farmer, to the soldier, to the racially oppressed, and to every common man and woman around the world whom Marx marginalized as the lumpen proletariat. This ecumenical outlook ultimately hamstringed the Progressive campaign, which did not appeal to a specific constituency or construct a politically shrewd strategy. Farmers, labor unions, progressives such as those in the Americans for Democratic Action (ADA), and African Americans by and large decided to stay with Truman and the Democratic Party rather than defect to a candidate with good intentions but vague promises. As Macdonald succinctly put it, "The friend of humanity in general turns out to be the friend of nobody in particular."[42]

In fact, Macdonald's most poignant critique of Wallace pointed to this very shortcoming. Macdonald disliked Wallace's association with Communists, to be sure, but his objection to the candidate's mixed company also stemmed from a frustration with Wallace's fuzziness, a style of impersonal and abstract rhetoric that Macdonald called "Wallese." "There is nothing personal about his writing," Macdonald concluded. "[He] never analyzes a problem; he barges around inside it, throwing out vague exhortations" like the "principal of a progressive school addressing a parent-teacher meeting."[43]

Vagueness plagued Wallace in the eyes of many potential supporters on the anti-Stalinist left and made his apologies for the Soviet regime even more conspicuous. Lewis Coser and Irving Howe referred to the Progressive candidate's "unbelievable capacity for high-sounding and musty generalization," dismissing him as a sincere but naïve man, "enveloped in a mist of progressive rhetoric yet uncertain as to his own ends."[44] Communists, they charged, also sensed the intellectual void and welcomed the opportunity to fill it with pro-Soviet propaganda. Macdonald also sounded a note for political precision in his 1947 critique, writing that Wallace deals in "rhetoric which accomplishes in fantasy what cannot be accomplished in reality." Such disparaging comments from those on the left were not just petty cuffs about the quality of semantics; they were potent expressions of a much deeper problem with Wallace. His saccharine generalizations undermined his radical credentials. Calling Wallace "a Man of Paper," Macdonald associated him with other superficial liberals, who wasted their time "habitually mistaking intentions for achievements, words for actions." Compared to true radicals such as Dorothy Day or Mahatma Gandhi, Wallace fell far short. "When Wallace wants people to do something, he makes a speech or writes a book," Macdonald explained. "When Gandhi does, he does it himself—as in his campaign against the salt tax."[45] Given Macdonald's positive assessment of Day and Catholic Worker, it is clear that he favored religious radicals who applied their idealism in daily life. Wallace, however, did not follow through.

Socialist Party leader Norman Thomas had similar complaints about Wallace's hypocritical record of direct action for the "common man." Acknowledging that socialists "would agree" with "many of the planks of the Progressive Party," Thomas chastised the former New Deal administrator for his foot-dragging aloofness to the plight of the Southern Tenant Farmers Union in the 1930s. While Wallace worked as secretary of agriculture, Thomas, Eddy, and the poor tenant farmers of Memphis appealed to the department for justice against discriminating white landowners. At that time, the secretary of agriculture played politics very well, refusing to rock the boat with his boss, Roosevelt, who needed to placate white southern anxiety about New Deal reform. Now, Wallace, as Progressive champion in 1948, had just completed a campaign tour of the South, bringing much-needed attention to the poverty and discrimination that blacks faced in segregated communities. For Thomas, however, Wallace's overtures were too little too late. He could not forget the "shameful mishandling of the problem of sharecroppers and field hands, the poorest Americans" in the 1930s when Wallace "lagged behind the better of his colleagues in serving the cause of racial equality."[46]

Despite Wallace's ardent calls for direct action in local communities, he participated very little, personally, at that base level. He did not "go to the people" or work alongside them like Day, sharing their struggles as equals in the fight for justice. When he did interact with the common man, he did so from a place of rank and privilege, as secretary of agriculture, vice president, or presidential candidate. He spoke to them and wrote to them as a sympathetic but distant spiritual statesman or prophet of the coming Kingdom. Wallace, in short, played the part of the elitist in his own anti-elitist philosophy. Macdonald said as much when he referred to the hero of progressive causes as an "oratorical gasbag." "Wallace as always made little connection between his general political philosophy and his specific policies," he wrote.[47] He failed, in the eyes of many potential supporters, to practice what he preached.

Though Wallace repeatedly promoted his ideals as practical planks (enumerated in the Progressive Party platform, for example), he seemed, at times, to be well aware of his limitations in the field of direct action. The "new frontier" or "new world" he so desperately wanted to see emerge from the matrix of hardship and hope in the 1930s required seaworthy, practical "vessels" to get there. Yet he left it up to the next generation to build them. "Few past the age of fifty like to think of building such vessels," he admitted. "That is left for youth. I think the youth of America is about ready to try it."[48] Wallace was more than willing to act as spiritual overseer, and he even hoped to plant a few seeds along the way. The hard work of cultivation, however, would take place at the local level, in the lives of ordinary men and women. In part, his understanding of democracy demanded such an arrangement. So did his respect for God's plan, which he saw as a longterm process of continuous human cooperation. One man could not expect to do all the work himself, but one man could inspire others to stay the course for the Kingdom of God. As he put it years later, "The common man is on the march, but it is up to the uncommon men of education and insight to lead that march constructively."[49]

Wallace did his best to offer the people a peaceful, constructive alternative to any future wars, but he spoke of "timeless truths" that were ultimately ahead of his time.[50] He knew this in 1933, in 1941, and in 1948, a fact that helps explain his lack of discouragement when confronted with the dismal political results of his bid for the presidency. The Progressive Party received only 1.1 million votes in November, finishing in fourth place behind Truman, Dewey, and the Dixiecrats. Wallace had failed to garner enough grassroots support from a broad range of people. Instead, he had his "Gideon's Army," a biblical reference to a small but mighty group of God's followers.[51] Wallace's following was indeed small, consisting primarily of those progressives associated with the *New Republic*, *PM*, the Progressive Citizens of America, and other independent voters. Of course, there were also the Communists, whose presence most contemporaries and historians have faulted for alienating non-Communist liberals and leftists from the campaign.[52] The Communist variable, in fact, makes it difficult to discern whether Wallace's message and the cause of spiritual socialism actually failed as a political platform. Voters saw red instead of a rose-tinted vision of Christian utopia that the Progressive candidate was trying to project.

Thomas choose not to clasp hands with the Progressive Party candidate for many reasons, including Wallace's poor record with tenant farmers in the 1930s, his interventionist position in the 1940s, and his reluctance to embrace a more radical position on national planning. Wallace's progressive capitalism, the Socialist Party president claimed, did not present a "definite philosophy of cooperation and integrated planning."[53] On this point, at least, Thomas acted a little unfairly. As early as September 1932, Wallace was urging then-candidate Roosevelt, via Henry Morgenthau Jr., to devote his time to crafting a major speech on the topic of national planning or, as he sometimes called it, "national coordination."[54] But Wallace stopped short of full federal ownership for the same reasons as Thomas, namely the threat to democracy and individual autonomy that such a top-heavy system posed. Neither candidate wanted to replicate the worst aspects of Soviet Communism in American society, though they insisted that social experimentation remained necessary. Communists, according to Wallace, were corrupt but redeemable, a belief that allowed him to continue working alongside them. Thomas was less certain.

Perhaps more than any other failing on the part of Wallace and his campaign, Thomas found this, the alliance with Communists, the most difficult to overlook. Instead of challenging their ethical blind spots, a willingness on the part of Wallace to completely forgive Communists their faults would only invite more aggression, Thomas claimed. Thomas, a staunch antiwar advocate if not absolute pacifist, also seemed to support

A. J. Muste's contention that the Roosevelt administration's way of war had ceded the moral high ground to the Communists in the postwar world, just as U.S. intervention had done during World War I. "[Roosevelt] dropped the inadequate idealism of the Atlantic Charter for the emotional ideal of unconditional surrender, a negative method of capitalizing on war's hates," Thomas argued, implicating Wallace. For Thomas, as well as for Muste, the knee-jerk reaction to join and then rationalize international violence represented a betrayal of moral values. Once those moral standards were dropped, Thomas lamented, it was nearly impossible to reclaim them as a stopgap against the worst tendencies of humankind. As he stated in *A Socialist's Faith*, "It was the kind of failure which, by blunting the idealistic and humanistic elements in democratic socialism and denying its claim as a living witness to world-wide fraternity, enormously handicapped its recovery and progress. This failure gravely injured those attitudes and convictions upon which democratic socialism depends. It gave weight to those factors in Marxism which emphasized social conflict in terms of amoral struggle for power."[55] In other words, Roosevelt and Wallace had sacrificed moral idealism on the altar of a "means to an end," thus giving free rein to Soviet Communists to act accordingly. Wallace, Thomas implied, felt bound to cooperate with Communists because he no longer occupied an ethically superior position from which to criticize them. The Socialist Party president, therefore, felt obligated to accept another nomination in the national arena in 1948 as a viable alternative to both hard power (Truman) and those soft on Communism (Wallace).

Thomas, however, could get caught up in his anti-Communism with language similar to that which Wallace deployed in his anti-Fascism. For instance, Thomas declared that "tolerance, liberty, decent respect for individuals, have been plants of slow growth. If they should be crushed in Western Europe and America, it will be long before they can grow again." By saying this, he was echoing the rationalization for force against Hitler that peppered Wallace's speeches on the need to defend democracy and the Kingdom of God. The difference hinged on Thomas's refusal to consider war and violence as suitable strategies. Instead, he called for a "positive policy of well-being which logically offers a constructive alternative to war."[56] For that enterprise, Thomas the erstwhile minister was willing to give religious values a chance to help redeem a world in peril.

Wallace's loss also exposed the Left's disarray, as independent, non-Communist radicals such as Irving Howe and the supporters of the Socialist

Party refused to bridge a coalition with Wallace and his campaign Communists. In failing to appeal to the non-Communist Left, Wallace also missed an important opportunity to inspire a religious-left movement that could have meshed nicely with his national politics. In fact, even secular socialists such as Howe and Thomas were open to the notion of religious values underpinning a socialist society. The popularity of Silone among independent radicals attests to the point. Silone, a literary theorist who prepared them to accept the radical potential of the civil rights movement, became a lodestar for leftists trying to realign around morals and grassroots action at midcentury.

Born at the turn of the twentieth century in the mountainous, and rather poor, southern region of Italy, the Abruzzo, Silone, orphaned after a devastating earthquake, was sent to a Catholic monastery, but he soon recoiled from the conservative, even corrupt, character of the Church, which failed to practice its professed principles. Instead, Silone found his "safety exit" from the "unbearable solitude" of moral powerlessness in the workers' movement, and he quickly climbed the ranks of the Communist Youth International.[57] By age twenty he was directing the publication of its weekly newspaper. A year later, 1921, he participated, along with Antonio Gramsci, in the founding of the PCI, or Italian Communist Party.

Although he suppressed his doubts about strict party ideology for the sake of solidarity, Silone found the "spiritual adaptation" or "conversion" to party organization "harsh and painful." "It was not easy," he later confessed, "to reconcile a spirit in moral mutiny against an unacceptable long-established social reality with the 'scientific' demands of a minutely codified political doctrine." Silone's loyalty to the Soviet-led party was eventually shattered by the party's degeneration from ethical standards. Liquidating dissent, consolidating power, and forging a war alliance with Hitler's Fascist regime were not the hallmarks of a new moral order. Along with thousands of other heartbroken radicals in the 1930s, Silone broke his allegiance to Stalin and ultimately to the Communists. "The day I left the Communist Party was a very sad one for me," he recalled. "It was like a day of deep mourning, the mourning for my lost youth."[58]

Silone soon realized, however, that the morals and ideals of his youth were not entirely lost and neither was his faith in the basic premises of socialism. He began to write about a reconstructed form of social solidarity and fellowship, expressed in social actions, not dogma. He wrote novels, such as *Fontamara* and *Bread and Wine*, featuring reformed radicals who discover the power of religious values. And he wrote essays like "The Choice of Comrades," which appeared in the winter 1955 issue of *Dissent*, encouraging disillusioned leftists to return to the roots of their beliefs, and begin again there. Addressing "The Choice of Comrades" to "certain kinds of people" who "find themselves in a state of spiritual vagueness and ambiguity," Silone called for a "reassessment" of "human behavior," a line of inquiry that Communists, in their political theorizing, had not thoroughly considered. Silone wanted to break the cycle of nihilism that had gripped so many radicals, even to the point of suicide. To do so, he argued that activists needed to place social success above political success. "Political regimes may come and go," he said, but "bad habits remain." In the same vein as the American spiritual socialists who grasped his meaning, Silone presented a vision of socialism in which one's comrades were not defined by occupation, party, or ideology, but instead were "human beings suffering and struggling against a common destiny."[59]

Conceiving of spiritual socialism from the bottom up, Silone contended that radicalism never really stemmed from "philosophical or scientific conviction," but from an "indestructible element deep-rooted in man" that manifests, at some point, in a "simple instinctive revolt against family or social surroundings," the crux of daily life. Consequently, he continued, the poor in rural Italy and elsewhere did not require Marxist-Leninist doctrine. They could glean their worldview from the soil of their farms, the problems of their communities, and the moral values of their religion.[60] Silone animated his literary narratives, therefore, with the everyday struggles and experiences of the Abruzzi peasants, the lumpen dregs of society, not the industrial proletariat romanticized by the Marxists. Factory workers, Silone insisted, were not the only oppressed members of society and they were not destined to serve as a morally pure vanguard. A true socialist society would develop only after all people, including peasants, were treated as equals. Silone acknowledged that most peasants were politically passive and, like anyone, morally imperfect. Yet he maintained that "when the occasion demands," ordinary folk "are capable of exceptional acts of generosity and courage."[61] In his 1933 book *Fontamara*, the unlikely hero, Berardo, "dies not for himself, but for others," inspiring his fellow villagers to discover their political agency and replace the fatalist "What did we do this for?" with an echo of Lenin's provocative question "What is to be done?"[62] Likewise, Luigi Murica, the Christ-like figure of *Bread and Wine*, convinces his comrades that "the beginning [of political revolution]" is "being together without being afraid."[63]

Evoking religious language and imagery, Silone maintained that "the union of the poor assumes an eschatological force." The Kingdom of God may not seem imminent, but, in the tradition of radical Christianity, "the expectation of a third age of the human race, the age of the Spirit, without Church, without State, without coercion of any kind . . . has never disappeared from Southern Italy." Conflating the Kingdom of God with socialist utopia, Silone remained committed to a prophetic vision: "an egalitarian society, sober, humble, benign, based on man's spontaneous charity."[64] "My faith in Socialism has remained more alive in me than ever. In its essence, it has gone back to what it was when I first revolted against the old social order . . . an extension of the ethical impulse . . . to the whole domain of human activity, a need for effective brotherhood, an affirmation of the superiority of the human person over all the economic and social mechanisms which oppress him . . . an intuition of man's dignity."[65] Scientific theories and political movements would come and go, Silone affirmed, but Christian values of human worth and fellowship provided permanent anchors for socialist solidarity. "I do not conceive Socialist policy as tied to any particular theory, but to a faith," Silone wrote in 1949. "On a group of theories one can found a school; but on a group of values one can found a culture, a civilization, a new way of living together among men." Expressing his hope that socialism would endure the traumas of the 1920s and 1930s, Silone concluded, "I do not think that this kind of Socialism is in any way peculiar to me."[66]

Silone's assumption proved prescient, as his testimonies of Communist corruption and spiritual redemption offered hope to thousands of demoralized socialists. By deconstructing socialism down to its fundamental roots in human experience, Silone revealed a naked moral impulse, a spiritual source so primal that it captured universal meaning "for a generation beaten and baffled, clinging with its fingertips to the edge of an ideal."[67] He taught radicals such as Muste, Day, Howe, and Staughton Lynd that in order to move forward and confront the dilemmas of radical politics one must first go back and reaffirm basic values—values that could dissolve boundaries of creed, class, or province, and guide political action when ideology failed. Anticipating a common theme among emerging New Leftists, Silone also addressed the "myth" of the proletariat, and the assumption that workers, as an abstract group, would implement a moral society. Some could be like "Christ," he acknowledged, while others behaved more like the criminal "Barabbas." With those odds, humanity could not put its faith in one particular group. Instead, it had to reach a broader base, at the very heart. "Since it is no longer class that decides, but conscience, we are back where we started," he wrote, in reference to the bedrock of basic values. Highlighting the fundamental belief of spiritual socialists, Silone claimed that "few people realize that the tyranny of means over ends is the death of even the noblest ends." In other words, the desired ideal must be practiced in the process of getting to it. Radicals would reap what they sowed.[68]

Howe, one of those refugees "belonging to no church or political party" in the 1950s, became one of Silone's most enthusiastic promoters in the United States, circulating his essay in the anti-Communist collection *The God That Failed* and publishing Silone's articles, such as "The Choice of Comrades," in *Dissent*, established in 1954.[69] In the 1950s, Howe and Silone discovered a shared desire to reclaim the moral core of socialism in the wake of Communist corruption. Howe had grown up in a Jewish neighborhood in the West Bronx, where he developed a commitment to working-class, secular politics. Yet the Italian novelist who wrote about Christian peasants in Italy spoke, in some fundamental way, to Howe's condition. "No more . . . than Silone could avoid the subjects that had chosen him, could I avoid his work once it had chosen me," Howe recalled in his memoirs. "His questions were also mine."[70]

Howe too wondered what could be done about socialism once the myths of Marxist theory had been revealed. The voice of Silone that resonated with him offered some insights, speaking of a socialism that seemed much more "organic" and "natural" to the problems of ordinary people in ordinary life. Done with dogma, Howe appreciated Silone's simplicity, his morality, his attention to values. Silone set his theoretical framework in the dynamic space between ideological doctrine and flimsy humanism, and his socialism went beyond compassion by suggesting social strategy—how to treat each other as family members and also perform the actions of compassion (what Day would call the works of mercy). In this way, Silone, according to Howe, provided a useful map or compass for wayward radicals, "theories" that were "indispensable for locating oneself," giving "the geography of society meaning and perspective." Of course, Silone's theories reduced to Christian values, and, though not a Christian, Howe did venerate these values in a concrete sense, just as he could respect Christ as a heroic human being dissolving the false dualism between means and ends. With his "pilgrimage of deeds" and religious sensibility, Silone helped Howe realize that the "tension between moral standards and practical behavior . . . can be resolved, if at all, only in practice."[71] And, as Silone argued, the means and ends of socialism amounted to primitive religious practice.

Though the *Dissent* editor admired all of Silone's works, it was Silone's second novel, *Bread and Wine*, first published in 1936, that stood out as the most inspiring. Howe called it Silone's "masterpiece."[72] Day and Lynd (see Chapter 5) also claimed it as a favorite. According to her diary, Day was reading *Bread and Wine* on June 15, 1937, about a year after opening the first hospitality house in Manhattan.[73] She remembered later feeling an intense "comradeship" with the Italian-Catholic novelist, whose trajectory from political to spiritual socialism so resembled her own. Silone's message also hit home, quite literally. In the Catholic Worker communities, she was practicing the values of primitive socialism and Christianity on a daily basis, in the breaking of bread and the sharing of wine. New York City was not rural Italy, and the Bowery poor were not peasants, but the conditions were similar. Most of the men who frequented the Catholic Worker houses were ragged and hopeless creatures leading miserable lives. Yet communion, for Day, had transformative powers in its amalgamation of spiritual and material intimacy. Suddenly, these destitute men were no longer strangers; they were like brothers. Day, therefore, understood Silone's message explicitly. It was of a socialism filtered through spiritual, not political, means. It was about the social side of socialism. And it was about the revolutionary potential of religion.

Even secular socialists such as Howe or Thomas did not reject religion outright. Though Thomas, a former minister, had long since relinquished his faith in a personal God or the Church as a progressive institution, he kept the door open for spiritual socialism. Writing in his 1951 book *A Socialist's Faith*, he pondered that "if, as an old professor of mine used earnestly to argue, 'religion is a deep sense of values transcending quantitative measurement,' then I think religion is necessary to the good life and to the good society." The "good society" he equated to socialist society, an ethical system based primarily in human values and the dignity of human personality, which needed to supplant the corruption of Communism and capitalism, two systems that mostly sowed conflict and hate. Democratic socialism, Thomas insisted, had to do better, facilitating better human relations in order to build a better world. That, he said, would begin with a basic recognition of man's spiritual capacities over their material motivations. "To meet [the challenge] requires a conscious acceptance of 'values transcending the material.' In so far as religion helps us to find, to measure, and to serve those values, it has a great role to play," he stated.[74]

Howe concurred, acknowledging the role that religious values could play as moral substance in a socialist society. His admiration for Silone and his spiritual socialist novels in the postwar period made it clear that religion, in a broad sense, was not the barrier keeping him and other independent leftists from supporting Wallace's campaign. In fact, Howe, in his memoir, accepted a positive connotation of religion similar to Thomas's use of the term in *A Socialist Faith*. "If by 'religious' one means here a faith for rational men and women, in behalf of which they can devote their best efforts even while remaining aware that the ultimate goal may never be fully realized, then yes, you can say a socialist belief has a 'religious' component," he conceded. "But then," Howe continued, "so does any other serious political view."[75] Howe's problem with Wallace pivoted instead on the issue of Communism and the Progressive Party candidate's seemingly naïve association with amoral radicals. The point is important, because it illustrates the disarray of independent leftists and a potential religious-left movement in the late 1940s. The religious Left and its fellow-travelers from the socialist ranks could not get their act together on issues of international relations, even when a self-appointed spiritual statesman like Wallace offered to lead them, as a Gideon's Army, into national influence. In the eyes of many, however, he seemed more like a false prophet leading progressives like lambs to the slaughter.

Eventually, Wallace did regret his choices. Two years after his failed presidential campaign, Wallace broke with the then openly pro-Soviet Progressive Party over the issue of war in Korea, which Communists blamed on U.S. aggression. Wallace held Russia equally culpable for the conflict. In fact, his public statements were increasingly critical of the regime he once commended as having peaceful intentions. While giving an Easter sermon in 1950, Wallace spoke of the resurrection of Christ as "the triumph of the spirit over force." "Neither Russia nor the United States has learned this lesson," he said. Both were using militant and material means to accomplish spiritual ends (relieving the suffering and oppression of the people). Eventually, he hoped, the state powers would realize their mistakes and recognize the value of religious agency; but he warned that the Russians might get there first. "Russia may yet put into practice more of the teachings of Jesus than the United States. . . . If so, all honor to the Slavs."[76]

After the loss of 1948, Wallace retired to his farm in New York. He did not, however, retreat into obscurity or abandon his political pulpit. Realizing that the Cold War era had made Jesus' message of peace and love "almost subversive," he continued to act as a spiritual socialist, calling for local action in the small towns, on the small farms, and in the modest homes of America.[77] "We must bring a much higher percentage of our population closer to the land so that the bulk of the children may be raised in closer contact with growing plants and animals," he advised. "Surely a small house molded by the loving care and artistic instincts of a woman is an approach to the Kingdom of Heaven on earth—as nearly as may be the human answer to the Lord's prayer. This is doubly true if this small house is not crowded up against other small houses in deadly uniformity."[78] He also continued to link local activism to international relations. "We lost Cuba in 1959 not only because of Castro but also because we failed to understand the needs of the farmer in the back country," he argued. The same mistakes, he said, seemed to be happening in Vietnam.[79]

Some observers, such as H. H. Wilson, writing the introduction to the 1965 publication of *Gideon's Army*, also made that connection, lamenting that a Wallace win in 1948 could have changed the global landscape for the better. "The Progressive party," Wilson stated, "was an attempt by some of the ablest, most conscientious and devoted Americans to make the country aware of the implications of Cold War policies." Afterward, he continued, open, public debate dried up into conformity while U.S. foreign policy "has brought us to the brink of disaster."[80] Wallace, who claimed a moral if not political victory for the Progressive Party, could only hope that the seeds he planted throughout his career would eventually bear fruit. He did not live to see the escalation of military involvement in Vietnam or the long-endured Cold War, dying as he did in 1965 from complications of crippling ALS (Lou Gehrig's Disease). As he had avowed years before, it was up to the next generation to cultivate the grass roots of spiritual socialism and advance the Kingdom of God on earth.

Wallace's fellow spiritual socialist Sherwood Eddy had died two years earlier, in 1963, at the age of ninety-two. Eulogies for the YMCA veteran extolled his lifelong mission, multiplying good works to make the world a better place. Senator Paul A. Douglas of Illinois praised him for his abundant acts of social justice.[81] A booklet memorializing him described his endeavors as reaching around the globe.[82] These contemporary admirers saw that Eddy's legacy would endure in the incremental ways he contributed to the coming Kingdom of God on earth, establishing churches in Asia or cooperative farms in the Mississippi Delta. He planted the seeds of a new social order with a "forward faith," knowing that he would never see the final product, in its full glory.[83]

One of the projects Eddy had helped establish, with a $200 start-up donation, was the Highlander Folk School, founded by religiously motivated activists Myles Horton, Don West, and James Dombrowski in Tennessee in 1932, around the same time that Dorothy Day and Peter Maurin were starting Catholic Worker in New York City. Inspired by the Danish rural folk-school movement and Christian socialism, the founders of Highlander hoped "to provide an educational center in the South for the training of rural and industrial leaders, and for the conservation and enrichment of the indigenous cultural values of the mountains." Much like Eddy's Delta Cooperative Farm, Highlander offered an alternative, cooperative space for practicing social justice and solidarity in the wake of capitalist collapse. Horton, West, and Dombrowski were committed to rebuilding the world and empowering the poor through community—an educational community that taught socialist values and encouraged its members to apply them wherever they lived or worked. Their mission was educational, economic, social, and also deeply religious. Starting the project in the early 1930s, around the same time as Catholic Worker, the Highlander folks laid the groundwork for a movement that Wallace had been unable to mobilize. They inspired a generation of New Leftists, including many religious radicals involved in the struggle for civil rights. The school's purposeful integration, a crucial cause for spiritual socialists, angered white supremacists in the community and provoked accusations of Communist-inspired infiltration. But Horton and the Highlander staff fought back with religious and democratic values, insisting that they were the ones living up to American ideals. They spoke of Jesus and democracy more than they did Marx or the Soviet Union.

Horton, who served as the school's director from 1932 to 1973, set spiritual socialism as the foundation of Highlander. He had developed an active interest in the radical potential of religious values at an early age. Born to school teachers in Savannah, Tennessee, in 1905, Horton grew up attending the Cumberland Presbyterian Church and the Young Men's Christian Association (YMCA), for which he worked as the student secretary of Tennessee in the late 1920s. His aim to apply Christian principles to practical problems, however, convinced him to look beyond formal institutions and theology. Debates about predestination, he learned from his mother, were merely "preacher's talk" that had little to do with daily life. "She had a very simple belief," Horton explained. "God is love, and therefore you love your neighbors. Love was a religion to her, that's what she practiced. It was a good nondoctrinaire background, and it gave me a sense of what was right and what was wrong."[84]

One summer in 1927, while conducting a YMCA vacation Bible school in the town of Ozone, Horton decided to invite the parents of his students to a session. The group talked about religion and the Bible for little more than five minutes before Horton began inquiring about their everyday lives and the issues that caused them the most concern. After some initial hesitation, the discussion shifted from Bible passages to socioeconomic topics, such as sanitation and cooperative farming. "It was a little awkward for all of us," Horton recalled in his memoir, "but the people finally started talking about their problems and what they were up against."[85] The experience inspired Horton to pursue this method of collective education more thoroughly. It also gave him more confidence to push the envelope in his capacity as YMCA secretary for Tennessee. After holding some interracial meetings without official YMCA approval, he was reprimanded and resigned his post. Formal religion would never again claim his loyalty, especially if it refused to confront ungodly issues such as racism. "I had grown up in a religious world and was trying to get beyond that to understand the broader economic, cultural, and social contexts in which things happened," he said. By the 1930s, he "was no longer interested in organized religion."[86]

However, Horton did not take a secular path from there on out. He merely made a distinction between institutional Christianity and applied, interpersonal Christianity. "I didn't have to understand theology, heaven and hell, any of those things," he claimed. "They all just faded out of my mind. But I did have love nailed down. My mother showed me the difference between the preachers and the churches, and Christian values. She showed me how to avoid mistaking the church for religion."[87] Retaining his belief that Christian practice could ameliorate socioeconomic problems, Horton was drawn to religious thinkers such as Harry F. Ward, whose book *Our Economic Morality and the Ethic of Jesus* he read just before enrolling at Union Theological Seminary in 1929. As Highlander Folk School historian John M. Glen wrote, Ward's anticapitalist critique "helped Horton mesh his own increasingly radical view of contemporary society with his strong religious values." He wanted to use "Christian ethics to change social conditions."[88] Those social conditions included economic inequality, racism, and subpar education for the poor.

Union Theological Seminary, Horton believed, offered him the best step in that direction, because it was a "radical place" that would grant him access to social gospel teachings in the classroom and social gospel projects throughout the poorer districts of New York City.[89] Horton was not quite sure what kind of educational project he wanted to build, but he considered his time at Union Theological, and later, at the University of Chicago, as training for it. He read books on labor organizing, the social gospel, socialism, and the pedagogy of John Dewey. Between coursework, he visited the Hell's Kitchen Boys' Club and the Henry Street Settlement House, and he attended political rallies in Union Square. He also traveled upstate to see the remnants of the Oneida cooperative colony as well as the operational methods of Brookwood Labor College, where Muste served as acting director. According to Glen, "Brookwood disappointed Horton. The college seemed too formally structured and not readily adaptable either to the rural South or to the educational approach that had seemed so promising in Ozone."[90] Perhaps Horton mistook the school for a proletariat training ground, not recognizing the broader mission that Muste had in mind. Horton may have also considered it too isolated from the rest of the world.

Utopian communities such as Oneida, in fact, were disappointing for Horton, who thought them too far removed from real life and real problems. "I took a hard look at utopian communes, which appealed to me because of their spiritual, religious and economic background," he stated. But "they don't demonstrate what you can do to change society. So I discarded [them] as escapist." These communes, Horton observed, were socially withdrawn, not socially active, and they did not address the needs of the whole of humanity. Consequently, Horton began to embrace socialism as his philosophy, a philosophy that could guide theory into practice and religious values into a way of life. "That's where I changed and became philosophically a socialist," he remembered. "I understood that you couldn't act alone, and that you couldn't withdraw into a utopian community. To deal with injustice you had to act in the world. You had to share what you knew. . . . Socialism seemed to me the only way to deal with the problems as I saw them."[91]

However, Horton, even in his radicalism, remained wary of any institutional affiliations. "I wasn't a socialist who was anti-Communist, but I couldn't be a Communist," he explained. "My strong mountain background of independence prevents me from pledging in advance to do what someone else decides for me. I could never do it." Though he did join the Socialist Party and the University of Chicago Socialist Club, he did not consider that action to be a pledge of political loyalty; rather, he thought these organizations were vehicles for an idea. "The Socialist party was a philosophical concept, and that was my philosophical bent," he said. "This wasn't unusual at a time when people like Niebuhr and John Dewey were socialists."[92] It also was not unusual at a time when spiritual socialism was gaining ground. Horton's trajectory resembled that of Day, Muste, or Eddy.

Instead of traditional, Marxist-based socialism, Horton crafted his grassroots, democratic version of socialism from a variety of different streams: his religious background; his union activism, which increased after the stock-market crash; and the Danish folk-school movement, which became the most influential model for the Highlander Folk School. "I was frustrated." Horton admitted. "Neither Chicago nor Union provided me with any model of how to work in Appalachia with poor and working people."[93] Horton traveled to Copenhagen in 1931 to learn more about Danish folk schools, many of which were founded in the early nineteenth century as adult educational sites for peasants who had been left out of traditional, elitist schools. Horton liked how the folk schools provided a place for working-class adults to meet and discuss issues of importance to them, similar to his short-lived experiment at the Ozone Bible School. He also appreciated the democratic approach to folk culture. While formal schools in Denmark taught classes in Latin and promoted the interests of the upper classes, the folk-school movement preserved peasant dialects and art forms, such as song and dance. The schools were also an expression of a religious philosophy, particularly that of pastor and polymath N. F. S. Grundtvig, whose religious views inspired him to support a more democratic, equitable, and creative Danish society, through education and political participation.

For men like Grundtvig, the folk-school movement represented a popular response to spiritual crisis in the nation of Denmark, but it was also an effect of economic and political conditions during the nineteenth century. Rapid industrialization unsettled many traditional folkways and identities, making it difficult for poorer people to understand their new place in society. The folk schools gave peasants an opportunity to express their views and apply their values to practical problems. Instead of high theory, book learning, exams, and earned degrees, the folk schools operated as informal meeting places to discuss daily life. As Grundtvig observed, the people of each community made every folk school unique.[94]

This feature of the folk schools was not lost on Horton, who realized that the central lesson of his efforts to find a model for an Appalachian equivalent in adult education was simply put: there is no model. On a sleepless night in Copenhagen, Horton channeled his epiphany into a plan of action: "What you must do is go back, get a simple place, move in and you are there. The situation is there. You start with this and let it grow. You know your goal. It will build its own structure and take its own form. You can go to school all your life, you'll never figure it out because you are trying to get an answer that can only come from the people in the life situation."[95] Here again, the grand theories of Grundtvig or even Marx seemed to have little bearing on daily life. Horton realized that his religious values had to unfold, unfettered from the moorings of any design.

Horton's belief in organic education meant that his education project, though inspired by the Danish folk schools, would never operate as a foreign import, propagating abstract ideas. Just as the movement in Denmark had emerged from local conditions and problems particular to time and place, so too the Highlander Folk School, which Horton cofounded on a small parcel of land near Monteagle, Tennessee, in 1932, was born to serve the needs of the Appalachian poor in the grips of the Great Depression. "I knew that people as individuals would remain powerless, but if they could get together in organizations, they could have power, provided they used their organizations instead of being used by them," Horton explained.[96]

Bolstered by his socialist beliefs and the spirit of the times, Horton initially identified industrial, unionized wage workers as his target audience. Communist doctrine, however, was never part of his agenda. Instead, he hoped that Highlander would inspire people to tackle problems on their own terms. "They were experts on their own lives and their own experiences," he said of his students. "And those experiences could have something to teach me even if I didn't see it at the moment." Horton had traveled far and read widely to find a method to match his philosophy. The movement that he helped cultivate in the American South, however, was homegrown. "The radical mood of this country at that time was just as influential," he acknowledged. "It wasn't very Marxian but grew instead out of more idealistic principles; a tremendous number of people had religious motivations, for instance."[97] As a spiritual socialist, Horton considered Marxism too limited for the universalism of the Kingdom of God on earth.

Many of those religiously motivated activists were former Union Theological colleagues, a sign that Horton's time in higher education was not ill spent. In fact, Highlander in its early years was largely funded and staffed by Union-affiliated alumni and professors, including cofounder Jim Dombrowski, organizer Zilla Hawes, and sponsor Reinhold Niebuhr. Another major sponsor, Sherwood Eddy, had also attended Union in the late 1800s. He heard about Horton's project after Niebuhr sent around a fundraising letter to potential donors. "One of the signers of this letter was Sherwood Eddy, then the international president of the YMCA, though he himself was a Christian socialist," Horton recalled. "All the people who signed the letter were socialists. Sherwood was independently wealthy, and at that time he was involved in leading tours to the Soviet Union. Reinie told Sherwood he should give some money to me, but I hardly knew him. Jim Dombrowski knew him, though, and arranged a meeting." According to Horton, Eddy donated start-up cash for the endeavor, which was then called the Southern Mountains School. He also agreed to serve on the advisory committee alongside Niebuhr and Norman Thomas, who later would become advisory board members for Eddy's cooperative farms in the mid-1930s.[98]

Possibly, Eddy's idea for the Delta farms was inspired by the Tennessee folk school and the opportunities it offered to put spiritual socialist principles into practice. The vision and mission for Highlander, in fact, resembled that of the Delta farms in several ways. As Niebuhr described in his fundraising letter, the founders of the folk school aimed to provide "education for a socialistic society" and "to enable those who otherwise would have no educational advantages whatsoever to learn enough about themselves and society, to have something on which to base their decisions and actions whether in their own community or in an industrial situation into which they may be thrown." Specifically, Niebuhr identified "southern mountaineers" in the coal and textile industries as the most likely folk-school participants because their needs were ill-served by both mainstream American Federation of Labor organizers and Communists. "Our hope," he wrote, "is to train radical labor leaders who will understand the need of both political and union strategy." "We are proposing to use education as one of the instruments for bringing about a new social order."[99]

Eddy's cooperative farms were not folk schools per se, and they did not train industrial workers. They were agricultural communes intended to provide displaced sharecroppers with a means of survival. However, the two projects did share a commitment to radical democracy, religious values, and "third-way" socialism in rural regions among rural people. The organizers hoped to foster a new social order from the bottom up, by empowering the people themselves to work together on common problems and solutions. Glen put it this way: "Instead of relying on missionaries for solutions to their ills, Horton wanted southern Appalachian residents to organize and use their own intellectual and material 'resources' to build better communities."[100] Eddy, who had altered his approach to missions while serving as the YMCA secretary for Asia, believed that top-down instruction was futile in the fight for a better world. He insisted that a socialist society must begin at the grassroots level, in small groups and communities that practiced Christian ethics. Such was the philosophy at Highlander. None of the founders believed in "hierarchical structures," Horton claimed.[101] Instead, he pitched Highlander as the start of a "new society embodying the ideals of democracy, brotherhood, and justice," a prefigurative implementation of social gospel principles that Eddy certainly would have appreciated.[102]

Yet Eddy, as Horton observed, was not the only Christian socialist involved in developing Highlander. Don West, who had grown up in Georgia and visited Denmark to learn more about folk schools, was also drawn to the project because of his socioreligious worldview. "Don was more or less a Christian socialist who had been a theology student of Alva Taylor at Vanderbilt University," Horton said.[103] Outspoken about his radicalism, West wrote of Highlander as a place that "educates for a socialized nation" in which "human justice, cooperation, a livelihood for every man and a fair distribution of wealth" would replace the "graft, exploitation and private profit" of the current, corrupt social order.[104]

Dombrowski also recognized the spiritual potential of socialism. During times when Highlander faced accusations of Communist affiliation, Dombrowski defended the school by citing its religious framework, convinced no doubt that religion would make Highlander's radicalism more palatable to its critics. In 1939, for instance, he explained that the school's staff wanted to "relate religious idealism to the social problems of today, particularly to relate the social aspirations of religion and the labor movement."[105] Dombrowski was not using smoke and mirrors. Religion had been part of the Highlander curriculum from the very beginning. The first residence term at Highlander in 1932–33, in fact, demonstrated the popularity of religious topics. Students wrote essays on the relationship between Christianity and socialism, and at the end of the first term in April, the staff decided to continue only one seminar, focusing on religion and social change.[106] Christian socialists such as Howard A. Kester, who was involved in the Fellowship for Reconciliation and would later help with the cooperative farms, spoke at the school that summer. In June, Highlander also hosted the Socialist Party state convention for Tennessee.

Then there was Niebuhr, one of the most prominent Christian socialists in the United States in the early 1930s. He supported Horton's vision, despite his growing misgivings about the possibility of achieving a perfect society in a fallen world. While at Union, Horton had taken Niebuhr's course on Christian ethics, structured around the core themes that later made its way into the 1932 bombshell *Moral Man and Immoral Society*. Instead of dismissing the book as a pessimistic polemic, however, Horton appreciated Niebuhr's insights into the seemingly perennial problem of enacting idealism in an immoral environment. "I went to Union because I had problems reconciling my religious background with the economic conditions I saw in society," Horton recalled. Niebuhr's realism helped ground the young dreamer to the certainty of hard, long-term struggle without dampening his desire for activism. "He . . . had a brilliant mind that gave off sparks," Horton said of Niebuhr. "He was young and radical and full of enthusiasm."[107]

Horton, like Eddy, admired Niebuhr but did not abandon the hope of approximating the perfect society, or the Kingdom of God on earth. "It made no sense," Horton said, "to work with poor people who had given up hope. Only people with hope will struggle. The people who are hopeless are grist for the fascist mill. . . . If they don't have hope, they don't even look for a path. They look for somebody else to do it for them."[108] Horton's idealism was bolstered by his belief in the inherent ability of ordinary people to make moral distinctions and govern themselves, given opportunities to do so. Long-term change, however, would take patience and discipline. While he insisted that "people have a potential for growth," Horton could also acknowledge that "growth is painful" and painstaking in its delicate, slow-moving process. Similar to Day, Muste, and Eddy, then, he placed strong emphasis on the matching of means and ends. "It's important to understand that the quality of the process you use to get to a place determines the ends," he explained, "so when you want to build a democratic society, you have to act democratically in every way. If you want love and brotherhood, you've got to incorporate them as you go along, because you can't just expect them to occur in the future without experiencing them before you get there."[109]

Success stories at Highlander reinforced Horton's optimism about the potential for comprehensive social change. Students solved problems cooperatively, respected each other's viewpoints, and acted democratically. They put moral theory into practice, at least in small, interpersonal groups of temporary duration. Horton was encouraged. Projecting an outlook very different from the one Niebuhr presented in *Moral Man and Immoral Society*, he sounded confident, but cautious. "Since I know those things can happen on a small scale, I assume that if we ever get wise enough and involve enough people, it could happen on a bigger scale." Contingency still weighed down any buoyant enthusiasm, as did a reluctance to predict final outcomes. "The goal I'm talking about is one that can never be reached. It's a direction, a concept of society that grows as you go along," Horton stated with a tinge of Niebuhrian pragmatism. "Goals are unattainable in the sense that they always grow. . . . That is why I say it's never completed. I think there always needs to be struggle."[110]

Horton's realistic assessment of the world did not dash his hopes for a new world order. The revolution eventually would come, he believed, but it "had to be made" "step by step" over the "long haul" of generations. True to his spiritual socialist philosophy, Horton talked at length about the need for a modified, but still radical approach to social change. "We reversed the usual process," he stated, "instead of coming from the top down and going from the theoretical to the practical, trying to force the theory on the practical, we learned you had to take what people perceive their problems to be, not what we perceive their problems to be." This give-and-take of practical problem solving, according to Horton, was what education was all about. It was a concept of cultivation. It was a concept of organic growth, a "yeasty" evolution that could "multiply" and thus "fundamentally change society." The small groups at Highlander, he believed, had exponential capacities, if students took what they learned at the school (the knowledge, the methods, and the behavioral practices) and implemented them in their own communities and workplaces, setting examples for others to follow. It could create, Horton hoped, a revolution from below, not merely a regime change but a completely different culture and new set of social norms. "I wasn't interested in resolving conflicts that would leave the same people in control and the same people powerless," he explained. Intent on building "strength from the bottom up instead of the top down," he made a conscious decision to "work with people from the bottom," including working people and those "exploited by class and by race."[111]

In the 1930s and 1940s, Highlander focused its efforts on educating union workers; however, racial issues were also at the heart of Horton's overall project, a constant concern that stemmed from his abiding belief in personalism, or the inherent dignity of all God's children. "Racism was a matter of not respecting people. It went against all my principles," he avowed.[112] Racial discrimination also obstructed Highlander's efforts to strengthen the labor movement. Glen wrote that "whenever they had tried to build unions, coalitions, or virtually anything else, they had eventually confronted the barrier of racism." Breaking off close collaboration with the Congress of Industrial Organizations in the late 1940s because of the federation's growing conservatism, Horton and the Highlander staff decided that "what was now needed was a program to unite black and white people in a struggle for common goals."[113]

Since the 1920s, Horton had experimented with interracial banquets and meetings, though he often faced opposition from those who claimed he was going too far too fast. By the mid-1950s, however, Horton sensed the time had come for a more radical approach to issues of race. Anticipating the 1954 Supreme Court decision *Brown v. Board of Education of Topeka*, Highlander set up a workshop on integrated education, gambling on the prospect that they would be on the cutting edge of a new era in southern social history.[114] The wager proved opportune. As Glen put it, "Highlander became the educational center of the civil rights movement during the 1950s and early 1960s." Reverend James L. Bevel, an activist in the Southern Christian Leadership Conference (SCLC), went so far as to call the school a "Father of the Civil Rights Movement."[115]

This is not to say that the civil rights movement sprang out of Highlander exclusively. The social gospel and spiritual socialism found its way into the movement through many channels, including the work of African American intellectuals and religious leaders such as Benjamin Mays, Howard Thurman, and Mordecai Johnson, who influenced Martin Luther King Jr. and other black activists.[116] Horton himself would not have claimed so much credit for Highlander, but he was thrilled to be on the cusp of a new and dynamic movement for social justice. On Labor Day weekend in 1957, Highlander celebrated its twenty-fifth anniversary with speeches by admirers such as Reverend King Jr., who lauded the school's role in building brotherhood in the South.

King and the newly formed SCLC were interested in using education to increase black voter registration, and Highlander already had the ball rolling in that direction. Its so-called Citizenship Education Schools, an extension program of Highlander on Johns Island off the coast of South Carolina, opened that year to teach literacy and civics to African Americans preparing for Jim Crow voting tests. "The first Citizenship School, which met twice a week for three months, grew from fourteen to thirty-seven students, and 80 percent of them graduated and got their certificates, that is, they registered to vote," Horton recalled.[117] Within a few years, the program had grown so large and popular that Highlander could no longer manage it without abandoning its work in Tennessee. The Citizenship Schools were thus handed over to the SCLC in 1961, continuing under the direction of Highlander alums such as Septima Clark, Esau Clark, and Bernice Robinson, who had taught on Johns Island. According to Glen, "The Citizenship Schools were Highlander's most significant contribution to the civil rights movement and perhaps the most important single program the staff ever developed."[118]

Yet literacy and voting, Horton realized, were not the sole remedies to racial discrimination. "We say, 'That's the first step, but it's only the first step,'" he stated with his characteristic vision of long-term, comprehensive change.[119] Highlander, in other words, had a multipronged approach to enhancing the lives of black Americans. In the late 1950s and early 1960s, the staff held interracial workshops on "social needs and social resources," which attracted dozens of ministers and lay activists interested in community welfare. Over one thousand people also enrolled in the ongoing residence program on integration, an experience that exposed participants to interracial cooperation, strategies of direct action such as sit-ins, and protest songs like "We Shall Overcome," an old hymn that Horton's wife, Zilphia, the musical director at Highlander, rearranged to express the resolve of labor and civil rights activism. "Highlander quickly became a place where student leaders could come to discuss the ideology, goals, and tactics of their protest," wrote Glen.[120] A workshop in the spring of 1961, entitled "New Frontiers for College Students," helped cultivate the grassroots leadership of Ella Baker, John Lewis, Bob Zellner, and Andrew Young, some of whom went on to form the Student Non-Violent Coordinating Committee later that summer. Julian Bond, Stokely Carmichael, and Rosa Parks also spent time at the school. "At Highlander, I found out for the first time in my adult life that this could be a unified society," wrote Parks of her experience in the mid-1950s. "It was a place I was very reluctant to leave. I gained there the strength to persevere in my work for freedom, not just for blacks, but for all oppressed people."[121]

Given his commitment to effecting change from the bottom up, Horton was pleased to see so many grassroots leaders emerging from Highlander programs. "The reason we chose to work on grassroots leadership," he explained, "was that when you're trying to break out of the conventional way of doing things, that is, a top-down authoritarian way, you have more chance of influencing someone who hasn't been molded into the hierarchical system, and hasn't already been socialized to operate from the top."[122] Horton's opinion of charismatic leaders like Martin Luther King Jr. hinged on this very point. He knew that movements were bound to produce strong and visible leaders, but he also believed that movements would lose steam without a reliable base of local organizers, who could keep the momentum going through inevitable highs and lows. "While some of the goals of the civil rights movement were not realized, many were," Horton concluded. "But the civil rights movement as it was then cannot and should not be imitated. It was creative, and we must be creative."[123]

The same held true for Highlander. In 1961, as state authorities were revoking the school's original charter, the staff moved to a new location in Knoxville, Tennessee, renaming the site the Highlander Research and Education Center under a new lease. The work of training social activists continued there until 1971, when it moved once again, this time to New Market, Tennessee. It continues to operate today as an education center for civil rights and social justice issues, environmentalism, workers' safety, and human rights. However, Horton, who retired as director in 1969 and passed away in 1990, insisted that the school could not be replicated throughout the nation and world as he originally had hoped. The issue, he realized through experience, was local culture and the unique context that it created for any grassroots organization. Highlander's home remained in Tennessee, where it could address the particular problems of the region and its people. To be sure, the focus on localism did not leave Highlander isolated from the rest of the world. Connections were forged through the sharing of spiritual values and democratic ways of life at what Horton called "islands of decency," places such as Catholic Worker or the Delta farms, where people were given opportunities to cooperate and practice socialism. According to

Horton, these "islands of decency" were laying the foundation for a new spiritual dispensation. "From Jesus and the prophets I had learned about the importance of loving people, the importance of being a revolutionary, standing up and saying that this system is unjust," he said. "Jesus to me was a person who had the vision to project a society in which people would be equally respected, in which property would be shared; he was a person who said you have to love your enemies, you have to love the people who despise you. . . . I don't live in that kind of world, but I want to help create one like it."[124]

Horton realized that his mission, in fact, was global, though his approach remained localized. Because capitalism, he reminded his readers, is not a nationally isolated system, but an international enterprise, activists would "have to learn to deal internationally with economic problems." "Unless you deal with world capitalism—transnationalism—the decisions you make are going to be very limited," he wrote.[125] Horton also realized that engaging with international economics meant engaging with international relations, including foreign policy, which remained a stumbling block for leftists in the 1940s and 1950s. He had supported Wallace in 1948, heralding the Progressive Party candidate as "the only strong voice speaking out against steps that will lead to war." Wallace's failure to inspire a broad-based movement and win Americans to his postwar vision of global cooperation proved disappointing to Horton and his fellow spiritual socialists. Let down by national parties and national politics, a feeling reinforced by Wallace's failure to build a New Left coalition, independent radicals found hope in community-building efforts and direct action, whether in Catholic Worker, the Highlander Folk School, or the civil rights movement. Spiritual socialists were prominent in all. Indeed, the civil rights movement that Horton helped activate in the South would open new and dynamic opportunities for the religious Left by the end of the decade, filling the void that Wallace's presidential campaign had left behind.[126]

CHAPTER 5

Socialism of the Heart

From his balcony seat at the 1948 Progressive Party convention in Philadelphia, Staughton Lynd gazed down on his Harvard professor, F. O. Matthiessen, as Matthiessen delivered the Massachusetts delegation's secondary nominating speech for the presidential candidacy of Henry A. Wallace.[1] The radical literary critic peppered his passionate, if lengthy, address with references to Emerson, Thoreau, Hawthorne, and Whitman—American forerunners, he suggested, to Wallace's democracy of the common man. "They felt," Matthiessen wrote in his 1941 tome *American Renaissance*, "that it was incumbent upon their generation to give fulfilment [sic] to the potentialities freed by the Revolution, to provide . . . literature for our democracy."[2] Democracy, according to Matthiessen, was a religious enterprise for the realization of true community, not merely a political system ruled by majority opinion.

Immersed in the radical writings of Ignazio Silone, A. J. Muste, and Simone Weil, Lynd could appreciate the spiritual message that Matthiessen professed. He had grown up among Marxists in the 1930s, but he never felt morally comfortable with the kind of aggressive party politics that most of them professed. Instead of apocalyptic social revolution spearheaded by a proletarian vanguard, Lynd wanted a brotherly way of life, rooted in religious ideals of love, peace, and cooperation, cultivated in grassroots communities, struggling in solidarity against oppressive institutions. This spiritualized form of socialism, Lynd argued, offered activists a moral alternative to violent revolution without relinquishing revolutionary ideals. Rather than relate to each other as competitors for resources in a market-based society, individuals were encouraged to interact as a family of equals, sharing resources, caring for those in need, and making decisions by consensus. Over time, Lynd hoped that these communal cooperatives would replace conventional institutions and form the foundation of a new, humane society. Dissenters, through a "daily practice of libertarian and fraternal attitudes in institutions of their own making," he wrote in 1968, "[keep] alive their faith that men [can] live together in a radically different way." Once corrupted structures began to crumble from decay, he prophesized, an "underground congregation" stood ready to "burst forth as a model for the Kingdom of God on earth, and an organ of secular 'dual power.'"[3]

Though Lynd located the source of the Kingdom of God in small, local communities, the newly refashioned Progressive Party gave him reason to hope that he had found a viable political vehicle for a transnational movement. Wallace inspired thousands of radicals in America and abroad by championing a New Deal for the world, grounded in human rights and social justice.[4] For those such as Lynd and Matthiessen, it was Wallace's spiritual spin on notions of equality, democracy, and peace that drew them into his orbit, even though his prophetic idealism failed to appeal to most American voters. The "People's Century" of the common man, however, did not die with the Wallace campaign, as some scholars have argued.[5] To the contrary, it continued to gain traction as insurgent campaigns for national liberation, civil rights, and human rights erupted in the 1950s and 1960s.

Race had always been part of spiritual socialists' concerns, though never foregrounded to the extent that it would be during the civil rights movement. At Sherwood Eddy's cooperative farms or Dorothy Day's Catholic Worker houses, racism was regarded as a component of the social malady, a condition that required attention. Their approach to race stemmed from their broad spiritual socialist worldview. Eddy and Day wanted not only a world in which blacks could vote and attend decent schools, but also a world in which every person lived a life of dignity, equality, and God-given potential. They considered individuals holistically, composed of more than the color of their skin, all the while knowing that color could mark a person for unfair treatment in a racist society. Many African American spiritual socialists seemed to agree that race did not stand alone. For Martin Luther King Jr. and Pauli Murray, for example, the civil rights movement was not just about black rights.[6] It was about integrating all members of the human family into a society that reflected the Kingdom of God. In the 1960s, Lynd and Murray both contributed to and criticized the civil rights movement for not going far enough and for not thinking of the whole person or the big picture. For instance, gender issues remained sidelined by civil rights activists and spiritual socialists before the late 1960s, an oversight that Murray, for one, felt determined to correct.

The civil rights movement was part of the New Left movements of the 1960s via the thread of spiritual socialism, a continuity crucial for understanding the emergence of a dynamic, non-Communist form of radical politics by the mid-twentieth century.[7] It is unlikely, in fact, that the New Left would have gained traction without the theoretical and practical groundwork that had been laid by Day, Muste, Eddy, Silone, Myles Horton, and even Wallace. Though not all New Leftists spoke in terms of religion, many of them, such as Lynd, Greg Calvert, and Murray, and scores of other civil rights activists did. More often than not, the language and ideology of ostensibly secular New Leftists matched that of spiritual socialists even when explicit religious content remained absent. In its 1962 manifesto, the Port Huron Statement, for example, Students for a Democratic Society (SDS) expressed their socialist beliefs in terms of human dignity, democracy, freedom, and the spiritual value of participation, applying the beliefs of spiritual socialists broadly to local and national politics. Though civil rights activists were linked to the New Left through shared liberal values and a commitment to democracy, the role of spiritual socialists in this book reveals that these overlapping movements also found common cause in a more radical vision of society: a socialist society.[8]

Unfortunately, Matthiessen would not live to see the upsurge of spiritual socialism across the nation for which he had long hoped. Biographer Frederick Stern noted the tragic irony of his subject's suicide a few years before the beloved community began to take shape in the form of the civil rights and New Left movements: "Had he lived longer, he would have been aware of many more Christians who developed radical social views than had been the case in his lifetime. One can imagine him in important conversations with the Fathers Berrigan and their radical Catholic allies, with Dr. Martin Luther King, Jr., with the other members of the black clergy who made of social action the primary evidence of their adherence to the Gospel, and with other such figures who emerged during the turbulent sixties."[9]

Matthiessen's student Lynd, for one, became a dedicated protégé of his mentor's spiritual socialist vision.[10] Soon after earning his Ph.D. in American history in 1961, Lynd began participating in New Left direct action for civil rights while teaching at Spelman College in Georgia with fellow radical scholar Howard Zinn. These New Leftists advocated an organic socialism cultivated through grassroots communities, intended not as moral gestures, but as powerful, parallel structures to rival traditional institutions. Yet the task of creating an alternative way of life required considerable patience and commitment to ideals. The struggle, in fact, met formidable resistance from conservatives and reticence from many liberals, thus causing confusion among radicals on issues of political program. As director of the Freedom Schools during the summer of 1964 (and earlier, as a member of the Macedonia Cooperative Community in Georgia), Lynd learned valuable lessons regarding the potential for and the limits of a beloved community and the Kingdom of God on earth. Everyone possessed an "Inner Light" or moral compass, the Quaker convert contended, but not everyone could agree on how to transform religious verities into practical politics. As Lynd told an audience gathered at a peace seminar in 1966, "We must say yes to our souls." The Quaker "spokesman for the New Left," as a *New York Times* reporter described Lynd, was always doing just that, exhorting radicals to "respond to what was deepest within" and approaching protest as "a moral action." Hoping to serve as a "translator" between the religious pacifist and socialist traditions, Lynd demonstrated that religion and radicalism were theoretically and functionally compatible.[11]

No wonder Wallace resonated so much with the young Lynd. "Fundamentally," Wallace once wrote a friend, "I am . . . a searcher for methods of bringing the 'inner light to outward manifestation.'"[12] While Wallace lost political momentum in the late 1940s, Lynd and his New Left comrades took up the task of illuminating America's spiritual path with a social approach to democracy. The radical lineage for Lynd, however, did not spring from Marxist circles, but had its source within a much longer history of religious dissenters in Europe and America. His story, therefore, helps decenter the Old Left–New Left genealogical debate by revealing the alternative spiritual socialist sources of 1960s radicalism. When the 1960s erupted into a debate about socialism, and its definition, form, and potential in the United States, spiritual socialists like Lynd helped set the terms of that debate. Lynd channeled every injustice he encountered, whether related to civil rights, war, or labor, into the following question: how can we build the Kingdom of God as a socialist alternative to Marxism? His answer typically involved some form of direct action, a way of living the process as though the Kingdom were already here.

As a child, Lynd had been politically precocious for his age. He had grown up absorbing the radical values of his parents and the Old Left "ambiance" of "the prevailing radical culture." Yet Marxist meetings, filled with little more than endless, empty talk, had always failed to fire young Lynd's imagination. During a visit to the New York City headquarters of the Socialist Party with one of his father's graduate students, Seymour Martin Lipset, in the early 1940s, however, Lynd was captivated by Lipset's tale of an anarchist in the Spanish Civil War who insisted on standing in a long lunch line with refugees. Though his comrades encouraged him to skip to the front, rationalizing that his time was too valuable, that he had to get back to the revolution, the anarchist remained in place, replying, "'This *is* the Revolution.'"[13]

This commitment to "acting out one's beliefs," Lynd recalled, represented a level of dedication that he rarely witnessed among his parents and their friends, who were rhetorically committed to revolutionary change, but spent their energies more on theory than action.[14] To Lynd, their brand of "bureaucratic, lifeless[,] . . . and repressive" Old Left–style Marxism "without 'spirit'" seemed cold and detached from the heart of human relations.[15] "Like so many young people in the 1960s," Lynd remembered, "I faulted my parents for talking a good game but not letting that disturb their comfortable lifestyle."[16] Lipset's simple anecdote of the anarchist's heroic example, however, symbolized something different. Instead of dictating directives and spouting dogma, these men *enacted* their socialist convictions as a way of life. Lynd found the approach irresistible. By putting theory into practice, by struggling alongside the poor and oppressed, they not only animated socialism for Lynd, but also planted the seeds for an entirely new worldview. In short, they "changed [his] life."[17]

Lynd's life began on November 22, 1929, the same year his parents, Robert and Helen Lynd, published their first sociological study about Middletown, which made them famous and financially secure. During the Depression, the Lynds lived comfortably in an eighth-floor apartment on Manhattan's West Side, four blocks from the Ethical Culture Society on West 64th Street, where Staughton attended school from pre-kindergarten to sixth grade.[18] The Ethical Culture schools were a product of a late nineteenth-century movement for the "reconstruction of religious thought" in an age of industrialization, theological skepticism, and scientific rationalism.[19] Demoralized by the Civil War, which had severely tested the nation's religious and political presumptions, and uncertain of the moral implications of Darwin's theory of evolution, many Americans struggled to stabilize the modern mind-set with firm but flexible pillars of thought. The challenge at the turn of the century, according to historian Howard Radest, was to "reintroduce the sacred into a world" with "a secularized future."[20] A young German Jew named Felix Adler set himself to the task. He founded the Society for Ethical Culture in 1876, which quickly developed into an international movement for moral education and social reform.

Though he rejected religious dogma and doctrine in the school's curriculum, Adler retained Reformed Judaism's emphasis on moral duty, social justice, holy community, and the eschatological Kingdom of God. "The last outlook that is opened," he prophesized, "is upon a perfect society, an ideal community of spiritual beings, a Kingdom of Heaven, a City of the Light."[21] However, according to Adler, Hebrew social thought and practice remained truncated by dogmatic theology and "the Father image as the symbol of Deity . . . which experience does not confirm." In place of a personal, individual, and unifying Godhead, Adler conceptualized a pluralistic ideal of God, a manifold "universe of spiritual beings interacting in infinite harmony." The fostering of practical, ethical human relations, based on the "recognition of the presence of something holy in each human being," became Adler's abiding philosophical project. "The appeal of the God in our neighbor is the substitute for the appeal in prayer to the God in heaven," he wrote. Adler made sure, however, to distinguish his ethical outlook from atheistic humanism. Although he underscored the importance of developing "sacred" individual "personality," Adler's ultimate aim transcended the temporal.[22] It was, he acknowledged, implicitly religious: "I believe in the supreme excellence of righteousness; I believe that the law of righteousness will triumph in the universe over all evil; I believe in the law of righteousness as the sanctification of human life; and I believe that in furthering and fulfilling that law I also am hallowed in the service of the unknown God."[23]

In 1895, Adler's free Workingman's School in New York City was renamed the Ethical Culture School as it began accepting enrollment from paying attendees of the middle and upper classes. Lynd spent his formative years there in the 1930s and 1940s, absorbing the spiritual idealism of its founder. The Society's motto, for example—"The place where men meet to seek the highest is holy ground"—written in large gold lettering above the auditorium stage, lingered long in Lynd's consciousness. In the early 1950s, as he applied for conscientious objector status, Lynd chose to recite these words to his draft board, claiming they "provided the best definition" of his "personal ethics and morality."[24] The adage, though ambiguous, reflects Adler's pragmatic approach to ethics devoid of specific religious content. Reluctant to affirm any explicit, and thus exclusive, statement of principle, Adler intended his thin description to embrace the infinite possibilities of communal experience. "The spiritual ideal itself must necessarily be conceived differently by different minds," Adler stated, "but the great general purpose will be the same, despite variations in shades of meaning and points of view."[25]

Echoing Adler years later, Lynd wrote of a "common religious experience that different persons might use quite different words to describe." A faith in the "inner light" or spiritual potential of every human being, acting in concert toward common ideals, also undergirded Lynd's defense of democracy: "We need each other because none of us can see the whole truth."[26] Throughout his life, Lynd would activate Adler's "elastic formula" of universal morality and pragmatic method, collective struggle and individual dignity, in his approach to radical politics.[27] Indeed, Lynd's education in Adler's brand of ethical pluralism, though it left him "almost completely unfamiliar with the New Testament" or the notion of a personal God, enabled him to find ecumenical affinity with Quakers, Buddhists, Catholics, Jews, and a whole host of self-identified secular radicals during his activist career.[28]

Lynd was immersed in Adler's particular leftist ideology while at school, but he also explored ideas about a spiritualized socialism on his own, especially in his extracurricular reading. Writing in his memoirs sixty years later, Lynd recalled, "My growing feeling that the revolution had to be, somehow, both Marxist and ethical, was articulated in a book." That book was Italian socialist Ignazio Silone's political exposé *Bread and Wine*, first published in 1937. "I shan't take time to narrate the whole plot of my favorite novel," Lynd continued. "Suffice it to say that a Communist revolutionary disguises himself as a priest, and in doing so is forced to consider how these two parts of his experience—the Marxist and the Christian—fit together. I too felt the need for such a synthesis."[29] As it had done for Day, Silone's use of Jesus as a model for moral action offered Lynd a spiritual alternative to dogmatic politics as well as an image for what he would later call "socialism with a human face," a form of community composed of simple, altruistic human actions.[30]

Lynd was too young to have experienced the disillusionment of Stalinist Communism. He had never subscribed to the party ideology. Still, Silone opened up a new world of radical possibilities for the fifteen-year-old socialist, who was, until then, unfamiliar with the social implications of Christianity. Devoid of specific historical and biblical content, the religious outlook of Lynd's parents and the Ethical Culturists hardly included the life of Jesus. Adler appreciated Christ as an ethical exemplar, but referenced him in terms of individual self-cultivation and virtue, not social reform. Unlike his social gospel acquaintance Henry George, who combined the material and spiritual, Adler considered it "a mistake to represent Jesus . . . as a kind of precursor of modern Socialism," because Jesus did not promote the pursuit of wealth at all, let alone wealth for all.[31]

Silone's *Bread and Wine* thus introduced Lynd to a radical, egalitarian, spiritual socialism for the first time, the ideas of which were very appealing to someone searching for a third way between the extremes of collectivism and individualism. Primitive Christianity, Lynd discovered, was the wedge on which radical activists could exert leverage, opening up a democratic space for social change. Indeed, the compassionate teenager felt stirred and "impressed by certain quotations from the Gospels" that Silone used to illustrate the inherent compatibility of Christianity and socialism.[32]

For Lynd, as much as for Silone, it became clear that the central message of Christ, in his preferential option for the poor and his moral resistance to the prevailing order, *was* a sort of democratic socialism based on religious values. "Jesus's program," Lynd wrote in an essay years later, "was empowerment from the bottom up, to rebuild peasant dignity and hope without waiting for God to do it."[33] The Kingdom of God was not some abstract, future utopia, Lynd concluded. To the contrary, it is "available here and now," within us and among us. It is enacted through love, compassion, and communion—the moral foundations of primitive Christianity —which, as Silone demonstrated, channel "worldly means to transcendent ends."[34] This correspondence between the material and the spiritual captured Lynd's imagination. Instead of awaiting the perfect society on the margins of hope, Lynd opted for enacting one's hope by applying spiritual truths to the social environment as a way of life. Throughout his career, in the face of setbacks and frustrations, Lynd would return to the core lesson learned from Silone: Christianity, given that its most basic principles of love, compassion, and communion are fully enacted, can provide "a new place to begin."[35]

A lingering question did remain in Lynd's mind: how does one *politicize* a radical religious worldview to effect fundamental social change? American pacifist A. J. Muste offered Lynd some strategic insights. Like Silone, Muste reaffirmed the superiority of his Christian convictions after a brief foray into revolutionary Marxism. Unlike Silone, however, the Protestant minister participated in direct, nonviolent resistance throughout his life. Direct action or civil disobedience, Lynd learned, was a crucial first step, necessary for exposing and opposing existing society as well as creating a space for new socialist structures to flourish.

By merging radical action with religion, Muste bequeathed to Lynd a live option for directing "the inner commandment of compassion" into prefigurative politics, an enactment of the ideal political society in real time.[36] The political potency of prefigurative social action, however, remained largely untested. Muste did not have any easy answers. He maintained his faith in the power of religious discipline, but acknowledged the need for "creative experimentation" in applying nonviolent methods to national social problems. Christ was the model. Perhaps more important than anything else, Muste introduced Lynd to Jesus' example of pacifist resistance, disputing the notion that pacifism means passivity. Jesus was not submissive, Muste argued: "No one could have been more un-submissive to human laws, institutions, and dignitaries than he." Instead, Christ represented a radical, uncompromising refusal to cooperate with evil. Mahatma Gandhi, Muste noted, was pacifism's most promising contemporary model, remarkable for his ability to modernize and universalize the Christian approach to power simply by engaging in direct resistance to colonial rule, using "no weapons but those of reason, love, humility, prayer, and willingness to die for . . . faith."[37] Muste expressed his hope that American activists would adopt such effective methods in the struggle for peace and racial justice.

In the early 1960s, Lynd began to experience firsthand the power of nonviolent resistance and direct action in the civil rights movement. In 1946, however, he was a sixteen-year-old freshman at Harvard College, searching for a career path that would allow him to practice his socialist convictions. This task was considerably complicated by Lynd's suspicion, reinforced by the example of his father, that the security of academia dampened the resolve for radicalism. Lynd dropped out of two different colleges in as many years. In 1948, a reading of Leon Trotsky's prophetic *Literature and Revolution* (1925), heralding a new "human type" of "self-educat[ed]" socialist man who would elevate art to its highest potential, provoked him to abandon his studies at Harvard and travel across the country.[38] He returned eastward, enrolled at Columbia University, but left again after seeing a film about Saint Vincent de Paul, who climbed down from his balcony seat next to the French king in order to take up the oar of an exhausted slave in a galley race. The scene crystallized the substantial difference that Lynd detected between radical intellectuals, like his parents, and active radicals. "However awkwardly," Lynd wrote, "one had to find a way to the place in society where ordinary people toiled at the oars, and assume a position beside them."[39]

Trotsky, just as he had for Muste, aroused at least partial admiration in Lynd, who found the Trotskyist organizations in college simultaneously "attractive" for their challenge to discredited Stalinism and "objectionable" for their reluctance to revise many Marxist-Leninist assumptions. In other words, Trotskyists made an admirable ethical leap by condemning the crimes of Stalin, but they remained too consumed by rigid doctrine and sectarian infighting to satisfy Lynd's search for moral foundations. While eating supper one night in Boston, Lynd stunned a group of Harvard Communists by affirming his belief in timeless ethical principles.[40] For them, ethical considerations obscured the serious struggle for political revolution. For Lynd, however, the practice of moral principles portended the revolution, a revolution in values necessary for lasting social or political change. Lynd's abiding loyalty to such principles prevented him from fully embracing Marxist ideology, no matter how reformed. To boot, his literary encounter with the brilliant spiritual socialist Simone Weil, and her devastating deconstruction of Soviet, Marxist, and even Trotskyist contradictions, shattered any residual hope he may have harbored for Old Left doctrine.

By emphasizing the immoral subjugation of individual freedom, Weil disputed Trotsky's defense of the bureaucratic Soviet regime as a degenerate workers' state in transition to true Communism. The party, she noted, showed no signs of relinquishing power to democratic Soviets. To the contrary, the "mere administrative mechanisms" of collective control relegated the working class to "its position as a passive instrument of production," thus sacrificing spiritually rich social relations for efficient material output. The root of the problem, according to Weil, originated with Marx, who placed his proletariat revolutionaries "above sin" and naïvely "omit[ted] spiritual factors" in his predictive vision of material necessity. As products of their flawed social and cultural environment, proletarians were bound to repeat the same cycle of depravity as in previous revolutions, Weil observed.[41] The task, then, was reduced to a "transformation of the fabric of human relationships." Advocating a social doctrine that was "nonviolent in practice but profoundly revolutionary in substance," Weil discovered the same denominator common to Silone and Muste: faithful socialists must nurture a revolution in social values instead of assuming that a historically inevitable catastrophe would generate spontaneous benevolence and goodwill among men. Such a transformation was possible, Weil wagered, if humans enacted social values as sharers in God—"a God *thought of* as ethical inspiration . . . a God who is *lived by*, an incarnate God," as her biographer explained.[42] For Weil, humane action on earth was an affirmation of supernatural grace, the abstract and impersonal made manifest through personal, concrete deed. Jesus, who personified God's truth in action, was thus the ultimate model for socialist society: "Such a society alone would be a society of men free, equal and brothers. Men would, it is true, be bound by collective ties, but exclusively in their capacity as men; they would never be treated by each other as things. Each would see in every workfellow another self occupying another post, and would love him in the way that the Gospel maxim enjoins."[43]

Although born Jewish, Weil "felt a great sympathy for Christianity," and she reportedly experienced encounters with Christ in mystical communion. Weil's faith in a transcendental truth, existing beyond space and time, led her to endorse a limited mystical correspondence. Her embrace of mystical experience through a particular religious lens also allowed her to universalize spiritual truths "by *analogy*," in the belief that most religious traditions provided access to God, so long as their advocates emphasized love, equality, and the inherent dignity of individuals. Devotion to a particular religion, she asserted, should help one to recognize these essential qualities in other religions. Likewise, a sense of self-awareness and self-worth should stir one to support the dignity of others. Weil's worldview began with personal experience and extrapolated to a universal value-system. Individual dignity, in short, precedes and provokes collective solidarity. The personal becomes political.[44]

Lynd considered Weil's concern for the individual worker, valued as more than a cog in the collective system, as her most insightful contribution to socialism. Summarizing the French theorist's significance decades after first encountering her work, Lynd wrote,

The thirst for democracy requires a prior affirmation of personal, individual dignity. Only when peasants and artisans came to believe in the priesthood of all believers did they begin to think of themselves as collectively capable of governing. We must, absolutely must, find a language in which to talk with one another about the way in which we are robbed of our selfhood when we are denied the opportunity to participate as fully as we are capable of doing in decisions affecting our work. Simone Weil came closer to finding that language than anyone else to date.[45]

According to Lynd, this was also the language of a particularly New Left dispensation, which Weil, Muste, and Silone, in their post-Marxist "effort to think things back to their beginnings," anticipated by at least two decades.[46] Marxist materialism, they insisted, was a false idol that blinded socialists to the spiritual needs of mankind and also smothered individuals with dogma and instrumentality. Yet "the true road exists," Weil assured, echoing Silone. "It is the transcendental bread mentioned in the original text of the Lord's Prayer," which speaks of communion and the correspondence between heaven and earth.[47]

Lynd saw Silone, Muste, and Weil, who longed for a reaffirmation of human values and ethical principles, as a radical triumvirate: "brothers and sisters of the spirit," as he called them.[48] Marxism remained useful as a *partial* analysis of the nature of capitalism—an economic system that corrupted human relations by substituting material self-interest for spiritual altruism—but it did not provide an adequate method or program for humane action. As Weil avowed, "Not even Marx is more precious to us than the truth"—a higher "truth" that was spiritual, even religious, in its reflection of God's existence through man's "perpetual straining after an unknown good."[49]

Renouncing rigid Communist ideology, Lynd began to construct a spiritual platform for securing and advancing an ecumenical socialist society, devoid of class exceptionalism. Persistent labor exploitation made workers an important constituency for radical activism; but labor organizing did not warrant the neglect of other oppressed groups, who could unite around shared values. "Workers are important not because the working class is destined to overthrow capitalism, but because their solidarity prefigures a better society," Lynd wrote after decades of labor activism.[50] The lesson he had first learned from spiritual socialists as a teenager was thus confirmed through later experience.

Already, Lynd knew he was not alone in his unorthodox convictions. The radicals in what he called "the first New Left," including Silone, Muste, and Weil, had prepared him to recognize his comrades in the "second New Left" in the 1950s and 1960s.[51] But, first, he had to contend with the Cold War and the commitments his country expected of him. Drafted at the behest of the Truman Doctrine for Communist containment in 1953 and summarily discharged from service as a result of the McCarthy Red Scare in 1954, Lynd yearned for a place to practice his spiritual values in peace. He and his wife, Alice Lynd, decided to visit the Macedonia Cooperative Community, a "commune" of conscientious objectors from World War II, who "were now trying to create a positive way of life expressive of their pacifism" on a thousand hilly acres near Clarkesville, Georgia. Lynd's disconcerting experience in the military added empathy to his curiosity about the Macedonia group, which soon extended into "a prolonged spiritual retreat," from November 1954 to September 1957.[52]

Grounded in the religious notion of inherent individual dignity (expressed by Quakers as the "Inner Light," or the moral conscience within every child of God) consensus decision makers at Macedonia presumed that "truth" aggregates from individual convictions. "Each of us is endowed with a conscience, and we need to use this conscience, to listen and be guided by it, to keep our hearts open," Lynd avowed. "At Macedonia we felt that any member of the group might perceive something that the rest of us were missing."[53] Reverence for individual dignity, therefore, meant recognizing the right of each person to use his or her "own voice" to participate directly in the decisions affecting their lives.[54] The result was what New Leftists would later call "participatory democracy."

Lynd had first been introduced to Quakerism through his wife and her parents, who were recent converts to the religion. Lynd and Alice, in fact, had been married at the Stony Run Friends Meetinghouse in Baltimore, Maryland, and though the newlyweds were not yet members of the meeting, the Quaker way of worshipping as a priesthood of all believers without ministerial authority or set program appealed to the young socialists.[55] In particular, the Quakers' consensus decision making reminded Lynd of the colonial New England town meeting, a "self-governing institution," in which he had become "intensely interested" while in college. As a model of community-based democracy, the town meeting offered Lynd a possible rejoinder to James Burnham's polemic against the prospects for alternative institutions in advanced capitalist society.[56] Would the egalitarian methods of the town meeting work in modern times, Lynd wondered?

The "Kingdom of God," as he acknowledged, "is available here and now," within and among us, and each person carries partial responsibility for its manifestation. Certainly, Lynd had been exposed to the Kingdom ethic in theory, primarily in works by Silone and Weil. Until Macedonia, however, he had never experienced it. The revelation held profound implications for Lynd's spiritual development and subsequent activism. Moral inquirers were moral *agents*, he realized. They need not wait or rely on some future, apocalyptic intervention to achieve peace and brotherhood. To the contrary, they could discover and apply religious truths to the immediate sociopolitical environment, despite occasional setbacks and disappointyments.[57]

Replete with such deep insights, the three years that Lynd spent prefiguring the Kingdom of God in the northeast Georgia commune turned out to be the most rewarding spiritual experience of his life. Group members were self-identified Christians, but not to the exclusion of other religious viewpoints. Like that of Lynd's Ethical Culture mentors, the community's "creed" amounted to an ecumenical recognition of social justice, regardless of faith or denomination. "We said that different persons might use quite different words to describe this common religious experience," Lynd explained. Making occasional trips to an Atlanta library, Lynd sought out a variety of religious sources, including the Hindu pacifism of Gandhi, the Zen Buddhism of Daisetz Suzuki, and the Jewish theology of Martin Buber. The diversity of Lynd's interest, however, did not imply spiritual caprice, but a focused faith in spiritual socialism. Convinced that the righteous were known by their fruits, not by empty labels or artificial dualisms such as "Christian" and "non-Christian," Lynd presumed that God, if he existed in personal form, would prefer the "unbeliever who does good deeds" to "the church member" who fails to convert religious rhetoric into practice.[58] On this point, Lynd found scriptural evidence in a parable from the gospel of Matthew, wherein God distinguishes his nominal followers (goats) from his true followers (sheep), declaring, "For I was hungry and you gave me something to eat, I was thirsty and you gave me something to drink, I was a stranger and you invited me in, I needed clothes and you clothed me, I was sick and you looked after me, I was in prison and you came to visit me. Then the righteous will answer him, 'Lord, when did we see you hungry

... or thirsty.... When did we see you sick and in prison and go to visit you?' To which God will reply, 'I tell you the truth, whatever you did for one of the least of these brothers of mine, you did for me.'"[59] In this pithy passage, which encapsulates Christ's social gospel, Lynd found a "standard of ethics" that he "affirm[ed] with all his heart and mind." "Those verses came to mean more and more to [me], first at Macedonia, and still more afterwards," Lynd confessed.[60]

Changes in the Macedonia Cooperative Community toward a more doctrinal understanding of Christianity, as well as a sense of restlessness in Lynd for direct action, precipitated his decision to leave the community in the late 1950s. In some ways, Lynd had felt the same kind of isolation from political activism at the rural commune that had so unsettled Muste at Brookwood Labor College. Consequently, Lynd chose to participate in public service at the University Settlement House on New York City's Lower East Side, a job that brought the radical nomad "into contact with poor people" and community organizers, who worked together resisting plans for urban renewal (and tenant displacement) in Cooper Square. By exposing Lynd to the possibilities of community coalition and direct action, the experience proved invaluable. In the end, however, the University Settlement House did not satisfy Lynd as a suitable substitute for Macedonia.[61] The campaign for housing rights, though important, focused on a single-issue fight against political power. It did not constitute a radical social alternative or cooperative community. Macedonia had demonstrated to Lynd that "people could live together in a manner *qualitatively* different from the dog-eat-dog ambience of capitalist society." It was this sense of fellowship that Lynd sought to re-create in all his subsequent pursuits, whether in the southern civil rights movement, in solidarity with rank-and-file laborers, or in Latin America alongside liberation theologians. "We found [the spirit of beloved community] in these other places because we were looking for it; because, after Macedonia, we knew it could happen," Lynd explained.[62]

In the early 1960s, these questions about race, nation, and democracy were still left unresolved. Lynd, "eager to participate in the civil rights movement then burgeoning in the south," figured he would have more opportunities to contribute to the fight against white supremacy by teaching at a southern institution rather than at an Ivy League college in the northeast. Consequently, he applied to only "Negro colleges," and he attended the American Historical Association conference in hopes of receiving a job offer from one of them. "About midnight," Lynd recollected, "there came across the floor in my direction a tall, skinny, dark-haired man, a few years older than myself, with such an offer in hand. It was Howard Zinn, chairperson of social sciences at a college for African-American women in Atlanta."[63]

Teaching together at Spelman College, Lynd and Zinn became not only fast friends, but also neighbors and political comrades. Just as Lynd had hoped, he was learning that one could "do history" and "do politics" at the same time, even if it appeared unconventional to colleagues. Zinn set an inspiring example. "Refusing to accept the idea that a teacher should confine his teaching to the classroom when so much was at stake outside it," the Spelman department chair served as an adult advisor to the Atlanta branch of the Student Non-Violent Coordinating Committee (SNCC).[64] It did not take long for Lynd to become involved in SNCC activities. The organization appealed to him, not only because of its focus on racial justice, but also because of its commitment to equality, nonviolence, and spiritual values. As the SNCC founding statement of 1960 read, "We affirm the philosophical or religious ideal of nonviolence as the foundation of our purpose, the presumption of our faith, and the manner of our action. Nonviolence as it grows from Judaic-Christian traditions seeks a social order of justice permeated by love. . . . Love is the force by which God binds man to Himself and man to man."[65]

Lynd, who upheld the spiritual emphasis on human brotherhood, identified with SNCC's philosophy. He was also drawn to the combination of social and political radicalism that SNCC offered as both a beloved community and a serious civil rights organization. These activists fought for reform while simultaneously struggling to build alternative institutions, such as the so-called Freedom Schools that began operating as part of the Mississippi Freedom Project in the summer of 1964. Lynd, with his background in higher education and community organizing, became a coordinator for the schools. "I came to be offered the task that turned out to be my major contribution to the southern civil rights movement," he wrote.[66]

Lynd, the radical with the religious worldview, found himself in company with scores of social advocates, whose sense of human solidarity brought back memories of Macedonia and beloved community. Writing to his wife, Alice, upon arrival in Mississippi, Lynd reported his experience as "a most moving time" with "wonderful people." "Over and over again I have been reminded of Macedonia," he remarked, referring to the southern civil rights movement's emphasis on alternative institutions and fellowship.[67] Not everyone in the movement, of course, subscribed to a spiritual socialist worldview. But many, such as Martin Luther King Jr., did combine religion and radicalism in a way that prefigured the Kingdom of God on earth. For King, the movement was about more than securing civil rights. He wanted to transform society into a brotherhood of man. "Beyond the calling of race or nation or creed is the vocation of sonship and brotherhood," he stated in his 1967 Riverside Church antiwar address.[68] Racism represented one of the most glaring components of oppression in America, King argued. To get to the Kingdom of God on earth, he encouraged activists to apply radical change comprehensively, not narrowly. In his 1963 collection *Strength to Love*, for example, King reaffirmed his belief that "the gospel at its best deals with the whole man, not only his soul but also his body, not only his spiritual well-being but also his material well-being."[69]

King has been called a democratic socialist and a radical social gospeler, but he was also instrumental in projecting the tradition of spiritual socialism into the national spotlight in the 1950s and 1960s.[70] Though he shied away from publicly embracing the label "socialist" because of its political liabilities, King shared the values and vision of spiritual socialists, who believed that applied Christianity could create the kind of society that God wanted: a society of love, cooperation, individual dignity, equality, and security. And though he pursued policy changes, court appeals, and legislation at the top echelons of politics, he also insisted that only grassroots community building, and the cooperative way of daily life, could alter social behavior and culture. People needed to be heard and helped, no matter their class or color.

The Freedom Schools conveyed that spirit of community. Equipped with years of experience in egalitarian social relations, Lynd was well suited to coordinate the schools, which operated with flexible curricula, designed to encourage student participation, input, and even direction. "Improvisation was the order of the day," Lynd remembered. Indeed, Freedom School education was built on the Highlander Folk School method of individual "experience" and collective construction, "in which the student would help to define and create what he or she needed to know."[71] This pedagogical approach, according to teaching volunteer Sandra Adickes, was a "revelation" to black youth, who "had never been permitted, let alone encouraged, to voice their own answers to questions and ask their own questions."[72] It was familiar territory, however, for a graduate of the Ethical Culture Society, founded on Adler's belief that "the object of education is not to develop the ability to adjust oneself to the environment, but rather the ability to change environment, . . . to forward the progress of the world."[73] Lynd brought Adler's essential outlook to the Freedom Schools, but with a more radical intention. As he stated, "Teaching in the midst of the civil rights movement brought home the aphorism (here slightly rephrased) of Marx's *Theses on Feuerbach*: The historians have interpreted the world; the thing, however, is to change it."[74]

Lynd found that the students attending the Freedom Schools, no less than those at Spelman College, approached history as "a medium for the discovery of personal identity."[75] Adickes agreed. She recalled that the black youth at her site showed particular interest in "Negro History," which "began with a synopsis of the Amistad mutiny" and included sections on the Constitutional Convention's consent to slavery, slave revolts, the abolition movement, the Civil War, and Reconstruction. Students were surprised to learn that blacks in the late nineteenth century had enjoyed the right to vote and hold office, but that the development of the Jim Crow system eventually repressed the political life of freedmen.[76] Thus Freedom School participants began to see that their reality in Mississippi was a product of historical contingency and custom and was not a fixed condition. Lynd, as coordinator of the schools, helped to make these connections between the present and the past explicit. At one site where teachers encountered difficulties sparking student interest, Lynd suggested doing voter registration work in the afternoons, a solution that "made historical material about the years after the Civil War when Mississippi had black state representatives seem suddenly relevant."[77]

Voter registration was certainly a crucial component in the struggle for southern black freedom, and Lynd valued it as a fundamental civil right. He had his doubts, however, that the issue could sustain a radical movement if pursued in isolation from broader goals. How long would activists continue to risk their lives for piecemeal reforms? How long could the struggle for a socialist society inspire commitment if short-term objectives were not connected to a long-term vision or higher purpose? Typically, advocates of practical politics motivated allies by directing them toward concrete, immediate, and winnable objectives. Lynd, however, argued that it was as impractical to limit the movement to single issues as it was to apply a Band-Aid to a tumor. The question, for Lynd, pivoted on whether SNCC wanted to achieve representative democracy, which would incorporate blacks into the existing, corrupt American system, or democratic socialism, which would restructure the American system to reflect not just civil rights but also indivisible human rights and social justice.

The solution, Lynd claimed, was socialism, a "forbidden word" that movement activists often danced around, but seldom embraced as a vocabulary for their vision. Lynd understood the "cultural prohibition" against the term, which had never received a fair hearing in individual-oriented American politics. The word's association with Old Left–style dogma also discredited it in the eyes of young, innovative activists. Yet socialism, as a structural affirmation of human dignity and cooperation, represented "the natural inheritor of the currents of dissent which have lately accumulated in America," Lynd insisted. Radicals in the movement spoke of democracy, but not democracy confined to "pulling a lever in a little curtained room." Instead, they demanded equality, liberty, and the pursuit of dignified livelihoods, all of which required comprehensive social and economic change.[78] Thus, while Lynd agreed wholeheartedly with SNCC leader James Forman's formulation of human dignity as an "umbrella concept" for the movement, he recognized, perhaps more clearly than many activists at the time, that the path to a humane society was paved with socialist substance.[79] "Equality requires a redistribution of wealth as well as the right to vote," he maintained, echoing King.[80]

Lynd offered a third way, combining the freedom faction's quest for beloved community with the structure faction's penchant for radicalism. Rejecting reliance on any "moral gesture only," Lynd supported "a determined attempt to transform the American power structure." However, he wanted to do so "without losing the spiritual exaltation" of interracial unity and direct moral action.[81] Community, Lynd argued, was the key. While centralized organizations oscillated to the rhythms of political expediency, communities endured "to face whatever life brings" in the "spirit of a family," "even at the cost of short-run tangible failures." Communities thus satisfied both the means and ends of radical vision: the creation of parallel institutions to rival and replace existing social and economic structures. As such, they provided an answer for those radicals intent on building a solid power base: "surely the ideological framework of brotherhood and community should make it easier to [do] so than one simply oriented to pragmatic goals," Lynd wrote. Such reasoning underlined Lynd's vision of spiritual socialism: cooperative communities "building . . . a brotherly way of life even in the jaws of the Leviathan" simply by heeding Jesus' call to love and care for one another. Prefigurative models of the Kingdom of God, however, were not intended to form isolated pockets, removed from the world and its problems. To the contrary, communal living packed considerable political punch. As Lynd explained, "It is conscientious objection . . . to the whole fabric of dehumanized society."[82]

The southern civil rights campaign, Lynd realized, was only one facet of an emerging New Left movement demanding a global revolution in values. At the University of Michigan in the early 1960s, for example, SDS began to develop a moral vision for a generation beset by Cold War realities. With its 1962 Port Huron Statement, SDS New Leftists, many of whom were civil rights volunteers, intended to provide an integrating framework for the radical regional and single-issue campaigns erupting throughout the nation and the world. These diverse dissenters shared a commitment to a common set of values, which directed action toward achieving basic human rights. The specific term "human rights" did not yet encapsulate their doctrine, but it was a key concept, shaping the contours of the Port Huron Statement and its expressed democratic alternative to Old Left and Cold War "indifference to human affairs." "Our own social values involve conceptions of human beings, human relationships, and social systems," the young radicals stated: "We regard *men* as infinitely precious and possessed of unfulfilled capacities for reason, freedom, and love. In affirming these principles, we are aware of countering perhaps the dominant conceptions of man in the twentieth century: that he is a thing to be manipulated, and that he is inherently incapable of directing his own affairs. We oppose the depersonalization that reduces human beings to the status of things—if anything, the brutalities of the twentieth century teach that means and ends are intimately related."[83]

Lynd recognized the Port Huron Statement, and its central, spiritualized concept of "participatory democracy," as a powerful expression of his radical worldview. Based on the inherent value of individual persons, the term "participatory democracy," Lynd sensed, appealed to the plight of ordinary, subjugated brothers and sisters all over the world, Communist or not. According to Lynd and his New Left allies, these voices needed to be heard. They deserved a chance to decide. Such was the reasoning behind the Assembly of Unrepresented People, a protest march held in Washington, D.C., on August 6–9, 1965, the anniversary of the Hiroshima and Nagasaki bombings, to present the U.S. government with a Declaration of Conscience, condemning national foreign policy. "The idea was that we did not support the undeclared war with Vietnam," remembered Lynd, who helped organize the event and participated in its march on the Capitol with Bob Moses, David Dellinger, and Muste.[84] In a Cold War climate, characterized by impersonal political and military maneuvering, these activists sought to humanize the enemy and remind policymakers that the world was one community in which universal values of democracy, individual dignity, and equality still applied. The trick was to keep things personal, yet universal. Religious intellectuals such as Reinhold Niebuhr had rejected as futile the attempt to transcend human nature. "The truth is that every immediate loyalty [to family, to country, etc.,] is a potential danger to higher and more inclusive loyalties," he wrote. "What lies beyond the nation, the community of mankind, is too vague to inspire devotion."[85] Lynd set out to prove the opposite: that loyalty to universal notions of humankind and human rights sustained moral interpersonal relations, regardless of cultural difference or geographic distance.

In 1965, Lynd voiced this message at several New Left antiwar demonstrations, including the massive SDS rally in Washington, D.C. Tom Hayden, the principal author of the Port Huron Statement, remembered "admiring Staughton as he chaired the event with authority and transfixed us with a comparison between suffering Vietnam and the Crucifixion."[86] Four months later, Lynd marched with the Assembly of Unrepresented People, who presented a Declaration of Conscience Against the War in Vietnam. "We believe," the statement read, "that all peoples of the earth, including both Americans and non-Americans, have an inalienable right to life, liberty, and the peaceful pursuit of happiness in their own way."[87]

By the late 1960s, however, the New Left *movement*, as a national and international manifestation of progressive political pressure, had started to fragment into factions, many of which aimed to forcefully overthrow the government, incite labor or racial discord, and bring the war home with domestic acts of terrorism. Lynd, like so many spiritual socialists before him, felt let down and left out by the people he had considered comrades in the struggle for a peaceful, cooperative society. The means to the ideal society no longer prefigured the ends. The New Left, it seemed to him, had abandoned its core values, the very spiritual values that made it humane, unique, and morally effective. "I found it embarrassing and shameful that the organizations created in the hopeful early years of the 1960s—first SNCC and then SDS—no longer existed ten years later," he confessed. Disillusioned and dejected by decade's end, Lynd "experienced something resembling Post-Traumatic Stress Disorder." For the rest of his life, he acknowledged, he would distrust any proposals for national organizations.[88]

Though the early 1970s were a "lonely and confusing time" for Lynd, he soon found reason for hope.[89] If *immediate* revolution, on moral terms, proved intractable, activists could remain faithful to the process of a long-term, *constructive* revolution, built on basic moral values and the spirit of community. Silone, recovering from his own disillusionment in the 1940s, had come to the same conclusion. "The fact that spiritual communion is possible," he wrote in an article for *Dissent* in 1955, meant that the "disillusionments of history" could never destroy the struggle for the Kingdom of God. "To be valid," Silone declared, "it does not need success."[90] Indeed, for many New Leftists, the fragmentation of the movement and its subsequent "cultural turn" did not necessarily denote the end of its collective struggle for an ethical new world order. New Left theorist Dick Flacks, for one, discerned the positive features of the movement's post-1960s fragmentation, which represented not defeat, but the perseverance of New Left values: "Basically, I think that the left in America is a cultural rather than a political force, defining 'political' as power-oriented. The claim that you are power-oriented is typically a sign that you are turning into a sect or that you are betraying the values that you once held. If that's true, the question for the left is what forms of organization are appropriate to being an intellectual, educative, moral force."[91]

Lynd called for "an alternative revolutionary strategy" to "change capitalism from below" "without taking state power."[92] "Solidarity unionism" became his new radical expression of labor-oriented spiritual socialism. Lynd acknowledged that this approach would take time, but he knew the value of simple, staid moral actions. "We are at that stage in organizing when what we are really doing is meeting people, making friends, building community in the one-on-one manner memorably described by Ignazio Silone in *Bread and Wine*," Lynd wrote in the early 1990s. Although he knew it was scandalous to assert it "among unreconstructed Wobblies," Lynd recognized that in the process of building socialism "there is also a religious dimension to what we will be doing."[93]

According to Greg Calvert, a former National Secretary for SDS, there had always been a religious dimension to the nominally secular New Left as well. "Spiritual values," centered on the concept of an "ego-transcendent community of love, brotherhood, and sisterhood," Calvert claimed, were implicit in the movement for participatory democracy. Explicit expressions of religious idealism, however, were "lacking" among New Leftists who often downplayed religion as a nonradical or nonpolitical approach to social problems. For Calvert, this failure to embrace the religious roots of the New Left's "democratic idealism" made the movement "vulnerable to attack from the materialisms of the Marxist or liberal traditions." In other words, many New Leftists turned to Marxist theory and dogma in the late 1960s because they had failed to develop their intuitive moral values into a practical political philosophy. Yet "there was one major effort to develop a framework in which New Left radicalism could find historical and philosophical roots in [a religious] idealist tradition," Calvert wrote. "This effort was the work of the New Left activist, thinker, and writer Staughton Lynd," who attempted to "legitimize the spiritual or religious intuitions and values of at least part of the New Left."[94]

There were, of course, still radicals who practiced spiritual values, a revelation that Lynd discovered during a trip to Central America in the 1980s. Traveling to Managua with the Inter-religious Foundation for Community Organization, Lynd and his wife intended to bear moral witness to activists who stood between Sandinista revolutionaries and the U.S.-backed "contra" forces.[95] Many of the peaceful dissenters, they learned, were liberation theologians, radical Catholics who supported the socialist revolution as a triumph for human dignity and brotherhood. "After years of feeling that in [the United States] I was too Christian for the Marxists and too Marxist for the Christians," Lynd wrote, "I went to Nicaragua and felt that everyone I met was like myself."[96] As Lynd learned during his five trips to Nicaragua in the 1980s and 1990s, liberation theologians shared many of his radical religious convictions. They believed, he explained, "that the Kingdom of God should be lived out here on earth" by struggling alongside the poor, confronting oppressive institutions, and building "base communities," where people could gather to "read the Gospel, and try to apply it in their . . . life."[97] Lynd devoted the rest of his life to the plight of industrial workers in eastern Ohio, where he worked as a labor lawyer.

The New Left movement that historians associate with the 1960s may have come and gone, but for Lynd the spirit of the New Left was still alive in the work of liberation theologians in South America, in the struggle for solidarity in U.S. factories, and in any place where people cooperated with each other for a more just, democratic, and peaceful society. The "New Left" approach, according to Lynd, predated the 1960s. It had existed in the work of "proto–New Leftists" such as Silone, Weil, and Muste, and it continued to thrive in local communities, where people could apply spiritual values to social situations.

"I remain, as I have been since age fourteen, a socialist," Lynd wrote in 1997.[98] He also remained a New Leftist on his own terms—a radical agent of social change accompanying the poor and persecuted, demonstrating humble leadership, building grassroots solidarity, resisting corrupt authority, and, in all ways, prefiguring the Kingdom of God on earth. Charles Eckert, reporting for the *Spectator* during a mock election for chancellor at Indiana University, put it this way: "In answer to the question 'What does being a radical mean to you?' Lynd gave an answer that revealed the strong Quaker-pacifist roots of his character. He likened himself to a Christian pilgrim, one who travels through the world 'diffusely and systematically at odds with the scheme of things.'"[99] Though the road was difficult and victories limited, Lynd refused to relinquish his faith in the potential for a better world based on ethical social relations. "Like the crucifixion of an obscure Jewish carpenter in the first century," he wrote, the fall of a movement might be only a "[seeming] failure," a temporary setback.[100] Despite the persistence of oppression, the spirit of New Left spiritual socialism, trusted Lynd, would continue to live on in the practice of humane social values all over the world.

In the early 1960s, Yale law student Pauli Murray was also grappling with the importance of democracy and social inclusion in America. However, Murray, a mixed-race individual dedicated to expanding civil rights and human rights, believed that many movement leaders had fallen far short of their professed egalitarian, religious, and democratic ideals, especially when it came to the status and treatment of women. Murray challenged Martin Luther King Jr. and A. Philip Randolph, for example, to recognize their patriarchal blind spots. Her sharp critique of left and liberal activists contained significant implications for spiritual socialism and the Kingdom of God, positing universal values without a universal subject and the notion of all-inclusive identity instead of the narrow identity politics emerging in the late 1960s and early 1970s.

Murray's multifaceted sense of self, in terms of race, gender, spirituality, and class, helped shape her response to progressive movements. Born on November 20, 1910, in Baltimore, Murray grew up in a close-knit family of "high ideals and strong religious values."[101] Her maternal grandfather, Robert Fitzgerald, half-white, had served in the Union Army during the Civil War and had volunteered to educate freedmen during Reconstruction. While in North Carolina, he married Cornelia, the daughter of a white plantation owner and a half-Cherokee house slave. Murray, adopted by an aunt at age three, lived amid this racial complexity in Durham, where some individuals in her family passed as white, though most were limited by Jim Crow segregation and racism to the social status of African Americans. At family functions, "it looked like a United Nations in miniature," Murray wrote, "ranging from fair-skinned, blue-eyed, red-haired, freckle-faced types through various shades of peach and olive to those with Indian copper skin, dark eyes, and heavy black hair."[102] Murray did not always feel comforted by the conditions of her in-betweenness. "In a world of black-white opposites, I had no place," she explained. "Being neither very dark nor very fair, I was a nobody without identity. I was too dark at home and too light at school."[103] Prejudice did not deter Murray from reaching her highest potential, though it did prevent her from attending the University of North Carolina, despite the decades of service and financial support her family had contributed to the institution. Instead, she moved to New York City to continue her education and escape the hindering and humiliating mores of the Jim Crow South.

Murray took the lessons of her youth north with her, particularly the multiracial heritage that had predisposed her to recognize "relatedness" over division and the inherent dignity of every individual as a special creation of God. As she wrote in her family memoir, *Proud Shoes*, in the mid-1950s, "the acceptance of the possibility of relatedness would do much to defuse the highly charged discussions on race. Ultimately, it might help to ease the transition to a more humane society."[104] There were plenty of examples of inhumane treatment in American society, including racial violence and the civil liberties abuses during the Red Scare. Murray's family pride and religious beliefs prompted her to rail against both. Her writings on her ancestry, she admitted, amounted to evidence of American belonging. And her theology was presented as proof of organic radicalism, unconnected to Communism. "Not Communism, but the ideals and influences within my own family had made me a life-long fighter against all forms of inequality and injustice," she insisted.[105]

Raised in an Episcopalian church, with influences from Quakerism and Presbyterianism via her grandfather, Murray learned from her family's faith that everybody is valued by God. "Each member of the household was made to feel important in the eyes of the Almighty and that he had his place in the universe."[106] Personalism, as it had for many spiritual socialists, formed the foundation of Murray's theology and politics. In 1932, she voted for Socialist Party candidate Norman Thomas, because "she could not bring [herself] to vote for a Democrat," the party of "apartheid" in the South. She also sold papers for the Urban League, taught remedial reading through the Works Progress Administration, marched in a Harlem picket line, and attended the New Workers School and Brookwood Labor College in the 1930s, all the while escaping the "morass of party influence" and ideology. Religious values, and the "religious fervor" of the labor movement, kept Murray moored to the personal experiences of her comrades more so than dogma. Before Brookwood, she "had never thought of white people as victims of oppression," but as she interacted with industrial workers, she "heard echoes of the black experience" in their tales of exploitation. "The study of economic oppression," she recalled, "led me to realize that Negroes were not alone but were part of an unending struggle for human dignity the world over."[107]

For Murray, Communism had nothing to offer the struggle. Religion and democracy, however, did. "I became convinced," she wrote, "that the alternative to communism was a democracy that could be made to work for all its people."[108] Conflating democracy with Christianity, Murray found the common denominator in God-given human dignity, which, by extension, formed the basis of political and social equality. Sarah Azaransky, in her study of Murray's political theology, makes this point well, arguing that Murray "grounded her calls for democratic transformation in Christian concepts of reconciliation and of the coming kingdom." Employing the term "democratic eschatology," Azaransky reveals how Murray tied democratic fulfillment to a future state of social harmony, analogous to the Kingdom of God on earth, wherein "people will be reconciled in their differences."[109] Murray's eschatology, then, resembled that of spiritual socialists, even if she felt less comfortable with the word "socialism" than many of her Kingdom-ethic comrades. Like most New Leftists in the 1950s and 1960s, she preferred to speak about democracy, which seemed more American and less ideological. That is not to say Murray was any less ideological or radical than her spiritual socialist counterparts. To the contrary, she challenged them to expand their vision and practice of inclusion by recognizing the acute discrimination of women in progressive movements as well as in society at large. She insisted that universal values of human equality and dignity did not dilute differences among people, but instead enhanced them.

The personal discrimination she faced at Howard University's law school, where she first felt her gender minority status and the lack of respect it held among her African American peers and mentors, opened Murray's eyes to the particular plight of women. She had intended to study law as a pacifist's weapon against Jim Crow and the prejudices of race, but "the discovery that . . . men I deeply admired because of their dedication to civil rights, men who themselves had suffered racial indignities, could countenance exclusion of women from their professional association aroused an incipient feminism in me long before I knew the meaning of the term 'feminism,'" she wrote. Once made sensitive to gender injustice, Murray noticed it everywhere, and she did not shrink from raising the issue and exposing the hypocrisy of civil rights leaders. At the celebrated 1963 March on Washington, Murray lamented that female activists received "little more than token recognition" on the program, despite their significant contributions to the movement. She also chastised Randolph for accepting an invitation to speak at the all-male National Press Club. These radical leaders, for Murray, were not radical enough. Their own male privilege blinded them from seeing the comprehensive, interrelated issues of human rights and equality that were necessary to address before democracy or the Kingdom of God could be achieved.[110] Years before a caucus of women submitted their Memo on Sex and Caste to the male leadership of SDS and SNCC in 1965, Murray had already diagnosed the gender disorder in early New Left movements. Even among spiritual socialists, not even Day focused on the unique conditions of women as oppressed. Instead, she folded her concept of human dignity into the universal concept that Christ is everyone. Day also criticized the Catholic Church on its failures to promote peace and workers' justice without calling special attention to the institution's strict patriarchal structure.

Murray demanded more commitment to equality, from liberals and leftists alike. Despite her burgeoning friendship with Eleanor Roosevelt, for instance, she called her and her husband, Franklin, to a higher standard of ethics than political expediency would allow. In 1952, when Murray's admiration for candidate Adlai Stevenson soured after his equivocating racial pronouncements, she faulted the former First Lady for continuing to support a Democrat who did not advocate more radical policies. "Not even Mrs. Roosevelt," Murray wrote, "seemed to appreciate fully the depth of our feeling that the subordination of the moral imperatives of our struggle to political expediencies was little short of betrayal by our friends."[111] For spiritual socialists, the primacy of morals above politics burned at the core of their opposition to both liberals and leftists, at least rhetorically. On issues of race and class, they strove to meet this standard. On issues of gender, they often fell short or ignored it altogether, as Murray was wont to emphasize. Murray insisted that gender injustice remained a glaring problem for those who claimed to cultivate progress toward the Kingdom of God or participatory democracy. There were those who told Murray that women's rights should remain subordinate to the more pressing causes of race or class. But Murray believed in the "interrelation of all human rights" and would not compromise on her all-inclusive vision.[112]

In essence, Murray's views on rights stemmed from her recognition of multiple, interrelated nodes of identity, at both the national and individual levels. A person, she argued, could not be reduced to a single identity, such as worker, woman, or Latino. Instead, each person contained many identifiers and, as such, should strive to express and defend them all, from the standpoint of an organic, undivided sense of self. A similar multiplicity held true, she insisted, for America's national identity, its history created by not only white men, but also women, workers, Asians, Africans, slaves, masters, and so forth. As Azaransky wrote, "Murray affirms that an American citizen is an identity formed in a web of relationships." Her own multiracial genealogy helped Murray see the nation as a large family unit, for better or for worse, struggling to prosper together.[113]

For Murray, the individual has importance, given the inherent dignity of each personality. Individualism, however, does not denote self-interest. An awareness of multiple identities entails multiple interests: not single-issue causes, but a variety of opportunities to connect with others who are also struggling for self-actualization. She favored broad coalition building in social justice movements as much more reflective of and responsive to the complexity of individual activists. In the early 1940s, as a traveling fundraiser for the Workers Defense League, she worked tirelessly to build a coalition of progressives on behalf of a black sharecropper, Odell Waller, imprisoned for shooting his landowner in a fit of desperation and sentenced to death in Virginia. Though she ultimately failed to free Waller, Murray made impassioned speeches across the country, highlighting the racial and economic discrimination that violated his rights and earning the ear and support of a variety of supporters, including attorneys for the National Association for the Advancement of Colored People, law school faculty, clergy, union leaders, and many activists associated with Eddy's Delta farms for sharecroppers.[114] Murray connected Waller's specific plight to more generalized stakes, including democracy, rights, and justice, thus allowing a broad coalition to see their own interests in Waller's case. As she put it a few years later, she learned that a "revolution in our individual thinking" is a prerequisite to social change. "It requires a moral ethic which reaffirms a fundamental kinship in all mankind," she wrote.[115] Instead of organizing for individual self-interest, activists, according to Murray, should locate a point of common interest and common humanity, which would help build coalitions for comprehensive social justice.

Murray's understanding of complex selves, identities, and solutions formed the crux of her ambiguity toward, if not outright rejection of, identity politics in the late 1960s and into the 1970s. Frustrated with the slow pace of change and the involvement of white leadership in New Left movements, many minority groups, whether racially, gender-, or class-based, began to advocate for an exclusive, empowered focus on the conditions particular to their identities. Consequently, organizations dedicated to Black Power, Chicano Power, American Indian rights, women's rights, and labor unions started to see their interests as separate and irrelevant to broad alliances or party politics. The development of these narrowing causes for each identity contributed to the fracturing of traditional coalitions on the left and made it particularly difficult for spiritual socialists to convince radicals that love, fellowship, and nonviolence remained worthwhile strategies for achieving social justice. The shift to particular group identities, however, should not have come as a great surprise, because, in some ways, spiritual socialists helped create the conceptual basis for identity politics to flourish. If one takes seriously the notion that every individual is a child of God, imbued with inherent dignity and singular worth, then an embrace of specialized characteristics would seem to follow. Practitioners of identity politics did not give up on social justice; they merely narrowed the field of collective association, casting aside abstract ideas of common humanity and universalisms for what they considered to be a more concentrated, intensive, and practical political focus.[116] This shift toward identity causes, of course, did not necessarily disrupt leftist unity. In many ways, identity politics helped keep leftists and liberals accountable to issues and minority demographics that were otherwise marginalized. However, identity politics fragmented the Left into single-issue groups that made it more difficult to find common cause. At best, identity politics fulfilled the leftist vision of radical democracy, but at worst, identity activists recycled the Left's most pressing internal problem: factionalism.

Murray, for one, lamented the turn to a new form of dogmatic single-mindedness, reminiscent of the sectarian splits that had crippled the Old Left. Black Power groups were active and vocal at Brandeis University, where Murray taught interdisciplinary Afro-American Studies courses. Students and faculty may have expected Murray to sympathize with the demands of minorities on campus, but she made her reservations clear. She resented the "crude sexism" that she perceived in the male-dominated movement for Black Power, as well as the self-induced ignorance of the experiences of those outside tribal parameters. Again, Murray could not separate the intertwined sources of herself, the multiple threads of identity that bound her to the human race in general. As she explained in her essay "Black Power for Whom?," "I stress human rights rather than Negro rights ... because I have a double minority status and ... achievements of Negro rights would leave me only partially protected. Nor do I believe that one set of rights must take priority over the other, but all must be achieved simultaneously or none will be permanently secured." Murray would not make the self-denying choice between her female or Negro identities.[117] As she declared in the preface to her book of poems, *Dark Testament*, "I speak for my race and my people—the human race and just people."[118]

Murray believed in universal human dignity, but she did not project a universal subject or identity, unlike many spiritual socialists, who spent little time discussing people's differences and kept their concept of common humanity rather abstract. Murray underscored the special circumstances of blacks and women (and especially black women) in the fight for justice. Employing the term "Jane Crow" to describe discrimination unique to women, she argued that African Americans could not achieve full civil rights without considering women's rights, and women's organizations such as the National Organization for Women, which she cofounded but later quit because of its white, middle-class preoccupation, could not make progress without equal attention to African Americans.[119] Again, identities, for Murray, were inseparable, to be justified simultaneously.

Movements that championed black pride to the exclusion of others did not arouse her support. Though Murray was pursuing theological training and ordination in Episcopal seminaries during the 1970s when black theology, feminist theology, and liberation theology were gaining traction, she equivocated on the conclusions of scholarship such as that of James Cone, author of 1969's *Black Theology and Black Power*, who conflated Christianity and Black Power, arguing that because Christ represented the condition and hope of the oppressed, and blacks in America constituted the group exposed to the greatest oppression, then Black Power reflected Christianity more than any other movement in the United States. Cone not only suggested that Black Power and Christianity were compatible, but he went so far as to say that "Christianity is not alien to Black Power; it is Black Power," derived from the premise that "if Christ is present among the oppressed, as he promised, he must be working through the activity of Black Power." Rather than herald love, fellowship, reconciliation, and nonviolence as the solutions to racial problems, as King had done, Cone supported any means that could help blacks cope and overcome white supremacy, including violence. In his rationale for violence as an extension of God through man, Cone wrote that "the attempt of some to measure love exclusively by specific actions, such as nonviolence, is theologically incorrect." He considered the outrage of blacks rioting in cities and taking up arms against white society not as a denial of God, but as an expression of existential being, confirming selfhood, and saying "yes to himself as a creature of God."[120]

Cone captured Murray's interest to some extent, especially given his concern with bolstering black pride and activism as expressions of God-given dignity (or theological personalism).[121] Murray, however, could not accept Cone's militant approach, his racial exclusivity, or his machismo. Cone's work, addressed to the "angry black man," was intended to "touch the souls of black brothers" and stir up a "revolutionary" response. He called for blacks to assume a "dominant" role in society, all the while separating black culture from white culture. And he outright rejected integration and reconciliation as worthy goals, dismissing them as irrelevant to black experience. "Black Power seeks not understanding but conflict; addresses blacks and not whites; seeks to develop black support, but not white good will," he stated.[122]

Adamant about the potential of human reconciliation despite differences, and the redemption of humanity through love and fellowship, Murray had more in common with spiritual socialists such as King than with Cone. Though she appreciated liberation theology in general with its preferential option of the poor, Murray's long-held pacifism kept her at odds with Cone's theological concepts and Black Power militancy. She had practiced nonviolent civil disobedience throughout her life, and despite her earlier criticism of King, she mourned the loss of his leadership in a nonviolent mission to reconcile blacks, whites, and all human beings into a brotherhood of mankind. King had "emphasized the moral and spiritual imperatives of the ongoing struggle for human dignity and had demonstrated the power of love to transcend divisions of race, sex, or class," she wrote.[123] Any notion of a discrete vanguard, favored to lead a violent struggle on behalf of all humanity, seemed sinful to her, grounded in Godless egotism, not God-given dignity. In a 1975 essay she wrote, "Black Theology: Heresy, Syncretism, or Prophecy?," she called Cone's theories a "desparate [sic] effort" mired in black pride, a handicap that would serve only to further alienate African Americans and thwart efforts of reconciliation.[124] She objected to any self-imposed segregation, considering it a step in the wrong direction and a sad reversal of the gains made by civil rights activists. It did not reflect dignity, for Murray, but shame and self-hatred. On these terms, she was not alone in her assessment. According to Anthony B. Bradley, a religious studies scholar at King's College in New York, "Black liberation theology actually encourages a victim mentality among blacks," similar to how Marx encouraged a victim mentality among workers who needed to first recognize and then challenge their oppressors.[125]

But Murray had the same issues with Cone that she had with Marx. Black Power advocates, Murray believed, did not seek to transcend divisions but to deepen them. Therefore, they could never serve as a useful model for social action. The notion of self-imposed segregation, Murray admitted, "grated upon [her] sensibilities," reminding her of the sectarian divisions of the Old Left more than the beloved community of the civil rights movement. "This emerging racial rhetoric smacked of an ethnic 'party line' and made absolutely no sense to me," she said. "I was uncomfortable in any environment that was not inclusive."[126] Cone's purpose certainly was not inclusive, and his notion of the coming Kingdom of God did not conform to that of spiritual socialists, who upheld the future ideal, the unrealized vision of perfect peace and love, as a guide to current action. "We are not living in what the New Testament called the consummated Kingdom," Cone wrote, "and even its partial manifestation is not too obvious. Therefore, black people cannot live according to what ought to be, but according to what *is*."[127] For Murray, such logic did not represent a fresh and empowering beginning for black determination, but a surrender to the evils of the world. Though spiritual socialists such as Eddy and Wallace had defended the need for a "just war" to eradicate evil forces such as Fascism and reset the conditions for the Kingdom of God, Cone's justification for violence did not strike Murray as a temporary aberration in service to the Kingdom, but as a long-term plan to marshal the worst traits of human nature for the sake of achieving sectarian power.

To a certain extent, Murray was making a value judgment not only about Black Power, but also about the decade, by dividing it into the "good" 1960s and the "bad" 1960s. As she explained it in her memoir,

> The earlier consensus, which had unified church groups, labor and liberal groups, and the major civil rights organizations around the goal of integration, was shattered in the mid-1960s, and interracial coalitions fell apart. Older leaders whose patient toil had made possible civil rights victories up to that time were being discredited and shunted aside by younger, embittered black nationalistic radicals. With the assassination of Martin Luther King, Jr., advocacy of the moral principle of nonviolent resistance to injustice coupled with the promise of racial reconciliation was quickly overtaken by the idea of black liberation by any means necessary and a mood of violent response to racial subjugation, real or imagined.[128]

The same sense of disillusionment gripped Lynd, who likened the perceived death of nonviolent activism in the late 1960s to a feeling of desperation on the verge of nervous collapse. Like so many spiritual socialists before him, he felt let down and left out by the people he had considered comrades in the struggle for a peaceful, cooperative society. The means to the ideal society no longer prefigured the ends. The New Left, it seemed to him, had abandoned its core values, the very spiritual values that made it humane, unique, and morally effective. Violence, for pacifists like Murray, Lynd, Day, and Muste, represented the antithesis to the brotherhood of man, wherein everyone is treated with love and respect. Dismissing Black Power advocates on a priori principles, these spiritual socialists could not hear them over their violent rhetoric, even as their failure to find fellowship with Black Power betrayed values of understanding and inclusion.

The issue with Cone, of course, was not limited to a fundamentalist pacifist position. It also involved conflicting visions about the Kingdom of God and socialism. According to Murray, Lynd, Day, Muste, and King, the means had to match the ends, not for moral reasons alone, but as a matter of practicality. They could agree with Cone's action-oriented eschatology to a degree, especially when he quoted Jürgen Moltmann, calling for a "love which institutes community, sets things right and puts them in order, becomes eschatologically possible through the Christian hope's prospects of the future of God's kingdom and of man." But Cone also demanded "the creation of new values independent of and alien to the values of white society," which were corrupted by racism, and a new social order defined by blacks' terms. Though Cone did not deny the aim of reconciliation as essential to Christian practice, he insisted that "the black community itself must lay down the rules of the game," and that white people must *become* black, not through skin color but through shared suffering and oppression.[129]

For many spiritual socialists, Cone's vision was too particularist and too much about power. They believed in creating a new order, adopting a new value system, and performing the cultural work of revolution. They did not believe, however, in elevating any particular group of people (defined by class or race) as a vanguard bent on achieving power at the expense of others. The crux of the matter came down to what kind of socialism one wanted: a top-heavy political force defined by dominance and (in many respects) retribution for past wrongs, or a grassroots culture of love, cooperation, and true equality. If the former, spiritual socialists could point to the Soviet Union and the problems that the Communist Party–centered system had yielded to the nation and the world. As for the latter, it had yet to be fully tried. And Black Power was not regarded as a step toward its development.

Not all spiritual socialists, however, rejected Black Power wholesale. Cornel West, the self-described "Chekhovian Christian" with a "Gramscian democratic socialism," did not divide the "good" 1960s from the "bad." Instead, he sought to find a point of connection and dialogue with proponents of Black Power and black theology, an extension of Christian fellowship that could offer an illuminating path around the impasse of identity politics for the religious Left, and for spiritual socialists in particular. West's propensity for theological and philosophical variety, drawing on traditions of pragmatism, Marxism, existentialism, black theology, and the social gospel, among others, might seem, at first glance, too equivocal for building a foundation for progressive religion. However, it is specifically West's willingness to engage with a wide range of worldviews that makes his political approach so powerful. Rather than dismiss any idea, individual, or identity group for deviating from his ideals, West strove to find value in everyone and everything. "My vision was surely based on my black Baptist foundation," he wrote in his memoir. "It had everything to do with Jesus Christ's mandate to love extravagantly and radically, but it also went in a dozen different directions."[130] By rejecting narrow dogmas and by projecting a language of shared values and practicing the politics of common ground, West operated with a flexibility, allowing him to find commonality in unlikely places. In short, he sought to transcend identity politics by deepening his engagement with diversity.

West's issues with black theologians like Cone, and Black Power advocates like Malcolm X, echoed those raised by Murray and Lynd. Committed to a Christian vision of universal brotherhood and reconciliation, West was "deeply suspicious of the politics of black nationalists." "I worked with them on antiracist issues," he wrote, "and we discussed, laughed and partied together weekly—but I always staked out my Christian version of democratic socialist values and politics."[131] The Black Panthers, headquartered in Oakland, California, near where West grew up, did not espouse a theology. In fact, they generally rejected religion as a means of oppression, utilized by centuries of slaveholders to keep blacks docile and focused on future rewards rather than present misery. West wanted to support such a strong black movement for liberation, but the "absence of a spiritual base" within the organization left him unsatisfied. "The more I read," he recalled, "the more I realized that black revolutionary nationalism didn't work for me. No nationalism did." For West, as for Murray, the cross of Christ dissolved all dichotomies and divisions and dogmatic lines. Liberation, according to West, would come from a spirit of love, a love that "saves us from the tyranny of chauvinism and its many manifestations."[132]

Criticisms notwithstanding, West found value in the Panthers and their constructive community programs, such as the breakfast program, which West helped with many mornings before heading to school. As he told his parents when they expressed misgivings about his extracurricular associations, the Panthers were not all bad. "I'd explain to my parents that, even as Christians, we could learn from the Panthers," especially since most Christians lacked a thorough "social analysis of capitalism." When West matriculated at Harvard the following year, he also defended the Panthers against the criticisms of his professors. "I disagree with them on many issues," he told Dr. Martin Kilson. "But on other issues they have something to say. We have a rich dialogue."[133]

At times, that dialogue could become quite tense, as West discovered after he openly disapproved of Elijah Muhammad's treatment of Malcolm X during a Nation of Islam event on campus. Fearing for his safety for weeks, West finally confronted a fellow student, who remained loyal to

Elijah Muhammad and had threatened West with retaliation for his disrespectful public comments. The two students engaged in a heated discussion, but eventually they earned each other's respect. "After a couple of hours of exploring each other's backgrounds, we got closer. Empathy overwhelmed anger." Enacting the Christian values that he espoused, West laid aside his self-righteousness and outrage in order to really listen to his opponent. "But that was only possible when I tried to put myself in his shoes," he explained. "Wasn't that I changed my mind or that he changed his. It was just a matter of giving each other space to be heard."[134]

Instead of dismissing an individual or viewpoint as unworthy of careful consideration, West chose to compartmentalize his differences with black nationalists, acknowledging the positive aspects he could while remaining true to his own beliefs. The same cannot be said for Murray or Lynd, whose unyielding condemnation of violence among Black Power militants kept them from reaching out in a spirit of fellowship. In this way, West *enacted* reconciliation, in deed as much as rhetoric, more authentically than many of his spiritual socialist comrades. He chose to transcend differences for the sake of diversity and coalition building, an approach that, in his mind, most reflected Jesus and also his greatest African American hero, Martin Luther King Jr. "I resonated with the sincere black militancy of Malcolm X, the defiant rage of the Black Panther Party, and the livid black theology of James Cone," West conceded. "Yet I did not fully agree with them. I always felt that they lacked the self-critical moment of humility I discerned in the grand example of Martin Luther King, Jr."[135]

Cone is a useful case in point. West could get behind the theology of Black Power, and no doubt he had appreciated Cone's Christian corrective to the brazen atheism he had encountered among the Panthers in Oakland. He also understood Cone's book as an existential outcry, a courageous attempt to inspire a commitment to life and radical change even unto death. In an 1998 essay written for the controversial book's thirtieth anniversary, West praised *Black Theology and Black Power* as "one of the first towering texts of modernity to wrestle with the question of what it means to be human in the face of death," and he referred to Cone as "a thinker who loves enough to attempt to tell the truth about himself as he tells the truth about others." Cone's blunt truth, above all, exposed the persistence of white supremacy, an ugly and hard truth that had to be confronted with one's entire being, "calling for us to die daily," as West put it. "It is no sunshine optimism," West knew, "but a blood-drenched hope" that African Americans could transcend their circumstances and gain the respect they deserved. It was, for West, a prophetic voice screaming for social atonement and a renewed Christian commitment to justice.[136] He did not regard Cone or Black Power as detrimental to democracy (or democratic socialism). Instead, he deemed it necessary to listen to the legitimate grievances of all members of society, especially those who feel marginalized and oppressed, to create democratic socialism and pay the high price of human cooperation that the Kingdom of God demanded.

Cone's lack of "humility," however, bothered West, and that kept him from completely endorsing the book, especially since King met the criteria for him, combining Christian love with prophetic courage. King, he wrote, "has always been not so much a model to imitate, but the touchstone for personal inspiration, moral wisdom and existential thought."[137] King taught blacks that they could critique society and individuals for all their sins, "while holding on to the humanity of those whom they opposed."[138] Cone, in contrast, resorted to stereotyping, dismissing all whites (referred to by the pejorative "Whitey" throughout his book) as irrelevant to black existence. King never went that far, and West noted the difference. "Love breaks down barriers," West contended, "so even when black rage and righteous indignation have to look white supremacy in the face . . . the language of love still allows black brothers and sisters to recognize that it's not all white people and it's not genetic."[139] Yet West could forgive Cone his anger and egotism, given the context of the book's creation. *Black Theology and Black Power* was written in the late 1960s, after the killing of black soldiers, of black rioters, and of King, and after the hope that liberalism could crack the callus of black poverty in America had disappeared. Despite all these odds, Cone retained the courage to fight on. And that meant the world to West.[140]

Cone's influence on West's work, particularly *Prophecy Deliverance! An Afro-American Revolutionary Christianity*, was profound. Cone helped orient West in a new paradigm of liberation theology, which opened the young scholar of philosophy to historical processes that put pressure on present political realities.[141] Already a proponent of pragmatism, West welcomed the works of Cone, Gustavo Gutiérrez, and Mary Daly as a significant supplement to the scholarship of neopragmatists such as Richard Rorty or Richard J. Bernstein, who, he argued, neglected history and strong political engagement in favor of academic rigor. Always one to mix and match the best components of each theory, viewpoint, or tradition, West wondered what a neopragmatic, prophetic philosophy of religion would look like. He took to the task in his first major published book, *Prophecy Deliverance!*, in the early 1980s, filling in the ahistorical gaps of neopragmatism with the historical, but philosophically weak, concepts of liberation theology. In short, West took what he had learned from Cone and tried to imbue it with more philosophical depth and less tribal egotism. "For many of us . . . Cone's Barthian Christocentrism was too thick—and [his] early one-dimensional social analyses were too parochial," he observed in 1985.[142] West, above all, wanted people to take radical religion seriously, and that meant African Americans recovering the Christian sources of their social activism, and philosophers recovering the religious roots of human experience. "My point here is not that American philosophers become religious, but rather that they once again take religion seriously, which also means taking culture and society seriously."[143] Religion, for one, had deep roots in human history, deeper than any secular tradition had established. As such, religion could give meaning and substance to existential struggle, the kind that thrives on hope to endure. "Secular traditions are indispensable, yet they have had neither the time nor the maturity to bequeath to us potent cultural forms of ultimacy, intimacy and sociality comparable to older and richer religious traditions," he explained. Given the complexity of society and its problems, West never subscribed to "one grand synthetic social theory," but sought to mix the best elements of human thought and practice. Religion, for him, held the vision and the values, while more secular philosophies provided the analytical tools to challenge economic injustice and political power.[144] All theories, however, were grounded in human experience and the historical processes that endowed them with truth. History, in short, gave radical theory its humanity and its hope.

Many spiritual socialists, in fact, turned to history to find hope in progress. Murray wrote memoirs such as *Proud Shoes* to reclaim her family's inspiring legacy. "I was part of a tradition of continuous struggle," she stated. "Each new attempt was linked with a previous effort, which, although unsuccessful, nevertheless had an impact on the forward movement."[145] Lynd too, in his 1968 monograph, *Intellectual Origins of American Radicalism*, traced the genealogy of democratic socialist discourse back to the American Revolution. The Declaration of Independence was not merely a Lockean political document, hailing the individual's right to life, liberty, and property, he contended. It was, for many "religious republicans" and "early American socialists," such as Thomas Paine and Joseph Priestly, an expression of the social message of Christ, which prioritized universal "human rights" over limited "property rights," and placed moral conscience above duty to the state, appealing not to the Constitution, but "to nature and nature's God." According to Lynd, this synthesis of the sacred and the secular represented the most potent political legacy of the late eighteenth-century intellectual tradition. "Having restored conscience to the center of man's experience, they generalized and secularized it," he commended. The result was a humanized, spiritualized answer to the problem of government that resembled the more recent New Left attempts to create democratic communities at home and abroad.[146] Academic historians, however, did not always appreciate Lynd's mining of a "useable past." In a scathing piece for the *New York Review of Books*, Eugene Genovese condemned *Intellectual Origins* as a "travesty of history," with "carefully selected" sources "plainly meant to serve political ends." Lynd's "glorification of the 'common man,'" Genovese wrote, sounded "strange since the passing of Henry Wallace."[147]

Genovese's linking of Wallace and Lynd was perceptive. Like Wallace, Lynd believed that a spiritualized form of socialism offered activists a moral alternative to violent revolution without relinquishing revolutionary ideals. If *immediate* revolution, on moral terms, proved intractable, activists could remain faithful to the process of a long-term, *constructive* revolution, built on basic moral values and the spirit of community. But they had to have hope for the long haul, as West reminded: "There's never any guarantee of victory in history. There never has been, there never will be. Nevertheless, if we can commit to loving, serving, and understanding each other—recognizing that we are far more alike than we are different—we have a chance," he said.[148] Day had spoken of a great chain of being throughout history. So did Murray. "If there were moments of deep despair in those years," Murray wrote, "there was also the sustaining knowledge that the quest for human dignity is part of a continuous movement through time and history linked to a higher force." It was, as she put it, "like running a relay."[149]

For many spiritual socialists, the failure of the movement and the conservative turn in the 1970s and 1980s did not denote the death of the collective struggle for a new world order. They continued, despite setbacks and disappointments, to build the Kingdom in small ways into the twenty-first century.

CONCLUSION

Spiritual Socialists in the Twenty-First Century

In light of the rise of the so-called religious Right or Moral Majority during the latter half of the twentieth century, many Americans have been puzzled by a legitimate question: what happened to the religious Left? The inquiry implies a declension narrative, an acknowledgment that a "religious Left" did exist at one time in American history, but has since ceased to garner attention as an organized, visible political group or social movement. However, leftists with a religious motivation have always been with us. And, as recent commentators have noted, they continue to organize in their communities and address the broader American public on issues of social justice in the twenty-first century.

The waning of religious activism on the left, as the story typically goes, began in the early 1970s, in tandem with the widely perceived moral degeneracy of the civil rights movement and New Left as well as the secularization of liberal and leftist organizations, who tied their sails to identity politics.[1] Yet religious voices, in tune with the antiwar and antipoverty proposals of radical New Leftists, did raise a ruckus in local and national politics throughout the 1970s. A November 1973 meeting of Evangelicals for Social Action at the Young Men's Christian Association in Chicago, for example, produced the "Chicago Declaration," detailing a left-leaning platform that the *Washington Post* predicted "could shake both political and religious life in America."[2] That same year, however, the Supreme Court in *Roe v. Wade* ruled in favor of legalized abortion, while the Watergate scandal heated up, and the Vietnam War wound down as a unifying issue for the Left.

Religious progressives did not die on the hills of the culture wars, but they were scattered and wounded without an overarching party or organization as refuge. In other words, no such national entity emerged in the

1980s to offer the religious Left a political vehicle equivalent to the Moral Majority's GOP. The Democratic Party, according to some scholars, deserves the blame for its increasingly neglectful treatment, even abandonment, of religious values and rhetoric. "Evangelicals could have taken a very different trajectory," as historian David Swartz concluded, "if in the 1970s there had existed an indifferent Republican Party and a welcoming Democratic Party."[3] And, as Jim Wallis wrote, "too many Democrats still wanted to restrict religion to the private sphere and were very uncomfortable with the language of faith even when applied to their own agenda."[4] In other words, religious leftists, unable to modify their universal values or ecumenical worldviews to fit into the narrow, "hardening" political affiliations of identity politics and party politics, found themselves "left behind" in the battle for national influence.[5]

Party realignments in this case mattered, positioning the Republican Party as a refuge for religious voters uneasy among seemingly "secular fundamentalists" across the aisle.[6] In fact, Republicans were only too happy to appeal to cultural conservatives and anti-abortion activists who provided the GOP with a coherent and recognizable religious base on which to claim the moral high ground. However, we must also consider the role of the media in highlighting those activists who made headlines in the 1970s and 1980s. Progressive Christians talking about loving thy neighbor and aiding the poor failed to garner the same level of attention that the religious Right was able to attract with its sensational attacks on abortion, welfare, and homosexuality. Perhaps because it seemed so contrary to the gospel of tolerance, the religious Right grabbed the spotlight in the latter half of the century by making intolerance appear mainstream and capitalism appear consistent with Christian doctrine.[7]

Of course, there are problems with relegating the fate of faith progressives to party politics. As Wallis reminds, "God is not a Republican or a Democrat, and the best contribution of religion is precisely not to be ideologically predictable or loyally partisan but to maintain the moral independence to critique both the Left and the Right."[8] Indeed, some of the most prominent religious leaders of the twentieth century, including Martin Luther King Jr., faulted both parties for failing to live up to American principles and universal human values. In the twenty-first century, such prophetic challenges continue, most notably in the Moral Mondays and Poor People's Campaign associated with Reverend William J. Barber II of North Carolina, president of the North Carolina National Association for the

Advancement of Colored People, who bridles at the label "religious Left." At a rally in Raleigh, Barber told his audience, "If you think this is just a left-versus-right movement, you're missing the point. This is about the moral center. This is about our humanity."[9] Rather than put spiritual voices into a rigid, political echo chamber, Barber gives religion room to run, right across the nation's political landscape.

For Barber and many religious progressives, the "moral center" does not correlate to centrist politics, a point that makes easy associations with the Democratic Party even more problematic. The Democratic Party does not represent, and historically has not represented, the radical Left, religious or secular, in its platforms and policies. Scholars, therefore, must look beyond formal politics to find radicals on the move, building grassroots coalitions in localized campaigns. As Swartz wrote, "Progressive social action outside of electoral structures stands as one of the principal legacies of the evangelical left. Its political relevance goes well beyond its marginal influence on the Democrats or Republicans. It has helped to launch engagement around a much broader array of issues . . . to which neither party pays much attention."[10] The list of such grassroots religious activism is extensive, if largely overlooked, including the Moral Mondays movement in North Carolina; the Amos Project in Cincinnati, Ohio; the Interfaith Coalition for Worker Justice in Madison, Wisconsin; and PICO (People Improving Communities Through Organizing), founded in California and now operating nationwide. As Barber put it, "If we're going to change the country, we've got to nationalize state movements. It's not from D.C. down. It's from the states up."[11]

These various efforts around the country have culminated over the past few decades into what commentators are calling a religious Left revival, or "religious resistance" movement, aimed at taking back the mic from the religious Right and challenging both political parties to support social justice in public policy. In June 2017, the *New York Times* ran a front-page story featuring Reverend Barber entitled "Religious Liberals Sat Out of Politics for 40 Years. Now They Want in the Game."[12] Earlier in the year, articles on the topic also appeared in *Dissent* magazine and were posted by Reuters, describing the phenomenon in terms of a "Moral Minority" or "Religious Left" emerging after decades of marginalization by politically powerful, conservative counterparts.[13] The authors of each piece echoed some common themes, acknowledging the strength of the religious Right, commenting on the disorganization of the religious Left, and expressing marked surprise that a left-leaning religious movement existed at all. As *Dissent* contributor Maxine Phillips put it succinctly, "In many ways, the decline of the Protestant left since the 1970s parallels what happened to the U.S. left more broadly. Before the fall of the Soviet Union, liberal churches were red-baited along with democratic socialists, civil rights activists, and student organizers. After the threat of godless communism disappeared, secularism, gays, and uppity women became the targets of choice for the moral-breakdown narrative of the religious right."[14]

Significantly, the narratives of these articles all share a common timeline, tracing the decline of progressive religion to the 1970s when conservatives took the political stage more prominently. They say nothing about the earlier history of the religious Left: its content, scope, or undulating influence throughout the twentieth century. The current rise of progressive religion, then, appears as a wonder without a past, born of a political Left without a legacy. Yet as Fordham University theologian J. Patrick Hornbeck II reminds us, "It's one of the dirty little secrets of American politics that there has been a religious left all along and it just hasn't done a good job of organizing."[15]

The crux of this statement is important for understanding the potential of a New Left movement as well as the potential pitfalls. And for such an endeavor, the history of spiritual socialism is especially instructive, given its roots in liberal piety, radical politics, and pragmatism, an all-American blend that produced an all-American alternative to secular, and largely discredited, forms of radical activism. If a revitalized Left has any chance of gaining traction in American politics, it must grapple with its ungodly image in the minds of many American citizens, who still equate radicalism with immorality and social justice with Soviet-style autocracy. It must project a language of values, make moral claims, and bridge the gaps of identity politics with common ground. To do so, scholars need to shift the initial question from "what happened to the religious Left in the late twentieth century" to "what happened to the moral underpinnings of social justice and economic equality in the late twentieth century?"

This is exactly the kind of shift that spiritual leaders like Reverend Barber and political leaders like Bernie Sanders are urging Americans to make. At first glance, Barber, an African American pastor, and Sanders, a secular Jewish politician, may not seem like easy allies. Sanders rarely speaks in religious terms, preferring instead to describe public policy as moral or immoral. However, he did make an exception when addressing the student body at Liberty University in 2015, an occasion for which he quoted directly and powerfully from the Christian gospels, reminding his audience that their faith should be directed, first and foremost, toward issues of social justice.[16] An unabashedly outspoken socialist, Sanders angles to promote a form of socialism with a strong moral foundation. Barber, an unabashedly outspoken Christian, seeks to revitalize a religious culture with a social gospel. In the Venn diagram of political theory and rhetoric, the tradition of spiritual socialism reveals their connection as comrades on a common front, entreating liberals, leftists, and conservatives to look homeward, angel, back to a time when political debate about morality and religious values was not monopolized by reactionary or conservative elements in American society. Indeed, resurrecting the history of progressive religious activism is crucial for both men and for anyone else, in fact, who hopes to galvanize support for political realignment around issues of social justice and economic equality without falling prey to fixed party formulas or ideological rigidity.

Spiritual socialists served as forerunners to precisely this kind of political project. They offered a way forward, around the dogmatic dogfights that divided the Left and discredited socialism in the minds of many Americans. But to understand how the current political climate developed, we must travel back further than the 1970s. We must consider the 1920s and 1930s, when progressive religious activists first began to challenge the Communist Party and Socialist Party (and their various spin-off groups) with questions of morality and values. From there, we can better trace the shifts on the left in the 1950s, when Stalinist disillusionment caused a crisis of faith for many socialists who began to doubt the moral viability of their beliefs. It was at this crucial juncture that spiritual socialists helped radicals reimagine leftist politics as a moral project, based on values such as human dignity, equality, civil rights, honesty, and community cooperation. When Irving Howe embraced the religious writings of Ignazio Silone, and Dorothy Day inspired Dwight Macdonald, we can witness the power that spiritual socialists exerted on a leftist world gone topsy-turvy, grounding secular radicals to a moral touchstone, to democratic principles, and, most importantly perhaps, to hope.

Like Barber or Wallis, they showed that socialism need not be secularized, narrowly political, or godless and un-American. They also illustrated that religion was not inherently conservative or purely personal, but also progressive and collective. Instead of an "ideologically predictable" radicalism and tired slogans, then, spiritual socialists insisted that nothing less than improving our social experience (the daily, interpersonal interactions that shape our social selves) would build a new world from the bottom up. Spiritual socialists, by bridging the secular and religious, the individual and collective, recognized that finding common ground politically meant finding common ground spiritually, even among outright atheists. They helped remind otherwise contentious radicals of their shared humanity and shared struggle.

In an age of divisive politics, the American Left today needs to recollect this common ground as much if not more so than it did in the 1950s, when beset by red-baiting, or in the 1930s, when torn by internecine battles. Notably, spiritual leaders like Barber have taken on the challenge, in both rhetoric and deed, of rebuilding a united movement for social justice in America. And he recognizes religion as a crucial component. "As much as the human being is a political animal," Barber wrote in his 2016 book, *The Third Reconstruction*, "I know that each of us is also a spiritual being . . . standing together where our values unite us and learning to respect one another where our traditions differ." For Barber, not only the Left, but the entire nation is facing the challenge raised by a "moral movement" for social justice in American politics, a "moral movement" that he insists "must study Scripture and sacred texts as well as state constitutions" in order to reclaim the "powerful language of faith" that "so-called conservatives" successfully "hijack[ed]" in the past few decades.[17] Observers such as Maxine Phillips know the task is tall, especially for many on the left. "It is precisely the right's hijacking not only of religious but of moral language more broadly that has made secular leftists wary and that has led so many progressive faith leaders to shy away from it when they reach outside their congregations."[18]

The Left, however, remains divided by more than lines of religion, a circumstance that Barber readily acknowledges and seeks to overcome. "Often the groups most impacted by injustice have been convinced that they are enemies," he wrote.[19] Implicitly, at least, Barber is referring to the problems associated with identity politics, which have fragmented the Left since the 1960s, as groups split off from broader coalitions to focus on a narrow set of issues pertinent to their particular race, ethnicity, gender, sexual orientation, or religion.[20] Rather than continue to fuel exclusivity among oppressed peoples, Barber calls for "fusion politics" or "fusion coalitions" built on "what we have in common" and "rooted in our deepest moral and constitutional values." Working together on a broader set of issues, however, does not mean ignoring the centrality of race, class, or any other identity-based problem, a point that Barber makes clear. When confronted with the question about whether race or class constitutes the driving agent of such change, he refuses to choose. "Yes, it's race *and* class," he insists.[21]

But how can progressives build fusion coalitions in an age of fracture and narrow truth claims? Drawing from decades of experience in North Carolina and elsewhere, Barber believes religion can help here too, and not just institutional religion, but "moral dissent" among activists for any cause. In the early 1990s, Barber, a young preacher, learned this lesson in Martinsville, North Carolina, where he helped organize African American clergy to support a unionization effort at a factory that was exploiting the labor of its black workforce. The clergy attended the banquet meeting on the topic, but refused to go much further. When Barber assessed the situation later, he realized that he had made the mistake of inviting only African American preachers, a small group that could be easily co-opted by the power elites. And that is exactly what happened.[22]

Since then, Barber has made sure to build an inclusive coalition with a variety of people, whether black or white or Latino, clergy or layman, poor or wealthy, finding strength in numbers as well as in diversity. Moral dissent, he insists, makes a difference, providing a common language to transform the conversation from a seemingly isolated, small cause to a broader struggle against oppressive measures that threaten everyone. Morality, fighting for what is right in the face of daunting opposition, also provides people with the will to continue together even when failure seems likely. As Barber wrote, "Moral dissent helped me to identify strategies and tactics to sustain people in their struggle, both in and beyond the church."[23] If religious values helped intensify identity politics in the mid-twentieth century by focusing on the dignity of each individual, they also help overcome the problems of identity politics by inspiring activists of every stripe to recognize a common humanity, a common struggle, and, crucially, the common sources of oppression. "We must learn how our issues intersect in a comprehensive moral agenda that demands transformation of everyone—not least, of us," Barber explained.[24] The strategy has worked in Barber's native North Carolina, where victories for voting rights and public education against neoconservative millionaires have set encouraging precedents for activists across the nation. And commentators on the left have noticed. Writing for *Dissent*, Phillips acknowledged that "Barber is perhaps the brightest star in the constellation. He is as adamant about reaching across racial, political, gender, and economic divides as he is about using moral and religious language. He insists on sharing platforms with anyone willing to listen to a moral argument."[25]

As stated in Chapter 5, the biggest challenge for religious activists like Barber might be human nature, especially the tendencies toward self-interest, which have plagued progressives throughout history. It remains far easier to organize people through impulses of fear and loathing than love and altruism. Reactionary politics have demonstrated this unfortunate fact time and again, from Cold War crackdowns on civil rights to more recent responses to immigration. But identity politics on the left also represent a form of self-interest as much as that of right-wing bigotry. The trick, and one Barber is trying to pull off, is to transform the self-interest of single-issue groups into a common interest, built on shared values that can reclaim the moral high ground from the so-called Moral Majority. Such unity is essential for progressive and defensive measures against the Right, which has long sought to divide and conquer protest movements or merely wait them out. The Right, rallied around the Republican Party, achieved more success translating its vision into policy in the last few decades than the Left.

For many longtime activists, the state of progressive politics in the twenty-first century has been discouraging, especially given the entrenchment of right-wing extremism, corporate capitalism, and neoliberalism in national policymaking. The election of Barack Obama in 2008 as the country's first black president marked a historic turning point, but not a political turning point for the Democratic Party, a frustration that spiritual socialists such as Cornel West have expressed. The persistence of capitalistic priorities, imperialism, warfare, and poverty, in fact, makes socialism seem an impossible dream. "I'm not an optimist at all," West stated during Obama's administration.[26] In the era of Trump, that optimism has dwindled more. "I was at the edge of hope when I wrote *Race Matters* 25 years ago," West said in a recent interview. "I have even less hope now." Yet West keeps faith. "As things become more hopeless, we have to fight more intensely because of issues of integrity, honesty, decency, truth, justice. You have to choose ways of being in the world, even when it looks as if you have very little chance of being victorious at the present moment."[27]

The resurgence of prophetic religious voices calling national attention to issues of injustice certainly has helped restore a measure of hope that a culture mired in "spiritual bankruptcy" has not completely collapsed.

"Thank God we've got William Barber and Liz Theoharis leading the poor people's campaign during the Trump years," West asserted, referring to Barber as "the closest person we have to Martin Luther King, Jr. in our midst." For West and a myriad of leftists, these models of moral courage buoy the best of social activism and keep progressive politics relevant. "Once we lose that, then we lose our moral credibility and our spiritual integrity, and we become nothing but just folk obsessed with power like everybody else. That's not who we are at our best," West warned.[28]

West was talking about society in general, but his remarks on moral authority also extend to the history of the Left. In an essay written for a special issue of *Monthly Review* in 1984, West chastised Marxists for neglecting religion, an inescapable facet of modern existence and a crucial element in the cultural struggle for socialism. Insisting that religion contains the potential to aid progressive movements as much as conservative backlash, he encouraged leftists to shed their "secular sensibilities" and channel religious impulses into a socialist challenge. "To extend leftist discourses about political economy and the state to a discourse about capitalist civilization is to accent a sphere rarely scrutinized by Marxist thinkers: *the sphere of culture and everyday life*," West wrote. "And any serious scrutiny of this sphere sooner or later must come to terms with religious ways of life and religious ways of struggle."[29]

West acknowledged Antonio Gramsci as well as advocates of liberation theology in Latin America, Africa, and Asia, who recognized religion as an important part of community building and cultural change. These non-American socialists, according to West, achieved a certain "desecularizing and deEuropeanizing of Marxist praxis" that overthrew the easy optimism of Hegelian philosophy in favor of a historicist struggle to bring abstract utopian theory down to earth, into people's daily lives. And, religion, for better or worse, remains a central part of many people's lives. Rather than dismiss religious impulses as reactionary, then, West suggested that socialists appreciate the potential to provide "a moral and political commitment beyond the self" that may well serve to "enhance and enrich the faltering and neglected utopian dimension of left theory and praxis." Instead of elevating abstract doctrine or power games among elites as the benchmarks of socialism, West envisioned a "society-in-the-making as manifest in the abilities and capacities of flesh-and-blood people in their struggles."[30]

Spiritual socialists in the United States made these connections and contributions to the American Left throughout the twentieth century. Unlike traditional Marxists, they did not focus exclusively on labor, political revolution, and the state apparatus. They saw socialism, instead, as a grassroots project to transform communities and culture. Like West, they could appreciate the economic analysis of Marxism while rejecting its shallow reach into the realities of everyday life. In their worldview, values were more vital than doctrine, and interpersonal relationships were more important than interparty rivalries. Macdonald recognized the difference and considered it an improvement on Marxism. He praised those like Day who denied the "rigid pattern [of] history" and worked "from the individual to society rather than the other way around." Ethics and values, he concluded, originated and developed at this level, the interpersonal level, rather than at the level of abstraction.[31] For Macdonald, spiritual socialists such as Day combined utopian vision with practical application. That is why they stressed the *practice* of socialism—the social and cultural dynamics that would create the new world order from the bottom up. Spiritual socialists gave the Left an interpersonal dimension and the existential roots that it lacked without a religious sensibility. They also endowed religion with revolutionary potential. As West observed in the mid-1980s, "The age of crude Marxist reductionist treatments of religion—along with European secular condescending attitudes that undergird them—is passing. Concrete social and detailed historical analyses of the relation of religion to revolutionary praxis is now a major issue on the agenda for contemporary Marxism."[32] Spiritual socialists had much to do with that change.

Yet their mark on history and society is unclear. One could blame the reactionary climate of the Cold War, the rise of conservative politics, identity politics, or the Left's religious refusal. But where did spiritual socialists go wrong in their program or vision? Despite their practicality, they failed to convince most Americans to take them seriously, to choose hope over fear, or to struggle patiently but ardently for a better day ahead. They lost millions of nominal Christians to the culture wars and single issues like abortion or antiwelfare policies even as the gospels remain replete with decrees about the plight of the poor and the evils of money lust. Do spiritual socialists bear the blame? Perhaps. Or maybe it comes down to the sheer magnitude of their mission. As Dan McKanan suggested in *Prophetic Encounters*, "I would like to leave open the possibility that American radicals failed not because they did something wrong but because they undertook a very difficult task. And I would insist that, this side of the Kingdom of God, every radical movement generates a tangled mix of success and failure."[33]

Though Barber, in a decided attempt to collapse binaries and ideology, does not identify with the terms "socialist" or "religious Left," he speaks the language of spiritual socialism, shares the mission of spiritual socialists, and faces the same problems building a movement around religious radicalism. "In the American struggle for justice and freedom," he wrote, "moral dissent has always seemed impractical when it began. Yet people of conviction have responded . . . by answering, 'Here I am. Send me.'"[34] Spiritual socialists, in short, keep showing up. They keep fighting even when the chances of success seem slim. They remind activists that faith and hope are as crucial to any revolution as theory and strategy. They build the Kingdom in their backyards. They run marathons across history. And they remain undaunted by how long it will take.

NOTES

Introduction

1. Dwight Macdonald, *The Root Is Man: Two Essays in Politics* (1946; Alhambra, CA: Cunningham Press, 1953), 18.
2. Editors, "A Word to Our Readers," *Dissent* (Winter 1954): 1.
3. Irving Howe, *Margin of Hope: An Intellectual Autobiography* (San Diego: Harcourt Brace Jovanovich, 1982), 194.
4. Ignazio Silone, *The Story of a Humble Christian* (London: Victor Gollancz, 1970), 33.
5. Ignazio Silone et al., *The God That Failed* (1949; New York: Harper and Row, 1963), 114. For more about the realignment of independent leftists in the mid-twentieth century, see Alan M. Wald, *The New York Intellectuals: The Rise and Decline of the Anti-Stalinist Left from the 1930s to the 1980s* (Chapel Hill: University of North Carolina Press, 1987).
6. See Maurice Isserman, *If I Had a Hammer: The Death of the Old Left and the Birth of the New Left* (New York: Basic Books, 1987); and Howard Brick and Christopher Phelps, *Radicals in America: The U.S. Left Since the Second World War* (New York: Cambridge University Press, 2015), 86–87. Isserman observed that many radicals were "no longer sustained by the comfortable orthodoxies of the past, some among them hoped that they were at last about to embark upon a truly 'American road to socialism'" (3).
7. The trajectory of spiritual socialists' radicalism and their relationship to Communism varied from individual to individual. Many were fellow travelers before realizing that their religious values were incompatible with Communism as practiced.
8. C. Wright Mills, "Letter to the New Left," *New Left Review* 5 (Fall 1960), https://www.marxists.org/subject/humanism/mills-c-wright/letter-new-left.htm.
9. Spiritual socialists were not necessarily "anti-Marxists." They did not reject Marxism wholesale as much as they tried to move beyond it, believing that they needed to expand Marx's cogent critique of capitalism to cover other aspects of injustice in society. The prevailing Marxists on the Left were not, for the most part, emphasizing the ethical, moral dimensions of Marxist theory or practice, though ethical considerations were not, of course, absent from Marx's writings. See, for example, Cornel West, *The Ethical Dimensions of Marxist Thought* (New York: Monthly Review Press, 1991).
10. See, especially, Leilah Danielson, Marian Mollin, and Doug Rossinow, eds., *The Religious Left in Modern America: Doorkeepers of a Radical Faith* (New York: Palgrave Macmillan, 2018), for an excellent overview of the history of the religious Left in the United States. See also Gary Dorrien, *The Democratic Socialist Vision* (Totowa, NJ: Rowman and Littlefield,

1986); Robert H. Craig, *Religion and Radical Politics: An Alternative Christian Tradition in the United States* (Philadelphia: Temple University Press, 1992); and Dan McKanan, *Prophetic Encounters: Religion and the American Radical Tradition* (Boston: Beacon Press, 2011). Craig and McKanan profile many radical activists with religious motives, but they do not analyze the interplay of socialism and religion, and they do not show how activists attempted to build socialism from local communities in a systematic way that combined religious belief with social reconstruction. They tell who, but not necessarily how. For more on the Protestant Left, see David Swartz, *Moral Minority: The Evangelical Left in an Age of Conservatism* (Philadelphia: University of Pennsylvania Press, 2014); Mark Hulsether, *Building a Protestant Left: Christianity and Crisis Magazine, 1941–1993* (Knoxville: University of Tennessee Press, 1999); and Heath W. Carter, *Union Made: Working People and the Rise of Social Christianity in America* (New York: Oxford University Press, 2015).

11. For examples of recent scholarship on conservative religion and politics, see Darren Dochuk, *From Bible Belt to Sun Belt: Plain-Folk Religion, Grassroots Politics, and the Rise of Evangelical Conservatism* (New York: W. W. Norton, 2012); Joseph Crespino, *In Search of Another Country: Mississippi and the Conservative Counterrevolution* (Princeton, NJ: Princeton University Press, 2007); Matthew Avery Sutton, *American Apocalypse: A History of Modern Evangelicalism* (Cambridge, MA: Belknap Press, 2014); Seth Dowland, *Family Values and the Rise of the Christian Right* (Philadelphia: University of Pennsylvania Press, 2015); and Neil J. Young, *We Gather Together: The Religious Right and the Problem of Interfaith Politics* (New York: Oxford University Press, 2015).

12. For more on religion and liberalism, see Matthew S. Hedstrom, *The Rise of Liberal Religion: Book Culture and American Spirituality in the Twentieth Century* (New York: Oxford University Press, 2012); and David Hollinger, *After Cloven Tongues of Fire: Protestant Liberalism in Modern American History* (Princeton, NJ: Princeton University Press, 2013).

13. For more on the "long civil rights movement," see Jacquelyn Dowd Hall, "The Long Civil Rights Movement and the Political Uses of the Past," *Journal of American History* 91, no. 4 (March 2005): 1233–63; and Nikhil Singh, *Black Is a Country: Race and the Unfinished Struggle for Democracy* (Cambridge, MA: Harvard University Press, 2005). For an explanation of why the neglect of religion is problematic in this scholarship, see Vaneesa Cook, "Martin Luther King, Jr. and the Long Social Gospel Movement," *Religion and American Culture: A Journal of Interpretation* 26, no. 1 (Winter 2016): 74–100. For an excellent exception to this general tendency, see David L. Chappell, *A Stone of Hope: Prophetic Religion and the Death of Jim Crow* (Chapel Hill: University of North Carolina Press, 2005).

14. In the introduction to *The Religious Left in Modern America*, the editors identify the 1930s to the 1950s as a period of "crisis, repression, and rethinking" for religious radicals beset by economic disaster, war, and anti-Communist hysteria. However, these decades were also a time of tremendous progress for the religious Left, as they made headway among secular radicals, who began to take religious values more seriously as a strategy and fundamental basis for making socialism viable in the United States. Radicals disenchanted with both Communism and anti-Communism at this time gravitated toward the religious Left or at least took them seriously for the first time. See Danielson, Mollin, and Rossinow, *Religious Left in Modern America*, 5.

15. For sources regarding the intersection of religion and politics more generally, see Matthew Avery Sutton and Darren Dochuk, eds., *Faith in the New Millennium: The Future of*

Religion and American Politics (New York: Oxford University Press, 2016); Andrew Preston, Bruce J. Schulman, and Julian E. Zelizer, eds., *Faithful Republic: Religion and Politics in Modern America* (Philadelphia: University of Pennsylvania Press, 2015); and R. Marie Griffith and Melani McAlister, eds., *Religion and Politics in the Contemporary United States* (Baltimore: Johns Hopkins University Press, 2008). While rich and valuable in their research, these collections offer case studies, not a seamless narrative, and they do not delve into the interplay of socialism and religion, in particular. Religious elements have also been incorporated into international and transnational histories. See Michael G. Thompson, *For God and the Globe: Christian Internationalism in the United States Between the Great War and the Cold War* (Ithaca, NY: Cornell University Press, 2015); Andrew Preston, *Sword of the Spirit, Shield of Faith: Religion in American War and Diplomacy* (New York: Knopf, 2012); and David A. Hollinger, *Protestants Abroad: How Missionaries Tried to Change the World but Changed America* (Princeton, NJ: Princeton University Press, 2017).

16. See Staughton Lynd, "Socialism Is a Dirty Word," in *From Here to There: The Staughton Lynd Reader*, ed. Andrej Grubacic (Oakland, CA: PM Press, 2010).

17. See Seymour Martin Lipset and Gary Wolfe Marks, *It Didn't Happen Here: Why Socialism Failed in the United States* (New York: W. W. Norton, 2000).

18. For more on the rise of the religious Right, see Kevin Kruse, *One Nation Under God: How Corporate America Invented Christian America* (New York: Basic Books, 2015).

19. See Joseph Kip Kosek, *Acts of Conscience: Christian Nonviolence and Modern American Democracy* (New York: Columbia University Press, 2009); and Patricia Applebaum, *Kingdom to Commune: Protestant Pacifist Culture Between World War I and the Vietnam Era* (Chapel Hill: University of North Carolina Press, 2009).

20. See Kosek, *Acts of Conscience*, 1.

21. See McKanan, *Prophetic Encounters*.

22. John R. Mott, *The Evangelization of the World in This Generation* (New York: Student Volunteer Movement for Foreign Missions, 1900), 1.

23. A. J. Muste, "Typewritten Notes for Course at New Brunswick Seminary," February 2, 1944, Reel 89.3, Papers of A. J. Muste, Microfilm edition, Swarthmore College Peace Collection, Swarthmore College (hereafter, Muste Papers).

24. Norman Thomas, *A Socialist's Faith* (New York: W. W. Norton, 1951), 11.

25. See Robert T. Handy, ed., *The Social Gospel in America, 1870–1920* (New York: Oxford University Press, 1966), 14, 6; and Charles Howard Hopkins, *The Rise of the Social Gospel in American Protestantism, 1865–1915* (New Haven, CT: Yale University Press, 1940), 3.

26. Thomas, *A Socialist's Faith*, 9.

27. Ibid., 122.

28. As examples of prominent declension narratives of both socialism and religious social radicalism in America, see Christopher Lasch, *The Agony of the American Left* (1966; New York: Vintage Books, 1969); and John P. Diggins, *The Rise and Fall of the American Left* (1973; New York: W. W. Norton, 1992). Many histories of religious social reform use World War I as their high-water mark, claiming that disillusionment during and after the war caused activists to retreat from reform and renounce their earlier optimism regarding moral progress. William Hutchison makes this point regarding American liberal Protestants. The Great War, he argues, dampened, if not destroyed, the "modernist impulse" by causing religious progressives to doubt the notion of progress toward Christian ethical ideals. See William R. Hutchison, *The Modernist Impulse in American Protestantism* (Cambridge, MA: Harvard University

Press, 1976). Donald B. Meyer has also highlighted the anxiety and insecurity of liberal religious reformers after World War I. See Donald B. Meyer, *The Protestant Search for Political Realism, 1919–1941* (Berkeley: University of California Press, 1960). Most work on the "social gospel movement" reinforces this idea of liberal religious decline after 1919.

29. My work contributes to historiography, most notably by Casey Nelson Blake and Michael Denning, that deals with cultural activism and community building in the 1920s and 1930s. Both Blake and Denning look at how cultural activism created communities with potent political implications for redefining self and society. However, neither author highlights the explicitly religious content of activists who worked to build communities prefiguring the Kingdom of God on earth. See Casey Nelson Blake, *Beloved Community: The Cultural Criticism of Randolph Bourne, Van Wyck Brooks, Waldo Frank, and Lewis Mumford* (Chapel Hill: University of North Carolina Press, 1990); and Michael Denning, *The Cultural Front* (London: Verso Press, 1997).

30. See William Inboden, *Religion and American Foreign Policy, 1945–1960: The Soul of Containment* (Cambridge: Cambridge University Press, 2010); and Andrew S. Finstuen, *Original Sin and Everyday Protestants: The Theology of Reinhold Niebuhr, Billy Graham, and Paul Tillich in an Age of Anxiety* (Chapel Hill: University of North Carolina Press, 2009).

31. Akira Iriye has made a very convincing case for the persistence of what he calls "cultural internationalism"—a network of cultural ambassadors who seek to create a transnational new world order through peace and fellowship—throughout the twentieth century, especially following World War I. As Iriye writes, "In many ways, cultural internationalists have viewed themselves as realists, comprehending the deeper springs of human intellect and emotions as a more solid base than armaments and collective national interests on which to build a stable world community." Iriye lays the theoretical groundwork for building connections between the local and the global, but he does not probe into the practical manifestations of this phenomenon. For example, he alludes to the role of religious reformers in this movement, but he does not focus on them. See Akira Iriye, *Cultural Internationalism and World Order* (Baltimore: Johns Hopkins University Press, 1997), 10. Alan Dawley also touches on some of these themes in his book *Changing the World*. He considers how progressive social reformers responded to international events, which shaped their approach to social problems at home and abroad. However, his concentration on progressives leads him to conclude that reformers largely abandoned their ideals and retreated from the world after World War I. Dawley does gesture to the post–World War I revitalization of what he calls "globalization from below" at the end of his study, but he does not historicize this concept apart from his narrative on the rise and fall of mainstream progressivism. See Alan Dawley, *Changing the World: American Progressives in War and Revolution* (Princeton, NJ: Princeton University Press, 2003), 357.

32. For examples of Jewish activists on the Left, see Tony Michels, *A Fire in Their Hearts: Yiddish Socialism in New York* (Cambridge, MA: Harvard University Press, 2005). For excellent essays on Jewish activists with religious inclinations, see David Verbeeten, "Judaism, Yiddish Peoplehood, and American Radicalism," and Doug Rossinow, "'The 1900-Year Crisis': Arthur Waskow, the Question of Israel/Palestine, and the Effort to Form a Jewish Religious Left in America, 1967–1974," in Danielson, Mollin, and Rossinow, *Religious Left in Modern America*.

33. For more on social Christianity in American history, see Gary Dorrien, *Social Ethics in the Making: Interpreting an American Tradition* (Malden, MA: Wiley-Blackwell, 2009).

34. Handy, *Social Gospel in America*, 11.
35. Muste, "Notes for Course at New Brunswick Seminary," 1.
36. A. J. Muste, "Sketches for an Autobiography," in *The Essays of A. J. Muste*, ed. Nat Hentoff (Indianapolis: Bobbs-Merrill, 1967), 135–36.
37. For examples of social gospel declension narratives, see Hopkins, *Rise of the Social Gospel in American Protestantism*; and Handy, *Social Gospel in America*. Efforts to identify social gospel strains in post–World War I America have been made, mostly, by theologians. See Christopher H. Evans, ed., *The Social Gospel Today* (Louisville, KY: Westminster John Knox Press, 2001).
38. Ronald C. White and C. Howard Hopkins, *The Social Gospel: Religion and Reform in Changing America* (Philadelphia: Temple University Press, 1976), xi. See Christopher H. Evans, *The Social Gospel in American Religion: A History* (New York: New York University Press, 2017); Evans, *Social Gospel Today*; and Swartz, *Moral Minority*.
39. For a very helpful chapter about the beliefs of Christian socialists in the United States in the early twentieth century, see Craig, *Religion and Radical Politics*, 83–129. Craig claims that they, along with their secular counterparts, subsumed racial issues under class issues.
40. Staughton Lynd, *Living Inside Our Hope: A Steadfast Radical's Thoughts on Rebuilding the Movement* (Ithaca, NY: ILR Press, 1997), 50.
41. The emphasis on bottom-up social work differs from leftists who advocated top-down party policy or even intellectual cultural institutions. See Hugh Wilford, *The New York Intellectuals: From Vanguard to Institution* (New York: Manchester University Press, 1995).
42. A. J. Muste, "Pendle Hill Lectures on the Peace Testimony," Lecture 7, May 1954, Reel 89.3, Muste Papers.
43. A. J. Muste, "Pendle Hill Lectures on the Peace Testimony," Lecture 5, April 28, 1954, Reel 89.3, Muste Papers.
44. Hollinger, *After Cloven Tongues of Fire*. See also Michael Kazin, *American Dreamers: How the Left Changed a Nation* (New York: Knopf, 2011).

Chapter 1

1. A. J. Muste, "Return to Pacifism," in *The Essays of A.J. Muste*, edited by Nat Hentoff (Indianapolis: Bobbs-Merrill Company, 1967), 200.
2. Leilah Danielson, *American Gandhi: A. J. Muste and the History of Radicalism in the Twentieth Century* (Philadelphia: University of Pennsylvania Press, 2014), 6.
3. See Kosek, *Acts of Conscience*; and Danielson, *American Gandhi*.
4. Muste, "Sketches for an Autobiography," 44. See also Jo Ann Ooiman Robinson, *Abraham Went Out: A Biography of A. J. Muste* (Philadelphia: Temple University Press, 1981), 8, 13–14.
5. Muste, "Sketches for an Autobiography," 43, 38.
6. Ibid., 43.
7. Walter Rauschenbusch, *Christianity and the Social Crisis* (1907; New York: Macmillan, 1913), 48.
8. A. J. Muste, "The Problem of Discontent," in Hentoff, *Essays of A. J. Muste*, 175–78.
9. Ibid., 177, 178.
10. Muste, "Sketches for an Autobiography," 44.
11. Ibid., 47.
12. Ibid.

13. Ibid., 46.
14. Ibid., 49–50.
15. A. J. Muste, "For Neutrality and Against Isolation," published radio address delivered at Station WEVD, New York, November 1, 1937, Reel 89.3, 78–80, Muste Papers, Swarthmore College Peace Collection (hereafter, Muste Papers).
16. Muste, "Sketches for an Autobiography," 56, 84, 56.
17. Ibid., 65, 64, 58, 77.
18. Robinson, *Abraham Went Out*, 31.
19. Muste, "Sketches for an Autobiography," 85–87.
20. Kosek, *Acts of Conscience*, 71.
21. Leilah Danielson noted that the Brookwood staff considered "their educational programs as counter-hegemonic institutions that would produce working-class meaning and knowledge." See Danielson, *American Gandhi*, 4.
22. Muste, "Sketches for an Autobiography," 85–87.
23. Danielson, *American Gandhi*, 13.
24. Robinson, *Abraham Went Out*, 32.
25. Muste, "Sketches for an Autobiography," 107.
26. Cara Cook, "Reminiscence," Reel 89.2, 115, Muste Papers.
27. Ibid., 106–7.
28. Ibid., 107, 112.
29. Muste, "Sketches for an Autobiography," 107.
30. A. J. Muste, "Press Release Protesting A. F. L. Action," August 9, 1928, Reel 89.1, Muste Papers.
31. A. J. Muste, "Press Release," January 29, 1929, Reel 89.1, Muste Papers.
32. *Daily Worker* (August 8–9, 1928).
33. A. J. Muste, "Press Release," January 29, 1929, Reel 89.1, Muste Papers.
34. Ibid.
35. John Dewey, "Address at a Meeting of the Local No. 5 of the American Federation of Teachers," 1928, Reel 89.1, Muste Papers.
36. C. Cook, "Reminiscence," 136.
37. Muste, "Sketches for an Autobiography," 155.
38. C. Cook, "Reminiscence," 106, 109.
39. A. J. Muste, "Reply to Staff," Reel 89.2, Muste Papers.
40. A. J. Muste, "Brookwood Policy" and "Statement of Purpose for Brookwood," 1933, Reel 89.2, Muste Papers.
41. A. J. Muste, "Resignation Statement to Brookwood Faculty and Students," February 11, 1933, Reel 89.2, Muste Papers.
42. "First Newsletter of the Brookwood Honor Roll Club," March 1933, Reel 89.2, Muste Papers.
43. C. Cook, "Reminiscence," 119.
44. Ibid., 209–10.
45. A. J. Muste, *New Republic* (February 8, 1933).
46. C. Cook, "Reminiscence," 209–10.
47. Muste, "Sketches for an Autobiography," 135–36.
48. Ibid.

49. Ibid., 137.
50. Muste, "Return to Pacifism," 198–99.
51. Muste, "Return to Pacifism," 201–2.
52. Sherwood Eddy, *Eighty Adventurous Years: An Autobiography* (New York: Harper and Brothers, 1955), 152–53. See also Sherwood Eddy to Brewer Eddy, January 28, 1931, Box 1, Folder 12, George Sherwood Eddy Papers, Yale Divinity School (hereafter, Eddy Papers).
53. Eddy, *Eighty Adventurous Years*, 153.
54. Sherwood Eddy, *The Kingdom of God and the American Dream: The Religious and Secular Ideals of American History* (New York: Harper and Brothers, 1941), 244, 307.
55. William R. Hutchison, most notably, has detailed the theological debates that reframed the scope and intent of foreign missions in the mid-twentieth century from a focus on biblical, Christ-centered conversions to a more ecumenical and culturally sensitive methodology. Eddy represents a significant figure in this shift. For example, Ian Tyrrell used Eddy as evidence of how field experiences abroad could sometimes soften the cultural imperialism of missionaries and transform their international worldviews. Michael Thompson's work also dovetails neatly with scholarship that traces the changing nature of mainstream missions in the twentieth century. See William R. Hutchison, *Errand to the World: American Protestant Thought and Foreign Missions* (Chicago: University of Chicago Press, 1987); Ian Tyrrell, *Reforming the World: The Creation of America's Moral Empire* (Princeton, NJ: Princeton University Press, 2010); and Michael G. Thompson, "Sherwood Eddy, the Missionary Enterprise, and the Rise of Christian Internationalism in 1920s America," *Modern Intellectual History* (October 2014): 1–2. For more on the role of missionaries in cultural imperialism in the early twentieth century, see Richard M. Gamble, *The War for Righteousness: Progressive Christianity, the Great War, and the Rise of the Messianic Nation* (Wilmington, DE: ISI Books, 2003); Emily S. Rosenberg, *Spreading the American Dream: Economic and Cultural Expansion 1890–1945* (New York: Hill and Wang, 1982); Preston, *Sword of the Spirit, Shield of Faith*; and Hollinger, *Protestants Abroad*. For more about the concept of cultural internationalism after World War I, see Iriye, *Cultural Internationalism and World Order*.
56. Eddy, *Eighty Adventurous Years*, 19. See also Rick L. Nutt, *The Whole Gospel for the Whole World: Sherwood Eddy and the American Protestant Mission* (Macon, GA: Mercer University Press, 1997), 11.
57. Eddy, *Eighty Adventurous Years*, 26–28.
58. Ibid., 27–28.
59. Sherwood Eddy, *A Pilgrimage of Ideas or the Re-education of Sherwood Eddy* (New York: Farrar and Rinehart, 1934), 162.
60. Ibid., 161.
61. Sherwood Eddy, *With Our Soldiers in France* (New York: Association Press, 1917).
62. Eddy, *Pilgrimage of Ideas*, 182.
63. Eddy, *Eighty Adventurous Years*, 103.
64. Eddy, *Pilgrimage of Ideas*, 16.
65. Sherwood Eddy to Mother, August 19, 1916, Box 1, Folder 2, Eddy Papers.
66. Sherwood Eddy, "Letter from the Salisbury Plains," September 30, 1916, Box 1, Folder 2, Eddy Papers.
67. Sherwood Eddy to Mother, August 21, 1916, Box 1, Folder 2, Eddy Papers.
68. Eddy, *Pilgrimage of Ideas*, 16.

69. Ibid., 211.

70. Ibid., 19. See also Sherwood Eddy, *Facing the Crisis: A Study in Present Day Social and Religious Problems* (New York: George H. Doran, 1922).

71. Eddy, *Pilgrimage of Ideas*, 16.

72. Eddy, *Eighty Adventurous Years*, 117.

73. See Meyer, *Protestant Search for Political Realism, 1919–1941*.

74. Eddy, *Eighty Adventurous Years*, 36.

75. Sherwood Eddy and Kirby Page, *Danger Zones of the Social Order: Facts Concerning Economic, International, Racial, Political and Moral Problems* (New York: George H. Doran, 1926), 81.

76. Doug Rossinow, *Visions of Progress: The Left-Liberal Tradition in America* (Philadelphia: University of Pennsylvania Press, 2008). See also Danielson, *American Gandhi*.

77. Eddy, *Kingdom of God and the American Dream*, 255.

78. Sherwood Eddy to Mother and Brewer Eddy, June 15, 1923, Box 1, Folder 5, Eddy Papers. See also Sherwood Eddy to Mother and Brewer, July 10, 1923.

79. Sherwood Eddy, *The New World of Labor* (New York: George H. Doran, 1923), 86, 88.

80. Sherwood Eddy to Mother and Brewer Eddy, September 12, 1923, Box 1, Folder 5, Eddy Papers.

81. Sherwood Eddy, *The Challenge of Russia* (New York: Farrar and Rinehart, 1931), vii.

82. Sherwood Eddy to Mother and Brewer Eddy, September 14, 1926, Box 1, Folder 8, Eddy Papers.

83. Eddy, *Challenge of Russia*; and Sherwood Eddy, *Russia Today: What Can We Learn from It?* (New York: Farrar and Rinehart, 1934). See also Sherwood Eddy, "Russia—Good and Evil," *Christian Century* 52 (September 18, 1935): 1171–72.

84. Sherwood Eddy to Josef Stalin, July 29, 1932, Box 2, Folder 83, Eddy Papers.

85. Brewer Eddy to Sherwood Eddy, December 18, 1923, Box 1, Folder 5, Eddy Papers.

86. Brewer Eddy to Sherwood Eddy, September 26, 1923, Box 1, Folder 5, Eddy Papers.

87. Eddy, *Pilgrimage of Ideas*, 155.

88. Sherwood Eddy to Brewer Eddy, June 25, 1924, Box 1, Folder 6, Eddy Papers.

89. Sherwood Eddy, *Religion and Social Justice* (New York: George H. Doran, 1927), 13, 73–74.

90. Brewer Eddy to Sherwood Eddy, October 31, 1929, Box 1, Folder 9, Eddy Papers.

91. Eddy and Page, *Danger Zones of the Social Order*, 32–33.

92. Sherwood Eddy to Brewer, June 23, 1930, Box 1, Folder 11, Eddy Papers.

93. Sherwood Eddy to Mother, June 4, 1930, Box 1, Folder 11, Eddy Papers.

94. Sherwood Eddy to Mother, December 4, 1929, Box 1, Folder 10, Eddy Papers. See also Sherwood Eddy, "India at the Crossroads," *Christian Century* 47 (January 8, 1930): 43–46.

95. Sherwood Eddy, "Gandhi—an Interpretation," *Christian Century* 40 (April 19, 1923): 489–94.

96. Ibid.

97. For more on the "Gandhian moment," see Kosek, *Acts of Conscience*, 85–111. See also Danielson, *American Gandhi*.

98. Sherwood Eddy, "Why I Believe in Foreign Missions," *Epworth Herald*, Box 6, Folder 114, Eddy Papers.

Chapter 2

1. Eddy, *Pilgrimage of Ideas*, 21.
2. W. E. B. Du Bois, "Socialism and the Negro Problem," *New Review* (February 1, 1913).
3. Robert Craig and Philip Foner profile black Christian socialists such as George Washington Woodbey, George W. Slater Jr., and Reverdy Ransom. See Craig, *Religion and Radical Politics*; and Philip S. Foner, *Black Socialist Preacher: The Teachings of Reverend George Washington Woodbey and His Disciple* (San Francisco, CA: Synthesis, 1983). Black social gospelers such as Howard Thurman and Benjamin Mays have also received attention in scholarship recently. See, for example, Gary Dorrien, *Breaking White Supremacy: Martin Luther King, Jr. and the Black Social Gospel* (New Haven, CT: Yale University Press, 2018), as well as his earlier work on the topic of the black social gospel, *The New Abolition: W. E. B. Du Bois and the Black Social Gospel* (New Haven, CT: Yale University Press, 2015). By bringing black scholars to the forefront of King's formative experience, Dorrien is making an astute intervention into King studies, particularly the debate over King's intellectual pedigree. While some biographers have insisted on the importance of the black church and southern culture in King's life, others have curbed black cultural influences in favor of northern white academics, an implication that the black church and highbrow scholarship are mutually exclusive. The social gospel, Dorrien rightly claims, formed the foundation for all of King's subsequent socialist and pacifist beliefs. But Dorrien collapses some binaries and raises another by drawing a color line across the history of the social gospel. Throughout the book, he refers to the "white social gospel" and the "black social gospel," a division that may reflect the historical truth of segregation, but undermines the power of social gospel universalism and eschatology. Vaneesa Cook, "The Social Gospel Roots of the American Religious Left," *Religion & Politics* (July 31, 2018).
4. For more on Christian socialism and race, see Craig, *Religion and Radical Politics*, 83–173. For more on socialism and race, see Philip S. Foner, *American Socialism and Black Americans: From the Age of Jackson to World War II* (Westport, CT: Greenwood Press, 1977). The social gospel movement has also been accused of neglecting racial issues. For more on this historiographical debate and a challenge to the trope, see Ralph E. Luker, *The Social Gospel in Black and White: American Racial Reform, 1885–1912* (Chapel Hill: University of North Carolina Press, 1991).
5. Dorothy Day, *Loaves and Fishes* (New York: Harper and Row, 1963), 87.
6. Dorothy Day, *The Long Loneliness* (New York: Harper and Row, 1952), 225.
7. Ibid., 216.
8. Brick and Phelps, in *Radicals in America*, identify this shift from Old Left to New Left politics in the 1950s, but spiritual socialists served as a vanguard of sorts already in the 1930s.
9. William D. Miller, a former historian at Marquette University in Milwaukee, Wisconsin, remains Day's primary biographer. Miller mentions the personalistic and distributionist features of what he calls Day's "non-collectivist" socialist worldview, but does not discuss it for more than two pages in *A Harsh and Dreadful Love: Dorothy Day and the Catholic Worker Movement* (New York: Liveright, 1973) or in *Dorothy Day: A Biography* (San Francisco: Harper and Row, 1982). For other examples of books on Day's Catholic legacy, written by authors with strong Catholic ties, see Mark and Louise Zwick, *The Catholic Worker Movement: Intellectual and Spiritual Origins* (New York: Paulist Press, 2005); and Jim Forest, *All Is Grace: A Biography of Dorothy Day* (Maryknoll, NY: Orbis Books, 2011). See also Geoffrey Gneuhs, "Radical Orthodoxy: Dorothy Day's Challenge to Liberal America," and Bill Kauffman, "'The

Way of Love'—Dorothy Day and the American Right," in *Dorothy Day and the Catholic Worker Movement: Centenary Essays*, ed. William J. Thorn, Phillip M. Runkel, and Susan Mountin (Milwaukee, WI: Marquette University Press, 2001), 205–33; and Eugene McCarraher, *Christian Critics: Religion and the Impasse in Modern American Social Thought* (Ithaca, NY: Cornell University Press, 2000). A notable exception is Dan McKanan, who devotes several pages to Day's religious radicalism in his book *Prophetic Encounters*, 160–61, 186–87, 218–19. However, he does not analyze her as a socialist.

10. Sherwood Eddy, "First Impressions of India: Report 3," March 1897, Box 3, Folder 50, Eddy Papers.

11. Tyrrell, *Reforming the World*, 183.

12. Sherwood Eddy to Friends, May 1, 1919, Box 3, Folder 50, Eddy Papers. See also Sherwood Eddy, *India Awakening* (New York: Missionary Education Movement, 1911); and Sherwood Eddy, *The New Era in Asia* (New York: Missionary Education Movement, 1913).

13. The timing of Eddy's shift to a "social gospel" understanding of missionary work is important, especially because historians such as Michael G. Thompson have identified Eddy's turn to social religion as an effect of World War I. I contend that his embrace of socialist theory and praxis developed earlier, during his missionary experiences. See Michael G. Thompson, "Sherwood Eddy, the Missionary Enterprise, and the Rise of Christian Internationalism in 1920s America," *Modern Intellectual History* (October 2014): 14–15.

14. Sherwood Eddy to Mother, December 27, 1914, Box 1, Folder 1, Eddy Papers.

15. Sherwood Eddy to Dear Friends, May 1, 1919, Box 3, Folder 66, Eddy Papers.

16. Sherwood Eddy to Margaret, February 21, 1919, Box 1, Folder 3, Eddy Papers.

17. Sherwood Eddy to Margaret, March 11, 1918, Box 1, Folder 3, Eddy Papers.

18. Sherwood Eddy to Dear Friends, 2–3.

19. Eddy, *Pilgrimage of Ideas*, 63.

20. Eddy, *Kingdom of God and the American Dream*, 307.

21. Eddy, *Pilgrimage of Ideas*, 256.

22. Eddy, *Eighty Adventurous Years*, 117.

23. Eddy, *Pilgrimage of Ideas*, 22.

24. Biographer Rick L. Nutt, for one, denied Eddy's socialist identity altogether, writing that "it is difficult to consider Eddy a true socialist, given that in his prescription for a reformed United States he does not call for public ownership of the means of production except in the case of utilities and a few 'key' unidentified industries. Much of his program reflected the Progressive movement and social gospel, decidedly moderate or liberal programs." More recently, Kip Kosek portrayed Eddy as a "social evangelist," who toured the country making speeches about nonviolence. He never mentioned Eddy's socialism. See Nutt, *Whole Gospel for the Whole World*, 272; and Kosek, *Acts of Conscience*, 57.

25. For more about the formation of the Southern Tenant Farmers Union, see H. L. Mitchell, *Mean Things Happening in This Land: The Life and Times of H. L. Mitchell, Cofounder of the Southern Tenant Farmers Union* (Montclair, NJ: Allanheld, Osmun, 1979); and Howard Kester, *Revolt of the Sharecroppers* (New York: J. J. Little and Ives, 1936). See also James R. Green, *Grass-roots Socialism: Radical Movements in the Southwest, 1895–1943* (Baton Rouge: Louisiana State University Press, 1978).

26. Sherwood Eddy, "The Delta Cooperative Farm: First Report of Progress," April 19, 1936, Box 4, Folder 82, Eddy Papers.

27. Sherwood Eddy, *A Door of Opportunity: An American Adventure in Cooperation with Sharecroppers* (New York: Eddy and Page, 1937), 38. See also Sherwood Eddy, "The Delta Cooperative's First Year," *Christian Century* 54 (February 3, 1937): 138–40; Sherwood Eddy, "The Future of the Sharecroppers," *Christian Century* 54 (December 22, 1937): 1590–92; and Sherwood Eddy, "Cooperative Farm No. 1," Box 4, Folder 82, Eddy Papers. Eddy's effort to gain the backing of politicians denotes an important point of difference between him and spiritual socialist Dorothy Day, who abhorred state intervention. Socialism, she believed, could not rely on top-down resources, dispensed by the establishment. Ever the pragmatist, Eddy believed, to the contrary, that the pandemic problem of poverty demanded economies of scale at the national level. He did not consider state aid as an interference with the Kingdom of God, but as a welcome windfall for its advancement.

28. Jonathan Daniels, *A Southerner Discovers the South* (New York: Macmillan, 1938), 155.

29. Eddy, *Door of Opportunity*, 33, 58.

30. Eddy, *Pilgrimage of Ideas*, 49–50.

31. Jerry W. Dallas, "The Delta and Providence Farms: A Mississippi Experiment in Cooperative Farming and Racial Cooperation, 1936–1956," *Mississippi Quarterly* 41 (1987): 283–305.

32. Daniels, *Southerner Discovers the South*, 155, 154.

33. Eddy, *Door of Opportunity*, 34.

34. Ibid., 59.

35. Sam H. Franklin Jr., "Early Years of the Delta Cooperative Farm and the Providence Cooperative Farm" (unpublished), 23.

36. Eddy, *Door of Opportunity*, 51.

37. Franklin, "Early Years," 23.

38. Dallas, "Delta and Providence Farms," 297. A recent scholar concurred, faulting the "lack of effort in developing indigenous leadership." See Fred C. Smith, *Trouble in Goshen: Plain Folk, Roosevelt, Jesus, and Marx in the Great Depression South* (Jackson: University Press of Mississippi, 2014), 139.

39. Scholar Fred C. Smith made much of Amberson's comment, arguing that a marked divide between political and religious (nominal) socialists existed from the very beginning of the enterprise and precipitated its demise. Accustomed to exercising leadership from the pulpit, Smith claimed that the "Christian Socialists found it difficult to allow popular or democratic governance." "Their notions of elitist guidance and superior knowledge," he continued, "placed them in direct opposition to the philosophy of their secular socialist colleagues." See Smith, *Trouble in Goshen*, 117.

40. Mitchell, *Mean Things Happening in This Land*.

41. Daniels, *Southerner Discovers the South*, 149.

42. Eddy, *Door of Opportunity*, 8.

43. Eddy, *Pilgrimage of Ideas*, 289, 268, 311.

44. Ibid., 94.

45. Senator Paul A. Douglas, "Symposium Honoring Sherwood Eddy," *Jacksonville (FL) Courier* (October 18, 1963): 3.

46. Young Men's Christian Association Sherwood Eddy Memorial, "Who Was Sherwood Eddy?," Box 20, Folder 214, Eddy Papers.

47. Day, *Long Loneliness*, 141.
48. Robert Coles, *Dorothy Day: A Radical Devotion* (Reading, MA: Addison-Wesley, 1987), 59–60.
49. Dorothy Day, *The Duty of Delight: The Diaries of Dorothy Day*, ed. Robert Ellsberg (Milwaukee, WI: Marquette University Press, 2008), 37.
50. Ibid., 40.
51. Dorothy Day, *From Union Square to Rome* (1938; Silver Springs, MD: Preservation of the Faith Press, 1942), 87, 150.
52. Robert Ellsberg, introduction to Day, *Duty of Delight*, x.
53. David J. O'Brien, "The Pilgrimage of Dorothy Day," *Commonweal* 107 (December 19, 1980): 711–15.
54. Mel Piehl, *Breaking Bread: The Catholic Worker and the Origin of Catholic Radicalism in America* (Philadelphia: Temple University Press, 1982), x.
55. Day, *From Union Square to Rome*, 26–27.
56. Day, *Long Loneliness*, 28–29.
57. Coles, *Dorothy Day*, 27.
58. Day, *Long Loneliness*, 62.
59. Day, *From Union Square to Rome*, 73.
60. Ibid., 74–75. Day also wrote pieces for the *Masses* in the last six months of its publication. Day's father was a sports journalist. The family moved with him from New York City to Oakland, California, and then to Chicago while Day was young.
61. Day, *Long Loneliness*, 73, 78, 81.
62. Day, *From Union Square to Rome*, 26.
63. Day, *Duty of Delight*, 572.
64. Day, *Long Loneliness*, 41.
65. Day, *From Union Square to Rome*, 7. For more on Day's reading of Russian literature and its effect on her radicalism, see Vaneesa Cook, "The Unaffiliated Revolution of Dorothy Day," *Raritan* (Spring 2018).
66. Day, *From Union Square to Rome*.
67. Ibid., 48.
68. Day, *Long Loneliness*, 33.
69. Leo Tolstoy, *The Kingdom of God Is Within You: Christianity Not as a Mystic Religion, But as a New Theory of Life*, trans. Constance Garnett (New York: Cassell, 1894).
70. Day, *From Union Square to Rome*, 143.
71. Day, *Long Loneliness*, 181.
72. Day, *From Union Square to Rome*, 149, 147.
73. Day, *Long Loneliness*, 41–42.
74. Day, *From Union Square to Rome*, 10.
75. Ibid., 120–22.
76. Ibid., 127.
77. Ibid., 24–25.
78. Day, *Long Loneliness*, 107.
79. Ibid., 139.
80. Ibid., 106.
81. For more on Day's ethics as a woman and mother, see June O'Connor, *The Moral Vision of Dorothy Day: A Feminist Perspective* (New York: Crossroad Publishing, 1991).

82. Day, *Long Loneliness*, 147, 138, 147–48.
83. Dorothy Day, "Pilgrimage to Mexico," in *Dorothy Day: Writings from "Commonweal,"* ed. Patrick Jordan (Collegeville, MN: Liturgical Press, 2002), 142.
84. Day, "A Reminiscence at 75," in Jordan, *Writings from "Commonweal,"* 165.
85. Day, *Long Loneliness*, 165.
86. Ibid., 166. Day was in Washington, D.C., on assignment for the Jesuit journal *America*.
87. Coles, *Dorothy Day*, 4.
88. Day, *Long Loneliness*, 166.
89. Ibid., 169.
90. Day, *Loaves and Fishes*, 7.
91. Ibid., 7, 100.
92. Day, *Long Loneliness*, 169.
93. Coles, *Dorothy Day*, 14.
94. Day, *Long Loneliness*, 244.
95. Day, *Loaves and Fishes*, 9.
96. Ibid., 95.
97. Day, "Reminiscence at 75," 167.
98. Day, *Duty of Delight*, 561, 143; Day, *Loaves and Fishes*, 9.
99. Dorothy Day, "Houses of Hospitality," in Jordan, *Writings from "Commonweal,"* 57.
100. Day, *Long Loneliness*, 170–71.
101. Day, *Loaves and Fishes*, 12–13.
102. Day, *Long Loneliness*, 171.
103. Day, *From Union Square to Rome*, 122.
104. Day, *Long Loneliness*, 81.
105. Ibid., 171, 217.
106. Day, *Loaves and Fishes*, 21.
107. John 15:16 (NIV).
108. Day, *Loaves and Fishes*, 4.
109. Ibid., 10–11.
110. *Catholic Worker* 1, no. 1 (May 1, 1933): 4.
111. Day, *Loaves and Fishes*, 11. The paper was printed by the Paulist Press for fifty-seven dollars. Day, *Long Loneliness*, 174.
112. Day, *Loaves and Fishes*, 18.
113. *Catholic Worker* 1, no. 1 (May 1, 1933): 4.
114. Day, *Long Loneliness*, 187–88.
115. Dorothy Day to Madeleine Sheridan, May 2, 1934, in *All the Way to Heaven: The Selected Letters of Dorothy Day*, ed. Robert Ellsberg (Milwaukee, WI: Marquette University Press, 2010), 76.
116. Dorothy Day to Madeleine Sheridan, March 1934, in Ellsberg, *All the Way to Heaven*, 71.
117. Anne Fremantle, "The Work of Dorothy Day in the Slums," *Catholic World* 170 (February 1950): 336.
118. *Catholic Worker* 1, no. 10 (April 1, 1934).
119. Jeff Dietrich and Susan Pollack, "Dorothy Holds Forth: An Interview with Dorothy Day," *Catholic Agitator* (December 1971): 1–2.

120. Coles, *Dorothy Day*, 82, 80.
121. Day, "Houses of Hospitality," 59.
122. Dorothy Day to the editor of *Interracial Review*, February 1935, in Ellsberg, *All the Way to Heaven*, 90.
123. Fremantle, "Work of Dorothy Day in the Slums," 336.
124. Day, *Loaves and Fishes*, 184.
125. Dorothy Day, "The Scandal of the Works of Mercy," in Jordan, *Writings from "Commonweal,"* 104.
126. Coles, *Dorothy Day*, 97, 109, 105.
127. Dorothy Day to Franz Weise, April 27, 1934, in Ellsberg, *All the Way to Heaven*, 75.
128. Day, *From Union Square to Rome*, 72.
129. Matthew 6:33 (NIV); Day, *Duty of Delight*, 234.
130. Day to Sheridan, March 1934, 71.
131. Dorothy Day, "The Diabolic Plot," *America* 49 (April 29, 1933): 82.
132. Dorothy Day to the New York City Police Commissioner, July 1935, in Ellsberg, *All the Way to Heaven*, 95.
133. "Why Write About Strife and Violence?" *Catholic Worker* (June 1, 1934): 2.
134. Dorothy Day to All Catholic Worker Houses, December 1941, in Ellsberg, *All the Way to Heaven*, 166.
135. Day, *Duty of Delight*, 42.
136. Day, *Long Loneliness*, 221.
137. Day, *Loaves and Fishes*, 174.
138. Ibid., 210.
139. *Catholic Worker* 1, no. 3 (July/August 1933): 8.
140. *Catholic Worker* 1, no. 4 (September 1933): 11.
141. Father Daniel Berrigan, S.J., "A Modest Proposal: A Day to Remember," *U.S. Catholic* 46 (May 1981): 30–32.
142. *Catholic Worker* 2, no. 1 (May 1934): 1.
143. Dwight Macdonald, "The Foolish Things of the World, Part I," *New Yorker* (October 4, 1952): 39. Part II of this two-part essay on Day was published on October 11, 1952.
144. Day, *Duty of Delight*, 212.
145. Day, *Long Loneliness*, 267. In the *Catholic Worker*, Maurin also used the term "Christian Communism" to describe his philosophy, saying he was "not afraid of the word communism." Socialism, however, seemed to connote state-centered control and reliance for Maurin. See "Easy Essays," *Catholic Worker* 1, no. 2 (June/July 1933): 4.
146. Dietrich and Pollock, "Dorothy Holds Forth," 1.
147. H. A. Reinhold, "The Long Loneliness of Dorothy Day," *Commonweal* 55 (February 29, 1952): 521–22.
148. Dietrich and Pollack, "Dorothy Holds Forth," 1.
149. Day, *Duty of Delight*, 396. See also Martin Buber, *Paths in Utopia* (1949; Boston: Beacon Press, 1958).
150. Dorothy Day to Brendan O'Grady, June 1954, in Ellsberg, *All the Way to Heaven*, 293.
151. M. Rubel, "The Uses of the Word 'Socialism,'" *Dissent* (Winter 1954).
152. Norman Thomas, Travers Clement, and Sebastian Franck, "The Use of the Word Socialism," *Dissent* (Summer 1954).

153. Lewis Coser and Irving Howe, "Images of Socialism," *Dissent* (Spring 1954): 138.
154. Day, *Loaves and Fishes*, 131.
155. Ibid., 15.
156. Day, *Long Loneliness*, 180.
157. Day, *Duty of Delight*, 493.
158. "Houses of Hospitality," *Catholic Worker* 1, no. 6 (November 1933): 7.
159. Day, *Loaves and Fishes*, viii.
160. Bruce Cook, "Dorothy Day and the Catholic Worker," *U.S. Catholic* (March 1966): 9.
161. Dwight Macdonald, "The Foolish Things of the World, Part II," *New Yorker* (October 11, 1952): 42.
162. Macdonald, "Foolish Things of the World, Part I," 42, 40.
163. Day, *Long Loneliness*, 190.
164. "Day by Day," *Catholic Worker* 2, no. 2 (June 1, 1934): 7.
165. Dorothy Day to Joe Zarrella, October 12, 1940, in Ellsberg, *All the Way to Heaven*, 153.
166. Day to New York City Police Commissioner, July 1935, 96.
167. Dorothy Day to Catherine de Hueck, July 1935, in Ellsberg, *All the Way to Heaven*, 98.
168. McCarraher, *Christian Critics*.
169. Macdonald, "Foolish Things of the World, Part I," 57.
170. Dietrich and Pollack, "Dorothy Holds Forth," 2.
171. According to historians such as McCarraher, they also prevented Day and her staff from making more fruitful inroads into the labor movement. Citing Day's "lack of prolonged experience in a factory," her aversion to state-centered politics, and her disdain for narrow trade unionism, McCarraher argued that Day "cultivated only tenuous links to labor." See McCarraher, *Christian Critics*, 87.
172. Fremantle, "Work of Dorothy Day in the Slums," 337.
173. Reinhold, "Long Loneliness of Dorothy Day," 522.
174. B. Cook, "Dorothy Day and the Catholic Worker," 7.
175. Father John Hugo, "Dorothy Day: Apostle of the Industrial Age," pamphlet, circa 1981, D8, Box 1, Catholic Worker Collection, Dorothy Day Papers, Marquette University (hereafter, Day Papers).
176. McCarraher, *Christian Critics*, 86–87.
177. Dorothy Day to "An Angry Subscriber," September 30, 1935, in Ellsberg, *All the Way to Heaven*, 103–4.
178. Macdonald, *Root Is Man*.
179. Dwight Macdonald, *Memoirs of a Revolutionist: Essays in Political Criticism* (New York: Farrar, Straus and Cudahy, 1957), 10–15, 17, 22–24.
180. Macdonald, "Foolish Things of the World, Part I."
181. Ibid., 369–73.
182. See Macdonald's short essay "Too Big," in *Memoirs of a Revolutionist*, 373–76, which ends with the Good Samaritan parable from the New Testament.
183. Macdonald, "Foolish Things of the World, Part I."
184. Day, *Long Loneliness*, 186.

Chapter 3

1. Day, *Duty of Delight*, 400–401.
2. Jordan, *Writings from "Commonweal,"* 158.
3. The literature referencing or analyzing Day as a pacifist is abundant. See Anne Klejment and Nancy L. Roberts, eds., *American Catholic Pacifism: The Influence of Dorothy Day and the Catholic Worker Movement* (Westport, CT: Praeger Press, 1996); Ira Chernus, *American Nonviolence: The History of an Idea* (Maryknoll, NY: Orbis Books, 2004); and Patricia McNeal, *Harder Than War: Catholic Peacemaking in Twentieth-Century America* (New Brunswick, NJ: Rutgers University Press, 1992).
4. Dorothy Day to a Priest Critic, July 24, 1941, in Ellsberg, *All the Way to Heaven*, 162.
5. Scholars have pondered over the logical necessity of this point. See Kosek, *Acts of Conscience*, 7.
6. Martin J. Corbin, "Dorothy Day," *The Lamp* 69 (January 1971): 16.
7. Dorothy Day to Gerry Griffin, January 21, 1943, in Ellsberg, *All the Way to Heaven*, 182–84.
8. Macdonald, "Foolish Things of the World, Part II," 54.
9. Dorothy Day, "Pilgrimage to Mexico," in Jordan, *Writings from "Commonweal,"* 145.
10. "Dorothy Day Has Made a Major Contribution to American Catholicism," *Today*, May 1, 1948, 6, D8, Box 1, Folder 1, Day Papers.
11. Dwight Macdonald, "Revisiting Dorothy Day," *New York Review of Books* (January 28, 1971): 12–17.
12. Corbin, "Dorothy Day," 16.
13. B. Cook, "Dorothy Day and the Catholic Worker," 6–7.
14. Coles, *Dorothy Day*, 109.
15. Ibid., 90.
16. "Christ the King Alone Can Reconstruct the World," *Catholic Worker* 2, no. 5 (October 1934): 1.
17. Day, *Loaves and Fishes*, 32.
18. Coles, *Dorothy Day*, 105, 109.
19. Day, *Duty of Delight*, 241.
20. Ibid., 529.
21. Coles, *Dorothy Day*, 89–90.
22. Day, *Loaves and Fishes*, 169.
23. Eddy, *Door of Opportunity*, 39–40.
24. Jonathan Mitchell, "Cabins in the Cotton," *New Republic* (September 22, 1937): 175–76.
25. Eddy, *Kingdom of God and the American Dream*, 1, 251.
26. Nutt, *Whole Gospel for the Whole World*, 274.
27. Reinhold Niebuhr, introduction to Eddy, *Eighty Adventurous Years*, 10.
28. Richard Wightman Fox, *Reinhold Niebuhr: A Biography* (Ithaca, NY: Cornell University Press, 1985), 140.
29. Reinhold Niebuhr, *Moral Man and Immoral Society: A Study in Ethics and Politics* (1932; New York: Charles Scribner's Sons, 1960), 21.
30. Franklin, "Early Years," 8.
31. Eddy became a great admirer of Niebuhr's social ethics and just-war theories, especially in the 1940s when Eddy refused to toe the line of absolute pacifism. Eddy dedicated his

book *The Kingdom of God and the American Dream* to him in 1941. The two also cooperated on a few written projects, such as the 1936 pamphlet "Doom and Dawn."

32. Eddy, *Eighty Adventurous Years*, 202.

33. Ibid., 106.

34. Eddy, *Pilgrimage of Ideas*, 303, 268.

35. Eddy, *Kingdom of God and the American Dream*, 301.

36. Eddy, *Pilgrimage of Ideas*, 303.

37. Ibid., 289, 268, 311 (emphasis added).

38. Henry A. Wallace, *Statesmanship and Religion* (New York: Round Table Press, 1934), 81, 132, 106.

39. "Mr. Wallace Is Busiest Vice President," *Sunday Star* (November 2, 1941).

40. Preston, *Sword of the Spirit*, 14.

41. Originally published as *Wallaces' Farmer and Dairy* in 1895, the owners/editors changed the name to *Wallaces' Farmer* in 1898. See John C. Culver and John Hyde, *American Dreamer: The Life and Times of Henry A. Wallace* (New York: W. W. Norton, 2000), 14–22.

42. Ibid., 26.

43. Ibid., 32–40. Wallace's first book, *Agricultural Prices*, was published in 1920.

44. For more on Wallace's life before politics, see Russell Lord, *The Wallaces of Iowa* (Boston: Houghton Mifflin, 1947); and Edward L. Schapsmeier and Frederick H. Schapsmeier, *Henry A. Wallace of Iowa: The Agrarian Years, 1910–1940* (Ames: Iowa State University Press, 1968).

45. Culver and Hyde, *American Dreamer*, 50.

46. Henry A. Wallace, *New Frontiers* (New York: Reynal and Hitchcock, 1934), 150.

47. Henry A. Wallace to Charles Roos, February 4, 1932, University of Iowa Digital Archives.

48. Ibid.

49. Henry A. Wallace to Charles Roos, n.d., 1932, University of Iowa Digital Archives.

50. Henry A. Wallace to Charles Roos, November 20, 1931, University of Iowa Digital Archives.

51. Henry A. Wallace to Charles Roos, April 7, 1932, University of Iowa Digital Archives.

52. Wallace to Roos, February 4, 1932.

53. Culver and Hyde, *American Dreamer*, 110–11.

54. Ibid., 104.

55. Wallace, *New Frontiers*, 94, 276.

56. Ibid., 11.

57. Wallace, *Statesmanship and Religion*, 120. Wallace's 1934 book derived from a series of lectures. The first three chapters are from the Alden-Tuthill Lectures at the Chicago Theological Seminary on January 30, 1934, while the fourth chapter is from a speech in front of the Federal Council of Churches in December 1933.

58. Ibid., 136.

59. Ibid., 71.

60. Ibid., 120–21.

61. Russell Lord, introduction to *Democracy Reborn* by Henry A. Wallace (1944; New York: Reynal and Hitchcock, 1973), 9.

62. Clifford Kennedy Berryman, "Henry, Who Called This Fellow Wilkie an Appeaser," *Evening Star* (Washington, DC) (September 21, 1940).

63. Westbrook Pegler, "Review of Wallace's Madison Square Garden Speech," November 12, 1942, Series X, Box 51, Henry A. Wallace Papers, Special Collections, University of Iowa (hereafter, Wallace Papers).

64. Because Wallace did not advocate an orthodox version of socialism as a top-heavy, centralized system that would immediately replace capitalism, many scholars tend to describe him as a liberal or even an economic conservative who wanted to save capitalism from radicals intent on destroying it. One scholar portrays him as a middle-path liberal (between left-wing Communism and laissez-faire advocates). See Norman D. Markowitz, *The Rise and Fall of the People's Century: Henry A. Wallace and American Liberalism, 1941–1948* (New York: Free Press, 1973).

65. Henry A. Wallace to Henry Morgenthau Jr., September 6, 1932, University of Iowa Digital Archives; Wallace, *New Frontiers*, 67, 8.

66. Wallace, *New Frontiers*, 29, 114, 183, 22.

67. Ibid., 259.

68. Henry A. Wallace, "We Are More Than Economic Men," *Scribner's*, December 1934, Series X, Box 2, Wallace Papers.

69. Henry A. Wallace to Mark Hyde, May 28, 1931, University of Iowa Digital Archives.

70. Henry A. Wallace, "We Must Save Free Enterprise," *Saturday Evening Post* (October 23, 1943): 12–13, 51–54.

71. Henry A. Wallace, "Where There Is No Vision, The People Perish," *Christian Herald*, March 1934, 11.

72. Wallace, "We Are More Than Economic Men."

73. Stanley High, "Will It Be Wallace?," *Saturday Evening Post* (July 3, 1937): 6–7, 84, 86.

74. Ibid., 86–88.

75. Henry A. Wallace, "The Price of Free World Victory," in Wallace, *Democracy Reborn*, 191, 196. For more on Wallace in the role of prophet during the war years, see Schapsmeier and Schapsmeier, *Prophet in Politics*.

76. Preston, *Sword of the Spirit*, 366.

77. "Hay Down," *Time* (December 19, 1938): 14–18.

78. Wallace, "Price of Free World Victory," 191–92.

79. Ibid., 195, 192.

80. Henry A. Wallace, "To Men at Arms," in Wallace, *Democracy Reborn*, 190.

81. Eric F. Goldman, in his negative assessment of Wallace's foreign policy proposals, portrayed Wallace as a sort of isolationist who did not want the United States to intervene against the Soviets in the world. See Eric F. Goldman, *Rendezvous with Destiny* (New York: Knopf, 1952); and Eric F. Goldman, *The Crucial Decade, 1945–1955* (New York: Knopf, 1956).

82. Dorothy Day to an English Catholic Worker, May 3, 1940, in Ellsberg, *All the Way to Heaven*, 147.

83. Henry R. Luce, "The American Century," *Life* (February 17, 1941): 61–65.

84. Wallace, "Price of Free World Victory," 191, 193.

85. Dwight Macdonald, *Henry Wallace: The Man and the Myth* (New York: Vanguard Press, 1948), 32, 12.

86. "Wallace," *Christian Century* (April 23, 1941).

87. Frank S. Mead, "The Last Best Hope on Earth: An Interview with Henry A. Wallace," *Christian Herald*, January 1943.

88. Henry A. Wallace, "Why Did God Make America?," June 8, 1942, Series X, Box 50, Wallace Papers.
89. "Wallace Declares U.S. 'Chosen of the Lord' to Lead World Peace," *Washington Star* (June 9, 1942).
90. Mead, "Last Best Hope on Earth."
91. Henry A. Wallace, "Practical Religion in the World of Tomorrow," March 8, 1943, Series X, Box 52, Wallace Papers.
92. Mead, "Last Best Hope on Earth."
93. A. J. Muste, "The World Task of Pacifism," in Hentoff, *Essays of A. J. Muste*, 218.
94. Ibid., 220.
95. A. J. Muste, "Pacifism and Perfectionism," in Hentoff, *Essays of A. J. Muste*, 317fn.
96. A. J. Muste, "Where Are We Going?," in Hentoff, *Essays of A. J. Muste*, 260, 259, 245.
97. A. J. Muste, "What the Bible Teaches About Freedom," in Hentoff, *Essays of A. J. Muste*, 288.
98. A. J. Muste, "Sketches for an Autobiography," in Hentoff, *Essays of A. J. Muste*, 37.
99. A. J. Muste, "Theology of Despair," in Hentoff, *Essays of A. J. Muste*, 302–7.
100. Ibid., 305.
101. Muste, "Pacifism and Perfectionism," 309.
102. Muste, "Theology of Despair," 302.
103. A. J. Muste, "Address to the Fellowship of Reconciliation," October 11, 1940, Reel 89.3, Muste Papers.
104. Muste, "Typewritten Notes for a Course," Reel 89.3, 13, Muste Papers.
105. Muste, "Address to the Fellowship of Reconciliation," 15.
106. A. J. Muste, "War Is the Enemy," in Hentoff, *Essays of A. J. Muste*, 277.
107. Ibid., 277.
108. Muste, "World Task of Pacifism," 225.
109. Muste, "Typewritten Notes for a Course," 13–14.
110. Mead, "Last Best Hope on Earth."
111. Wallace, *New Frontiers*, 278, 196, 270.
112. Wallace, "Where There Is No Vision," 10.
113. Wallace, *Statesmanship and Religion*, 121.
114. Wallace, *New Frontiers*, 276, 138.
115. Preston, *Sword of the Spirit*, 323.
116. Wallace, *Statesmanship and Religion*, 82.
117. Ibid., 78.
118. High, "Will It Be Wallace?," 7.
119. Henry A. Wallace, "Protestants and Social Action," *Christian Century* (January 29, 1936): 187–89.
120. Wallace, *New Frontiers*, 274.
121. Wallace, "Where There Is No Vision," 11.
122. Wallace, "We Are More Than Economic Men."
123. Wallace, *New Frontiers*, 19.
124. Wallace, "We Are More Than Economic Men."
125. Wallace, *New Frontiers*, 275.
126. Wallace, *Statesmanship and Religion*, 8.

127. Wallace, *New Frontiers*, 277.

128. Frank S. Mead, interview, "The Last Best Hope on Earth," *Christian Herald*, January 1943.

129. Muste, "Return to Pacifism," 196.

130. Muste, "World Task of Pacifism," 221.

131. Muste, "War Is the Enemy," 275, 267.

132. Wallace, *New Frontiers*, 10.

Chapter 4

1. Henry A. Wallace, *Statesmanship and Religion* (New York: Round Table Press, 1934), 135, 132, 111.

2. Ibid., 132.

3. Biographer Norman D. Markowitz makes this point in his rather sympathetic study of Wallace, but he does not fully unpack Wallace's religious vision for building the Kingdom of God on earth. Markowitz portrays Wallace as a failed social democrat who could not overcome his interest in preserving capitalism or his fascination with the Soviet Union. The author never reconciles these two tendencies in Wallace's worldview in large part because he does not place Wallace within a longer tradition of spiritual radicalism. See Norman D. Markowitz, *The Rise and Fall of the People's Century: Henry A. Wallace and American Liberalism, 1941–1948* (New York: Free Press, 1973). For more on the New Deal as a global project of American liberals, see Elizabeth Borgwardt, *A New Deal for the World: America's Vision for Human Rights* (Cambridge: Belknap Press, 2005).

4. See Brenda Gayle Plummer, ed., *Window on Freedom: Race, Civil Rights, and Foreign Affairs, 1945–1988* (Chapel Hill: University of North Carolina Press, 2003) and *Rising Wind: Black Americans and U.S. Foreign Affairs, 1935–1960* (Chapel Hill: University of North Carolina Press, 1996). See also Carol Anderson, *Eyes Off the Prize: The United Nations and the African American Struggle for Human Rights, 1944–1955* (Cambridge: Cambridge University Press, 2003).

5. Wallace's 1948 campaign vision was rational and consistent with his views as a spiritual socialist. He did not disagree with Truman because of a political grudge or because of an eccentric, irrational personality disorder which scholars such as Arthur M. Schlesinger, Jr. have implied. See Arthur M. Schlesinger Jr., *The Age of Roosevelt*, 3 vols. (1958; Boston: Houghton Mifflin, 2003); and Arthur M. Schlesinger Jr., "Who Was Henry A. Wallace: The Story of a Perplexing and Indomitably Naïve Public Servant," *Los Angeles Times* (March 12, 2000).

6. Wallace was not only vice president during the war, but also chairman of the Board of Economic Warfare.

7. For more on the Roerich Affair, see John C. Culver and John Hyde, *American Dreamer: The Life and Times of Henry A. Wallace* (New York: W. W. Norton & Company, 2000), 130–46.

8. Gardner Jackson, "Henry Wallace: A Divided Mind," *Atlantic Monthly* (August 1948): 27–33.

9. Henry A. Wallace, "Interview with Stanley Dixon," August 5, 1943, Series X, Box 53, Wallace Papers, Special Collections, University of Iowa, Iowa City (hereafter, Wallace Papers).

10. Henry A. Wallace, "We Must Save Free Enterprise," in *Democracy Reborn* (1944; New York: Reynal & Hitchcock, 1973), 249–53.

11. Borgwardt, *A New Deal for the World*.
12. *New York Times* (January 24, 1944).
13. Curtis D. MacDougall, *Gideon's Army* (New York: Marzani and Munsell, 1965), 57.
14. Wallace, "Russia," in *Democracy Reborn*, 200.
15. Henry A. Wallace, Madison Square Garden Speech, 12 September 1946, Wallace Papers.
16. James A. Hagerty, "Wallace Warns On 'Tough' Policy Toward Russia," *New York Times* (September 13, 1946).
17. Peter Kihss, "Wallace Calls for Peace with Russia as Truman Policy," *New York Herald Tribune* (September 13, 1946).
18. Joseph and Stewart Alsop, "Tragedy of Liberalism," *Life* (May 20, 1946): 68–69.
19. Henry A. Wallace, "America Must Choose," World Affairs Pamphlet, January 1934, Series X, Box 1, Wallace Papers.
20. Henry A. Wallace, *New Frontiers* (New York: Reynal & Hitchcock, 1934), 286, 275.
21. Ibid., 278.
22. Russell Lord, introduction to Wallace, *Democracy Reborn*, 15.
23. Wallace, *Statesmanship and Religion*, 81.
24. Wallace, "Price of Free World Victory," 193–94.
25. Henry A. Wallace, "Statement Regarding Mexican Labor in California," September 29, 1942, Series X, Box 50, Wallace Papers.
26. Henry A. Wallace, "Soil, Food, and the People," October 17, 1942, Series X, Box 51, Wallace Papers.
27. Henry A. Wallace, "America Tomorrow," in Wallace, *Democracy Reborn*, 238–45.
28. Macdonald, *Henry Wallace*, 69.
29. Introduction to "What We Fight For," by Henry A. Wallace, reprinted in *New Republic* (September 20, 1943) (emphasis added).
30. Wallace, *New Frontiers*, 283.
31. Wallace, "Russia," 199.
32. Henry A. Wallace, "Meet the Press," radio interview, Mutual Broadcasting System, January 10, 1947, Wallace Papers.
33. Wallace, *Statesmanship and Religion*, 80.
34. Wallace, "Russia," 196–200.
35. Macdonald, *Henry Wallace*, 101, 105. Historians have addressed Wallace's alignment with Communists. In his recent study of Communist influence in the 1948 campaign, Thomas W. Devine offered a balanced view, arguing that while the far Left filled the ranks of the New Party (later Progressive Party) and attempted to control its agenda, they did not control its candidate. "To be sure," Devine wrote, "Wallace himself was not subject to Communist discipline. . . . [H]e continued to follow an independent political trajectory." See Thomas W. Devine, *Henry Wallace's 1948 Presidential Campaign and the Future of Postwar Liberalism* (Chapel Hill: University of North Carolina Press, 2013), 34.
36. Jackson, "Henry Wallace: A Divided Mind," 27–33.
37. Henry A. Wallace, "Thoughts at Christmas," *New Republic* 117 (December 22, 1947): 12–13. Wallace was offered a post at the *New Republic* as an editor-contributor, which he accepted and began in 1946.
38. Wallace, "Protestants and Social Action," 189. See also "Three Philosophies," in Wallace, *Democracy Reborn*, 219–27.

39. See Devine, *Henry Wallace's 1948 Presidential Campaign*, 45–46, 57.

40. Ibid., 90, 141.

41. Mead, "Last Best Hope on Earth."

42. Macdonald, *Henry Wallace*, 137.

43. In addition to the full-length work on Wallace, see also Dwight Macdonald, "A Note on Wallese," in *Memoirs of a Revolutionist: Essays in Political Criticism* (New York: Farrar, Straus and Cudahy, 1957), 299–300.

44. Irving Howe and Lewis Coser, *The American Communist Party: A Critical History, 1919–1957* (Boston: Beacon Press, 1957), 470–71. See also Devine, *Henry Wallace's 1948 Presidential Campaign*, 46.

45. Macdonald, *Henry Wallace*, 23, 27, 139, 134.

46. Norman Thomas, "Speech on the Progressive Party," September 19, 1948, Series IV, Box 11, Wallace Papers.

47. Macdonald, *Henry Wallace*, 49, 65, 82.

48. Wallace, *New Frontiers*, 7.

49. Henry A. Wallace, "Corn and People," October 14, 1964, Wallace Papers.

50. As Norman Markowitz wrote, "The cooperative commonwealth (the secular expression of the Kingdom of God on Earth) had not flowed freely from the hearts of the people." Wallace, therefore, was left with a plan that "was never seriously tried." Markowitz, *Rise and Fall of the People's Century*, 312, 328.

51. Wallace referred to Gideon's Army in his speech announcing his candidacy in December 1947. It is also the title of Curtis D. MacDougall's three-volume account of the Progressive Party campaign (see note 13 of this chapter).

52. Karl M. Schmidt has argued that Wallace accepted the support of Communists more by default than design because he could not persuade other major segments of left-liberal constituents, including African Americans and labor unions, to cast their lot with him instead of Truman. The fact still remains, however, that Wallace failed to convince these potential supporters with his vision of a spiritual socialist approach to domestic and foreign policy. See Karl M. Schmidt, *Henry A. Wallace: Quixotic Crusade* (Syracuse, NY: Syracuse University Press, 1960).

53. Thomas, *A Socialist's Faith*, 179.

54. Henry A. Wallace to Henry Morgenthau Jr., September 6, 1932, University of Iowa Digital Archives; Wallace, *New Frontiers*, 67, 8.

55. Wallace, *New Frontiers*, 101, 133–34.

56. Ibid., viii, x.

57. Ignazio Silone, "Emergency Exit," in *The God That Failed*, ed. Richard Crossman (New York: Harper and Row, 1949), 98.

58. Ibid., 98, 101.

59. Ignazio Silone, "The Choice of Comrades," *Dissent* (Winter 1955): 7, 9, 11.

60. Ibid., 12–13.

61. Silone, *Story of a Humble Christian*, 17, 22.

62. Ignazio Silone, *Fontamara*, trans. Eric Mosbacher (New York: New American Library, 1984), 157, 164.

63. Ignazio Silone, *Bread and Wine*, trans. Eric Mosbacher (New York: Signet Classics, 2005), 261.

64. Silone, *Story of a Humble Christian*, 25.
65. Silone, "Emergency Exit," 114.
66. Ibid., 101–2.
67. Irving Howe, introduction to Silone, *Fontamara*, 4. For more on Silone's spiritual influence on Howe and the independent Left, see Vaneesa Cook, "Eighty Years Since *Bread and Wine*: Ignazio Silone's Christian Socialism," *Dissent* (online), May 6, 2016.
68. Silone, "Choice of Comrades," 15–16.
69. Ibid., 18.
70. Howe, *Margin of Hope*, 194.
71. Irving Howe, "Silone and the Radical Conscience," *Dissent* 3 (Winter 1956): 69–71.
72. Irving Howe, *Politics and the Novel* (New York: Horizon Press, 1957), 5.
73. Day, *Duty of Delight*, 25.
74. Thomas, *A Socialist's Faith*, 122, 128. For more on Thomas and his life's trajectory from minister to Socialist Party leader, see W. A. Swanberg, *Norman Thomas: The Last Idealist* (New York: Charles Scribner's Sons, 1976). Swanberg says that Thomas gave up on organized religion and the notion of a personal God. However, Thomas's writings indicate that he still held respect for religious values, especially when they dovetailed with a socialist program.
75. Howe, *Margin of Hope*, 346.
76. Henry A. Wallace, "Easter Sermon," April 9, 1950, Series 10, Box 76, Wallace Papers.
77. Ibid.
78. Henry A. Wallace, "The State Exists for Man, Not Man for the State," Series 10, Box 77, Wallace Papers.
79. Wallace, "Corn and People."
80. H. H. Wilson, introduction to MacDougall, *Gideon's Army*, xii, vii. Richard J. Walton also regarded the election failure as a lost opportunity that could have changed the course of the Cold War. See Richard J. Walton, *Henry Wallace, Harry Truman, and the Cold War* (New York: Viking Press, 1976), 355.
81. Senator Paul A. Douglas, "Symposium Honoring Sherwood Eddy," *Jacksonville (FL) Courier* (October 18, 1963): 3.
82. Young Men's Christian Association Sherwood Eddy Memorial, "Who Was Sherwood Eddy?"
83. Dr. Gordon E. Michalson, "Speech at the Sherwood Eddy Memorial Service," March 6, 1963, Box 20, Folder 212, Eddy Papers.
84. Myles Horton, *The Long Haul: An Autobiography* (New York: Doubleday, 1990), 7.
85. Ibid., 22.
86. Ibid., 26, 28.
87. Ibid., 26.
88. John M. Glen, *Highlander: No Ordinary School, 1932–1962* (Lexington: University of Kentucky Press, 1988), 9.
89. Horton, *Long Haul*, 33.
90. Glen, *Highlander*, 10. A. J. Muste was still involved with Brookwood until 1933, when he resigned. It is unclear whether Horton met Muste when he visited in 1929–30, as Muste was traveling often for the Conference for Progressive Labor Action and League for Independent Political Action during those years and dealing with the American Federation of Labor's controversial accusations of Communist activity at Brookwood.

91. Horton, *Long Haul*, 30.
92. Ibid., 36.
93. Ibid., 48.
94. N. F. S. Grundtvig, *Selected Writings* (Minneapolis, MN: Fortress Press, 1976).
95. Horton, *Long Haul*, 55.
96. Ibid., 49.
97. Ibid., 20, 43.
98. Ibid., 60.
99. Reprinted in ibid., 62.
100. Glen, *Highlander*, 19.
101. Horton, *Long Haul*, 65.
102. Glen, *Highlander*, 20.
103. Horton, *Long Haul*, 63.
104. Glen, *Highlander*, 20.
105. Ibid., 61.
106. Ibid., 22.
107. Horton, *Long Haul*, 35.
108. Ibid., 44.
109. Ibid., 133, 184, 227.
110. Ibid., 227–28.
111. Ibid., 81, 140, 57, 46, 146, 44.
112. Ibid., 24.
113. Glen, *Highlander*, 127.
114. Horton, *Long Haul*, 84–85.
115. Glen, *Highlander*, 2.
116. For more on the "black social gospel," see Dorrien, *Breaking White Supremacy*.
117. Horton, *Long Haul*, 103.
118. Glen, *Highlander*, 155.
119. Horton, *Long Haul*, 104.
120. Glen, *Highlander*, 145.
121. Rosa Parks remembrance, reprinted in Horton, *Long Haul*, 150.
122. Horton, *Long Haul*, 146.
123. Ibid., 120.
124. Ibid., 133, 27.
125. Ibid., 171.
126. Ibid., 104.

Chapter 5

1. Staughton Lynd, e-mail message to author, December 22, 2010.
2. F. O. Matthiessen, *American Renaissance: Art and Expression in the Age of Emerson and Whitman* (New York: Oxford University Press, 1941), xv.
3. Staughton Lynd, *Intellectual Origins of American Radicalism* (1968; London: Wildwood House, 1973), 173.
4. For more on Wallace's vision of a New Deal for the world, see Norman D. Markowitz, *The Rise and Fall of the People's Century: Henry A. Wallace and American Liberalism, 1941–1948* (New York: Free Press, 1973).

5. Norman Markowitz, for example, concluded that "The common man had failed. The new social machinery had not been perfected," in *The Rise and Fall of the People's Century*, 312.

6. Nikhil Singh, in *Black Is a Country*, wrote: "The [civil rights] movement that he had come to personify was never limited to securing the rights of black people." Singh saw King's global mission as a radical restructuring for social and political equality, though he did not connect this vision to the Kingdom of God. See Nikhil Singh, *Black Is a Country: Race and the Unfinished Struggle for Democracy* (Cambridge, MA: Harvard University Press, 2004), 2.

7. For more on the New Left as broadly conceived, see Van Gosse, *Rethinking the New Left: An Interpretive History* (New York: Palgrave Macmillan, 2005), and Van Gosse, *The Movements of the New Left, 1950–1975: A Brief History with Documents* (Boston/New York: Bedford/St. Martin's, 2004).

8. For more on the religious connections between the civil rights movement and the broader New Left, see Doug Rossinow, *The Politics of Authenticity: Liberalism, Christianity, and the New Left in America* (New York: Columbia University Press, 1998). Scholars such as Christopher Phelps and Howard Brick, who have traced the continuity of earlier independent radicals in the 1940s and 1950s with the later New Left, do not highlight the spiritual approach to socialism that formed the core of that continuity and underlay discourse about democratization. See Phelps Brick, *Radicals in America*.

9. Frederick C. Stern, *F. O. Matthiessen, Christian Socialist as Critic* (Chapel Hill: University of North Carolina Press, 1981), 17.

10. Staughton Lynd dedicated his sourcebook on nonviolence in America to Matthiessen in 1966. See Staughton Lynd, ed., *Nonviolence in America: A Documentary History* (Indianapolis: Bobbs-Merrill, 1966).

11. John Corry, " 'We Must Say Yes to Our Souls': Staughton Lynd, Spokesman for the New Left," *New York Times* (January 23, 1966): 12.

12. Henry A. Wallace to L. E. Johndro, October 24, 1931, University of Iowa Digital Archives. See also Culver and Hyde, *American Dreamer*, 82.

13. Alice Lynd and Staughton Lynd, *Stepping Stones: Memoir of a Life Together* (Lanham, MD: Lexington Books, 2009), 29–32.

14. Ibid.

15. Staughton Lynd, "The Once and Future Movement," in *Living Inside Our Hope* (Ithaca: ILR Press, 1997), 15.

16. Lynd and Lynd, *Stepping Stones*, 29.

17. Ibid., 32.

18. Lynd later attended the Fieldston Ethical Culture School in Riverdale from seventh to twelfth grade.

19. Horace L. Friess, *Felix Adler and Ethical Culture: Memories and Studies* (New York: Columbia University Press, 1981), 2.

20. Howard B. Radest, *Toward Common Ground: The Story of the Ethical Societies in the United States* (New York: Frederick Ungar, 1969), 13.

21. Felix Adler, "The Distinctive Aims of the Ethical Culture School: Incidental Versus Systematic Moral Teaching," fourth address in *The Ethical Record: Society for Ethical Culture*, vol. 3 (New York: Society for Ethical Culture, 1904), 208.

22. Felix Adler, *An Ethical Philosophy of Life* (New York: D. Appleton, 1929), 23, 126, 43, 352, 7.

23. Felix Adler, "Address on Atheism," quoted in Radest, *Toward Common Ground*, 35.
24. Lynd and Lynd, *Stepping Stones*, 23.
25. Adler, *Ethical Philosophy*, 341.
26. Lynd, "Liberation Theology for Quakers," in *Living Inside Our Hope*, 49–50.
27. Adler, *Ethical Philosophy*, 344.
28. Staughton Lynd, e-mail message to author, March 8, 2010.
29. Lynd and Lynd, *Stepping Stones*, 33.
30. Lynd, "The Once and Future Movement," 15.
31. Adler, *Ethical Philosophy*, 37.
32. Staughton Lynd, e-mail message to author, March 8, 2010.
33. Lynd, "The First New Left . . . and the Third," in *Living Inside Our Hope*, 68; Lynd, "Liberation Theology for Quakers," 62.
34. Irving Howe, introduction to *Bread and Wine* by Ignazio Silone, vi.
35. Lynd, "The First New Left," 68.
36. A. J. Muste, "Sketches for an Autobiography," in *The Essays of A. J. Muste*, ed. Nat Hentoff (Indianapolis: Bobbs-Merrill, 1967), 18.
37. Muste, "The World Task of Pacifism," 225, 223, 228; A. J. Muste, "What the Bible Teaches About Freedom," in Hentoff, *The Essays of A. J. Muste*, 283.
38. Leon Trotsky, *Literature and Revolution*, ed. William Keach (1925; Chicago: Haymarket Books, 2005), 207.
39. See Lynd and Lynd, *Stepping Stones*, 33–34; Staughton Lynd, "Father and Son," in *Living Inside Our Hope*, 21.
40. Lynd and Lynd, *Stepping Stones*, 33.
41. Simone Weil, *Oppression and Liberty* (London: Routledge and Kegan Paul, 1958), 4, 20, 158, 164, 153.
42. Gabriella Fiori, *Simone Weil: An Intellectual Biography*, trans. Joseph R. Berrigan (Athens: University of Georgia Press, 1989), 194.
43. Weil, *Oppression and Liberty*, 100.
44. Fiori, *Simone Weil*, 54, 204.
45. Lynd, "First New Left," 77.
46. Lynd, *Living Inside Our Hope*, 74. For more on Lynd's conception of the New Left, see his introduction to Priscilla Long, ed., *The New Left: A Collection of Essays* (Boston: Extending Horizons Books, 1969), 1–13. By identifying Silone, Muste, and Weil as proto–New Leftists in an Old Left milieu, Lynd reinforces, in some ways, the thesis of Maurice Isserman, who argued that the New Left developed from a variety of Old Left sources and connections. However, Lynd also insisted that these proto–New Leftists were decidedly different from their typical Old Left counterparts in that they focused on human values and community building more than politics and power. See Isserman, *If I Had a Hammer*.
47. Weil, *Oppression and Liberty*, 157.
48. Lynd, "First New Left," 70.
49. Weil, *Oppression and Liberty*, 6, 173.
50. Lynd, "Once and Future Movement," 14.
51. Lynd, "First New Left," 68–70.
52. Lynd and Lynd, *Stepping Stones*, 34–35, 45. Before moving to Macedonia, the Lynds had lived in Chicago, where Staughton studied regional planning under Rexford Tugwell at

the University of Chicago and Alice worked as a secretary in the Education Department of Roosevelt University.

53. Ibid., 47.

54. Lynd, "Liberation Theology for Quakers," 49.

55. Lynd and Lynd, *Stepping Stones*, 2.

56. See James Burnham, *The Managerial Revolution: What Is Happening in the World* (New York: John Day, 1941), in which Burnham argued that capitalism was adaptable and thus difficult to eradicate. Lynd read this book as a teenager, and he was inspired to challenge Burnham's claims about capitalism's resistance to alternative economic and social systems. See Lynd and Lynd, *Stepping Stones*, 32–33.

57. Lynd, "Liberation Theology for Quakers," 64.

58. Lynd and Lynd, *Stepping Stones*, 49–50.

59. Matthew 25:35–45. Lynd quotes this as one of his favorite biblical passages in Lynd and Lynd, *Stepping Stones*, 49–50.

60. Lynd and Lynd, *Stepping Stones*, 50.

61. Ibid., 54–56, 61–64.

62. Lynd, "Liberation Theology for Quakers," 50.

63. Lynd and Lynd, *Stepping Stones*, 3, 65.

64. Ibid., 21.

65. SNCC Statement of Purpose, in Doug McAdam, *Freedom Summer* (New York: Oxford University Press, 1988), 30.

66. Lynd and Lynd, *Stepping Stones*, 67.

67. Staughton Lynd to Alice Lynd, June 24, 1964, quoted in Carl Mirra, *The Admirable Radical: Staughton Lynd and Cold War Dissent, 1945–1970* (Kent, OH: Kent State University Press, 2010), 49.

68. Martin Luther King Jr., *Testament of Hope: The Essential Writings and Speeches of Martin Luther King, Jr.*, ed. James Washington (New York: HarperCollins, 1991), 234.

69. Martin Luther King Jr., *Strength to Love* (Philadelphia: Fortress Press, 1963), 150.

70. For more on King's religious radicalism, see V. Cook, "Martin Luther King, Jr. and the Long Social Gospel Movement"; Dorrien, *Breaking White Supremacy*; Michael K. Honey, *Going Down Jericho Road: The Memphis Strike, Martin Luther King's Last Campaign* (New York: W. W. Norton, 2007); and Chappell, *Stone of Hope*. For more on King as a democratic socialist, see Douglas Sturm, "Martin Luther King Jr. as Democratic Socialist," *Journal of Religious Ethics* 18, no. 2 (Fall 1990): 79–105; and Singh, *Black Is a Country*. It is crucial that any study of King give equal attention to his radical politics and his religious worldview, though the scholarship is often split on these grounds. Understanding him as a spiritual socialist is the best way to capture his radical religious vision.

71. Lynd and Lynd, *Stepping Stones*, 68, 70–71. The Highlander Folk School was cofounded in Tennessee by innovative educator Myles Horton in 1932 to "train" social reformers through an organic process of interpersonal experience. More like an education center than a formal school, Highlander operated without a set agenda or curriculum. Instead, students and teachers explored issues in an egalitarian environment intended to prefigure a radical new society based on democracy and brotherhood. In the early 1960s, the school hosted a series of college workshops on strategies for building a biracial civil rights movement, in the spirit of the recent sit-ins. A session offered in 1960 entitled "The New Generation Fights for

Equality" attracted over eighty students, many of whom joined the newly founded SNCC that year. During the 1962–63 voter registration drive, SNCC initiated workshops at Highlander that attracted more than 1,500 participants. The idea for Freedom Summer took shape there. For more on SNCC and the Highlander Folk School, see Glen, *Highlander*, 148–54, 211–12.

72. Sandra E. Adickes, *The Legacy of a Freedom School* (New York: Palgrave Macmillan, 2005), 58.

73. Felix Adler, "The Distinctive Aims of the Ethical Culture School," third address in *Ethical Record*, 165.

74. Staughton Lynd, "A Profession of History," *New Journal at Yale* 1, no. 3 (November 11, 1967): 10.

75. Ibid.

76. Adickes, *Legacy of a Freedom School*, 44–45.

77. Lynd and Lynd, *Stepping Stones*, 70.

78. Staughton Lynd, "Socialism: The Forbidden Word," in Grubacic, *From Here to There*, 60–67.

79. Staughton Lynd, "Remembering SNCC," in Grubacic, *From Here to There*, 70.

80. Lynd, "Socialism: The Forbidden Word," 61.

81. Staughton Lynd, "The New Radicals and 'Participatory Democracy,'" in Grubacic, *From Here to There*, 95, 93.

82. Ibid., 94, 93, 94.

83. Students for a Democratic Society, Port Huron Statement, 1962, available at http://www.h-net.org/~hst306/documents/huron.html (accessed December 11, 2011).

84. Staughton Lynd, "The Cold War Expulsions and the Movement of the 1960s," in Grubacic, *From Here to There*, 101.

85. Niebuhr, *Moral Man and Immoral Society*, 47, 91.

86. Tom Hayden, foreword to Lynd and Lynd, *Stepping Stones*, viii.

87. Declaration of Conscience Against the War in Vietnam, in Lynd, *Nonviolence in America*, 377.

88. Lynd and Lynd, *Stepping Stones*, 176.

89. Ibid., 90.

90. Silone, "Choice of Comrades," 12, 19.

91. Dick Flacks, quoted from an interview in James Miller, *Democracy Is in the Streets: From Port Huron to the Siege of Chicago* (New York: Simon and Schuster, 1987), 323.

92. Staughton Lynd, "Speech at the IWW Centennial," in Grubacic, *From Here to There*, 243, 245.

93. Staughton Lynd, "Internationalization of Capital and Labor's Response," in Lynd, *Living Inside Our Hope*, 203, 204.

94. Greg Nevala Calvert, *Democracy from the Heart: Spiritual Values, Decentralism, and Democratic Idealism in the Movement of the 1960s* (Eugene, OR: Communitas Press, 1991), xii, xv, 210, 212.

95. Lynd and Lynd, *Stepping Stones*, 125.

96. Lynd, "Internationalization of Capital and Labor's Response," 204.

97. Lynd, "Liberation Theology for Quakers," 45, 47, 46.

98. Lynd, "Once and Future Movement," 15.

99. Charles Eckert, *Spectator*, 8, Lynd Papers.

100. Staughton Lynd, "The Webbs, Lenin, Rosa Luxemburg," in Lynd, *Living Inside Our Hope*, 230.
101. Pauli Murray, *Song in a Weary Throat: An American Pilgrimage* (New York: Harper and Row, 1987), 3.
102. Ibid., 28. For more on Murray's family history, see her first autobiography, *Proud Shoes: The Story of an American Family* (New York: Harper and Row, 1956). See also a recent biography, Rosalind Rosenberg, *Jane Crow: The Life of Pauli Murray* (New York: Oxford University Press, 2017).
103. Murray, *Proud Shoes*, 271.
104. Ibid., xvi.
105. Ibid., viii.
106. Ibid., 73.
107. Murray, *Song in a Weary Throat*, 93, 103–7.
108. Ibid., 107.
109. Sarah Azaransky, *The Dream Is Freedom: Pauli Murray and American Democratic Faith* (New York: Oxford University Press, 2011), 3–4. For more on Murray's aversion to Communism, see Azaransky, *Dream Is Freedom*, 15.
110. Murray, *Song in a Weary Throat*, 184, 238.
111. Ibid., 308–9. For more on Murray's relationship with Eleanor Roosevelt, see Patricia Bell-Scott, *The Firebrand and the First Lady: Portrait of a Friendship: Pauli Murray, Eleanor Roosevelt, and the Struggle for Social Justice* (New York: Knopf Doubleday, 2017).
112. Azaransky, *Dream Is Freedom*, 3.
113. Ibid., 69, 48.
114. Ibid., 25–26.
115. Quoted in ibid., 30. The original text is Pauli Murray, "Negroes Are Fed Up," *Common Sense* (August 1943): 274–75.
116. See Grant Farred, "Endgame Identity? Mapping the New Left Origins of Identity Politics," *New Literary History* 31, no. 4 (Autumn 2000): 627–48; and Linda Martín Alcoff et al., *Identity Politics Reconsidered* (New York: Palgrave Macmillan, 2006). Identity politics is not confined to the Left, but has also been embraced by the far Right. See Francis Fukuyama, *Identity: The Demand for Dignity and the Politics of Resentment* (New York: Farrar, Straus and Giroux, 2018).
117. Quoted in Azaransky, *Dream Is Freedom*, 83. The original source is Pauli Murray, "Black Power for Whom?" (August 26, 1968), Box 2, Folder 30 in the Pauli Murray Papers, Arthur and Elizabeth Schlesinger Library, Radcliffe Institute for Advanced Study, Harvard University.
118. Pauli Murray, *Dark Testament: And Other Poems* (Norwalk, CT: Silvermine Press, 1970).
119. Azaransky, *Dream Is Freedom*, 70, 83.
120. James H. Cone, *Black Theology and Black Power* (1969; Maryknoll, NY: Orbis Books, 1997), 38, 48, 55.
121. Ibid., 30.
122. Ibid., 2–3, 32, 1, 18, 16.
123. Murray, *Song in a Weary Throat*, 416–17.
124. Azaransky, *Dream Is Freedom*, 88–95. The author points out that Murray was more accepting of the theories of Deotis J. Roberts, who challenged James Cone in *Liberation and*

Reconciliation: A Black Theology (Philadelphia: Westminster Press, 1971). See also Pauli Murray, "Black Theology: Heresy, Syncretism, or Prophecy?," 7, April 16, 1975, Box 23, Folder 472, Pauli Murray Papers, Arthur and Elizabeth Schlesinger Library on the History of Women in America, Radcliffe Institute, Harvard University.

125. Anthony B. Bradley, "The Marxist Roots of Black Liberation Theology," Acton Institute, April 2, 2008, https://acton.org/pub/commentary/2008/04/02/marxist-roots-black-liberation-theology.

126. Murray, *Song in a Weary Throat*, 396, 391–92.

127. Cone, *Black Theology and Black Power*, 17.

128. Murray, *Song in a Weary Throat*, 394. On not dividing Black Power from the "good" 1960s, see Peniel E. Joseph, *Waiting 'til the Midnight Hour: A Narrative History of Black Power in America* (New York: Henry Holt, 2006).

129. Cone, *Black Theology and Black Power*, 126–27, 145, 151.

130. Cornel West with David Ritz, *Brother West Living and Loving Out Loud: A Memoir* (Carlsbad, CA: SmileyBooks, 2009), 88.

131. Cornel West, *The Cornel West Reader* (New York: Basic Civitas Books, 1999), 6.

132. West, *Brother West*, 48–50.

133. Ibid., 58, 49, 61.

134. Ibid., 69.

135. West, *Cornel West Reader*, 3.

136. Cornel West, "Black Theology and Human Identity," in *Black Faith and Public Talk: Critical Essays on James H. Cone's "Black Theology and Black Power,"* ed. Dwight N. Hopkins (1999; Waco, TX: Baylor University Press, 2007), 11–19.

137. Cornel West, "The Making of an American Radical Democrat of African Descent," in West, *Cornel West Reader*, 4.

138. Cornel West, *Hope on a Tightrope: Words and Wisdom* (Carlsbad, CA: Hay House, 2008), 73.

139. Ibid., 161.

140. West, "Black Theology and Human Identity," 12.

141. Cornel West, "The Historicist Turn in Philosophy of Religion," in West, *Cornel West Reader*, 366. For more on West's prophetic religious philosophy and his treatment of Black Power and Malcolm X, see Cornel West, *Prophecy Deliverance! An Afro-American Revolutionary Christianity* (Philadelphia: Westminster Press, 1982). See also Cornel West, *Race Matters* (Boston: Beacon Press, 1993); and Cornel West, *Black Prophetic Fire* (Boston: Beacon Press, 2014).

142. West, "Historicist Turn in Philosophy of Religion," 367. "Cone's religious claims reek of hermetic fideism," West also stated.

143. Ibid., 368.

144. West, *Cornel West Reader*, 369–70. See also West, *Hope on a Tightrope*, 73.

145. Murray, *Song in a Weary Throat*, 128.

146. Lynd, *Intellectual Origins of American Radicalism*, 132, 27, 89, 7, 18, 30–31.

147. Eugene Genovese, "Abolitionist," *New York Review of Books* 11 (September 26, 1968): 69–74.

148. West, *Cornel West Reader*, 158.

149. Murray, *Song in a Weary Throat*, 232.

Conclusion

1. See Jim Wallis, *God's Politics: Why the Religious Right Gets It Wrong and the Left Doesn't Get It* (New York: HarperCollins, 2005).
2. For more on evangelical left-liberals in the 1970s, see David R. Swartz, *Moral Minority: The Evangelical Left in an Age of Conservatism* (Philadelphia: University of Pennsylvania Press, 2012).
3. Ibid., 265.
4. Wallis, *God's Politics*, xxi. For more on the cultural turn toward conservative ideas, see Daniel T. Rodgers, *Age of Fracture* (Cambridge, MA: Belknap Press, 2011); and Andrew Hartman, *A War for the Soul of America: A History of the Culture Wars* (Chicago: University of Chicago Press, 2015).
5. Historian David R. Swartz put it bluntly in his book *Moral Minority*, in which he argues that the ascendency of the religious Right in the 1970s, culminating in the 1980s, was not a foregone conclusion, but a product of political maneuvering. "Identity politics sabotaged [a] nascent progressive coalition of evangelicals," he wrote. Tracing the diversity and dispersion of evangelicals in the post–World War II era, Swartz offers many examples of continued social justice activism for evangelical left-liberals. See Swartz, *Moral Minority*, 6, 1, 254.
6. Wallis goes so far as to claim that the Democratic Party has been captured by "secular fundamentalists." See Wallis, *God's Politics*.
7. See Kevin M. Kruse, *One Nation Under God: How Corporate America Invented Christian America* (New York: Basic Books, 2015).
8. Wallis, *God's Politics*, xxiii.
9. Quoted in Maxine Phillips, "Moral Minority," *Dissent* (Winter 2015), https://www.dissentmagazine.org/article/moral-mondays-protestant-left-usa.
10. Swartz, *Moral Minority*, 263.
11. Laurie Goodstein, "Liberals Fighting for Their Faith," *New York Times* (June 11, 2017).
12. Ibid. See also the online version, "Religious Liberals Sat Out of Politics for 40 Years. Now They Want in the Game" (June 10, 2017), https://www.nytimes.com/2017/06/10/us/politics/politics-religion-liberal-william-barber.html.
13. Phillips, "Moral Minority"; Scott Malone, "'Religious Left' Emerging as US Political Force in Trump Era," Reuters, March 27, 2017; Cleve R. Wootson Jr., "Reverend William Barber Builds a Moral Movement," *Washington Post* (June 29, 2017).
14. Phillips, "Moral Minority."
15. Quoted in Malone, "'Religious Left' Emerging."
16. Vaneesa Cook, "Bernie Sanders and the Spiritual Case for Socialism," *Dissent* (November 2015).
17. William J. Barber II with Jonathan Wilson-Hartgrove, *The Third Reconstruction: How a Moral Movement Is Overcoming the Politics of Division and Fear* (Boston: Beacon Press, 2016), xv, 128.
18. Phillips, "Moral Minority."
19. Barber, *Third Reconstruction*, 129.
20. See Hartman, *War for the Soul of America*; Rodgers, *Age of Fracture*; John P. Diggins, *Rise and Fall of the Left* (1973; New York: W. W. Norton, 1992); and William L. O'Neill, *New Left: A History* (Wheeling, IL: Harlan Davidson, 2001).

21. Barber, *Third Reconstruction*, 129, 128.
22. Ibid., 15–19.
23. Ibid., 24.
24. Ibid., 129.
25. Phillips, "Moral Minority."
26. West, *Hope on a Tightrope*, 15.
27. Hope Reese, "Cornel West: Neoliberalism Has Failed Us," *JSTOR Daily* (December 25, 2017), https://daily.jstor.org/cornel-west-interview/. In late 2017, West sparked a national debate over his critical review of Ta-Nehisi Coates's book *We Were Eight Years in Power*, which West panned as a neoliberal apology for the Obama administration and Obama's preoccupation with corporate capitalism and military power. West argued that the reaction against Obama is not explained by white supremacy and racism alone, but also stems from Obama's failure to effectively address issues of poverty, labor, and warfare for the American public. See Cornel West, "Ta-Nehisi Coates Is the Neoliberal Face of the Black Freedom Struggle," *Guardian* (December 17, 2017), https://www.theguardian.com/commentisfree/2017/dec/17/ta-nehisi-coates-neoliberal-black-struggle-cornel-west.
28. Reese, "Cornel West." See also Wootson Jr., "Rev. William Barber Builds a Moral Movement"; and West, *Black Prophetic Fire*.
29. Cornel West, "Religion and the Left," in West, *Cornel West Reader*, 372. This essay originally appeared in 1984 in the *Monthly Review* as "Religion and the Left." In another essay in the *Cornel West Reader*, West wrote, "Marxism is not and cannot serve as a religion. And if it is cast as a religion, it is a shallow secular ideology of social change that fails to speak to us about the ultimate facts of human existence. To put it charitably, Marxist thought does not purport to be existential wisdom—of how to live one's life day to day." See "The Making of an American Radical of African Descent," in West, *Cornel West Reader*, 13.
30. West, "Religion and the Left," 378–79.
31. Macdonald, *Root Is Man*, 16.
32. West, "Religion and the Left," 375.
33. McKanan, *Prophetic Encounters*, 14.
34. Barber, *Third Reconstruction*, 22.

INDEX

Addams, Jane, 12
Adickes, Sandra, 186–87
Adler, Felix, 175–77, 186–87
á Kempis, Thomas, 72
Alinsky, Saul, 94
Alsop, Joseph, 139
Alsop, Stewart, 139
Amalgamated Textile Workers (ATW), 22, 30, 32
Amberson, William R., 62, 66
American Federation of Labor (AFL), 22, 34–37, 162
American Federation of Teachers, 34–35
American Revolution, 207
American Seminar. *See* Sherwood Eddy, American Seminar
Americans for Democratic Action (ADA), 145
American Workers Party (AWP). *See* Conference for Progressive Labor Action (CPLA)
Amos Project, 211
anarchism, 59, 71, 75, 79, 85–86, 90–91, 94
anticommunism. *See* Communism, and anticommunism
anti-imperialism, 14, 45, 53–54, 99–100, 121, 140–42, 216
Appleseed, Johnny, 69
Atlantic Charter, 137, 149
Australia, 88
Austro-Hungary, 46
Azaransky, Sarah, 195, 197

Baker, Ella, 167
Baptist church, 11, 203
Barber, William J., II, 11, 19, 210–19
Barth, Karl, 207

Batterham, Forster, 75
Belloc, Hilaire, 90
Bernstein, Richard J., 206
Berrigan, Daniel, 85, 172
Bevel, James L., 166
Bible/Scripture, 4, 14, 18, 71–72, 89, 107, 123, 183; and literalism, 24, 27
Black Panthers, 204–5
Black Power, 198–206
black radicalism, 4, 56–57, 198. *See also* Black Power; civil rights movement
black theology, 203–4, 229n3. *See also* Cone, James; liberation theology
Bliss, W. D. P., 12
Bolshevik Revolution (1917), 34, 49, 86
Bond, Julian, 167
Bradley, Anthony B., 201
Brandeis University, 199
Brookwood Labor College, 11, 22–23, 30–39, 43, 91, 98, 159, 184, 195
Browder, Earl, 114
Brown v. Board of Education (1954), 166
Buber, Martin, 86, 183
Buddhism, 14, 121, 176, 183
Burnham, James, 183
Byrnes, James, 139

Call, The, 69, 71
Calvert, Greg, 172, 191–92
capitalism: problems of, 15–16, 25–26, 28–29, 35, 42, 45–46, 53, 104, 112; and progressive alternative, 115–16, 136, 148, 210
Carmichael, Stokely, 167
Catholicism, 11, 73, 84, 94, 101, 121, 150, 192. *See also* Day, Dorothy
Catholic University of America, 84

Catholic Worker (newspaper), 80–88, 100, 102
Catholic Worker movement, 2, 11, 82, 87–94, 96, 100–102, 146, 154, 157, 168, 171. *See also* Day, Dorothy
Catholic World, 90
Chesterton, G. K., 90
Chicago Theological Seminary, 112
China, 43, 60, 121, 141
Christian Century (magazine), 54, 121, 128
Christian Herald, 116, 121, 126, 130
Christianity: dogma, 12, 14–15, 24, 73, 158; ethics, 12, 21, 152–53, 158–59, 164, 176, 183; institutional/formal, 2–3, 9, 46, 73, 158; and political theory, 4, 9
Christian realism, 10, 98, 105, 122–23. *See also* Niebuhr, Reinhold
Christian socialism, 14, 20, 41–42, 157, 163–64
civil liberties, 4, 144, 194
civil rights movement, 4, 157, 166–69, 171–72, 188, 193, 196, 201–2, 209, 212, 216; and Freedom Movement, 185–88; and religion, 9, 13, 134, 150, 169, 186
Clark, Esau, 167
Clark, Septima, 167
class/proletariat, 4, 6, 8, 14–16, 21, 41, 71, 81–83, 90–93, 145, 151, 179–81, 195–97, 215
Coates, Ta-Nehisi, 252n27
Cogley, John, 101
Cold War, 10, 19, 42, 131–34, 144–45, 156, 182, 189–90, 216, 218
Coles, Robert, 69, 101–3
Columbia University, 24, 179
Commons, John R., 31
Commonweal magazine, 75, 77, 82–84, 90, 96
Commonwealth College, 31
Communism: and anticommunism, 34, 82, 92, 132–69, 214; and atheism, 3, 8, 22, 34–35, 40–41, 48, 51, 71–76, 80–84, 89, 195, 212, 217–18; and reception in the United States, 1, 50–51, 83, 92, 99, 133–69; and sectarianism, 11, 15, 19, 22, 32, 38, 92, 199, 201, 213–14; and totalitarianism, 2, 8, 23, 51, 86, 115, 132–35, 203, 212; and utopianism, 20, 41. *See also* Marxism; socialism
Communist Party (general/international), 1, 10, 40, 49, 150

Communist Party USA, 3, 37, 58, 76, 114, 213
Cone, James, 199–207
Conference for Progressive Labor Action (CPLA), 22, 32, 36–40
Congregational church, 11, 27, 44, 70
Congress of Industrial Organizations (CIO), 166
Cook, Bruce, 101
Cook, Cara, 32–33, 35, 39–40
Cornell, Tom, 101
Cort, John, 101
Coser, Lewis, 1, 12, 87, 146
Cuba, 156
culture wars, 209–10
Culver, John C., 108, 111

Daily Worker (newspaper), 82–83
Dallas, Jerry W., 64
Daly, Mary, 206
Daniels, Jonathan, 63, 65, 67
Danielson, Leilah, 32
Darwin, Charles, 175
Day, Dorothy, 2–3, 8, 12, 15, 135, 146, 154, 208, 213; background of, 69–73; and Catholic Church, 11, 58–59, 74–78, 83–85, 196; and conversion, 58–59, 73–76; and daughter, 74–77; founding of Catholic Worker movement, 11, 57–58, 69, 80–95, 102–3, 154, 157, 171; opposition to the state, 58–59, 77, 81–87, 98, 119, 129; peace activism, 96–101, 106; scholarship on, 5, 58–59, 89–91, 96–97, 235n171; socialist identity, 59, 85–86, 93, 154
Day, John, 70
Debs, Eugene V., 26–27, 61
Dell, Floyd, 71
Dellinger, David, 100, 189
Delta Cooperative Farm(s), 11, 53, 56–57, 62–69, 82, 90–91, 94, 103–5, 162–63, 168, 171, 197
de Lubac, Henri, 86
Democratic Party, 26, 76, 109, 114, 133, 135–39, 145, 195, 210–11, 216
democratic socialism, 3, 19, 58, 86, 133, 149, 154, 177, 186–87, 203–7. *See also* revival of, 5, 210–19; socialism, and democracy
Denmark (Danish Folk Schools), 160–61
de Paul, Saint Vincent, 179
Detroit, MI, 104

Dewey, John, 24, 35, 159–60
Dewey, Thomas, 148
direct action, 3, 6, 23, 41, 98, 147, 169, 172–73, 178
Disciples of Christ, 11
Dissent (magazine), 2, 86–87, 135, 151, 153–54, 191, 211–12, 215
Dombrowski, James, 157, 162–63
Dorrien, Gary, 229n3
Dostoevsky, F. M., 72–73
Douglas, Paul A., 69, 156
Du Bois, W. E. B., 56
Dutch Reformed Church, 11, 22–27

East, Clay, 62
Eastman, Max, 71
Eckert, Charles, 193
ecumenicism, 12, 14–15, 18, 121, 140, 145, 176, 181–83, 199
Eddy, Brewer, 51–53
Eddy, Sherwood, 3, 8, 12, 26, 143, 162; and American Seminar, 23, 43–44, 48–53, 56, 104, 162; background of, 43–44; death of, 68–69, 156; and Delta Farms, 56, 62–69, 103–5, 146, 157, 162, 171; and missionary work, 45, 48–49, 53–55, 59–62, 66, 68, 119; and racial issues, 63, 66–68; and Reinhold Niebuhr, 104–6, 164, 236n31; scholarship on, 43–44, 227n55, 230n13; socialist identity, 11, 42–55, 58, 61, 230n24; and World War I, 21, 43–48, 60, 67; and World War II, 99, 106–7, 125
education. See *Brown v. Board of Education*; Denmark (Danish Folk Schools); Freedom Schools; Highlander Folk School
Ellsberg, Robert, 70
Emerson, Ralph Waldo, 24, 109, 170
English, Jack, 101
Episcopalian church, 11, 70, 127, 194, 199–200
Espionage and Sedition Acts (1917–18), 27
Ethical Culture Society, 174–77, 183, 186
Evangelicals for Social Action, 209
existentialism, 203, 205–6, 218

Fascism, 81, 99, 106–7, 112, 115, 118–19, 123, 126–29, 145. See also Hitler, Adolf
Fellowship for a Christian Social Order, 48, 104

Fellowship of Reconciliation (FOR), 27, 29, 64, 164; and Comradeship, 29–30
Fincke, Helen, 31
Fincke, William, 31
Flacks, Richard (Dick), 191
Fordham University, 212
Forest, Jim, 101
Forman, James, 188
Fortune (magazine), 92
Four Freedoms, 137
Fox, Richard Wightman, 104
France, 45–46
Franklin, Sam, 62, 64–66, 105
Freedom Schools, 173, 185–88

Gandhi, Mahatma, 41, 53–55, 93, 146, 178, 183
gender issues, 4, 14, 18, 172, 193, 196–200, 214–16
Genovese, Eugene, 208
George, Henry, 177
Germany, 46, 49, 119, 123–24
Glen, John M., 158–59, 163, 166–67
Goldman, Emma, 75
Graham, Billy, 10
Gramsci, Antonio, 150, 203, 217
Great Britain, 46, 49, 53–54
Great Depression, 36, 38–39, 53, 56–57, 76–81, 88, 110, 112
Great War. See World War I
Grundtvig, N. F. S., 160–61
Gutierrez, Gustavo, 206

Handy, Robert, 12
Harding, Warren G., 108
Harrington, Michael, 101
Harvard University, 170, 178–79, 204
Hawes, Zilla, 162
Hennacy, Ammon, 101
Henry Street Settlement House, 159
Herron, George, 12
High, Stanley, 116–17, 127
Highlander Folk School, 11, 31, 43, 104, 134, 157–69, 186, 247n71. See also Horton, Myles
Hill, Joe, 16
Hillman, Sidney, 138
Hinduism, 15, 121
Hitler, Adolf, 106, 117, 119, 123–24, 149–50
Hope College (MI), 23–25

Hornbeck, J. Patrick, II, 212
Horton, Myles, 3, 8, 12, 15; background of, 157–58; death of, 168; founding of Highlander Folk School, 11, 104, 134, 157–69; and race issues, 57; socialist identity, 159–62
Horton, Zilphia, 167
Howard University, 195
Howe, Irving, 1–6, 10, 12, 58, 80, 87, 135, 146, 149–50, 153–55, 213
human nature, 7–8, 16, 18, 22, 27, 105–6, 113, 116, 123, 134, 216
human rights, 189, 193, 197, 199, 208
Humphrey, Hubert, 143
Hyde, John, 108, 111

identity politics, 193, 198, 203–4, 209–18, 251n5
independent leftists, 10, 43, 48, 58, 85, 135, 146, 149–55, 160, 169, 172, 194, 210
India, 43, 53–56, 59–62, 121, 141
Indiana University, 193
individualism, 5, 18, 48, 197
Interfaith Coalition for Worker Justice (ICWJ), 211
International Workers of the World (IWW), 24, 71
Interracial Review, 82
Iowa State College, 108
Islam, 121; and Nation of Islam, 204–5
isolationism, 22–23, 49, 102, 119

Jackson, Gardner, 136, 143
James, William, 24, 109
Jane Crow, 199
Jesus Christ: disciples of, 11; revolutionary image of, 54, 93, 156–57, 169, 176–80, 193; and Sermon on the Mount, 26, 47, 68–69, 83–84, 111, 113, 129; social message of, 12, 14–18, 25, 47, 76, 128, 144, 153, 177, 203
Jewish radicals, 11–12
Jim Crow, 167, 187, 194–96
Johnson, Mordecai, 166
Jones, Jesse, 135–36
Jones, Mother, 75
Jones, Rufus, 26
Judaism, 11–12, 15, 121, 212; Reformed, 11, 175
"just war" theory, 26, 99, 105–6, 201

Kester, Howard, 56–57, 62, 64, 66, 164
Kilson, Martin, 204
King, Martin Luther, Jr., 8, 134, 166–68, 171–72, 186, 188, 193, 200–202, 205–6, 210, 229n3
Kingdon, Frank, 138
Korean War, 42, 96
Kosek, Kip, 31
Kropotkin, Peter, 70, 72, 77–79, 86

Labor Age. See Conference for Progressive Labor Action (CPLA)
Labor Party (Great Britain), 37, 49
Labor Temple, 11, 98
LaFarge, John, 73
La Follette, Robert, 109, 119
Latin America, 141. See also liberation theology
Lawrence, MA strike, 22, 29–30, 96
leftist historiography, 9–10, 19, 23, 43, 89–91, 94, 209, 211, 214, 217
Lenin, Vladimir, 141
Lerner, Max, 138
Lewis, John, 167
liberalism, 2, 4, 21, 35, 48, 76, 99, 105, 139, 206, 213. See also neoliberalism; New Deal
liberal religion, 10, 13–14, 18, 21, 25, 40, 94, 209–12, 216–19
liberation theology, 192, 199–200, 206–7, 217
libertarianism, 59, 85
Liberty University, 213
Life (magazine), 119–20, 139
Lippmann, Walter, 136
Lipset, Seymour Martin, 174
Lisieux, Saint Thérèse, 70, 103
Locke, John, 207
London, Jack, 72
Lord, Russell, 113, 140
Luce, Henry R., 119–20
Lynd, Alice, 182
Lynd, Helen, 174
Lynd, Robert, 174
Lynd, Staughton, 3, 5, 8, 12, 15, 154; background of, 170–82; ecumenical vision of, 15, 33, 176, 181, 183; and A. J. Muste, 178–82; and New Left history, 11, 152, 173, 182, 189, 192–93, 207–8, 246n46; and peace activism, 189–90, 202, 205; race

issues, 57, 172, 185–89, 205; and Henry A. Wallace, 170–71, 173
Lyrical Left, 59

Macdonald, Dwight, 1–6, 92, 135; and Dorothy Day, 58–59, 80, 85, 88–89, 91–94, 100–101, 146, 213, 218; and Henry A. Wallace, 120–21, 141–43, 145–47
Macedonia Cooperative Community, 173, 182–86
MacLean, Donald A., 84
Marciniak, Ed, 101
Marx, Karl, 4, 145, 157, 161, 179, 181, 187, 201, 203
Marxism: problems of, 1–4, 8, 15–16, 20–21, 91–93, 105, 115–16, 151, 162, 174, 179, 189, 217–18, 221n9, 252n29; violence, 16, 40–41, 58, 73, 92–93, 112, 115, 141, 149, 170. *See also* Communism; socialism
Masses, The, 69, 71
materialism, 5, 8–9, 16, 22, 82, 113, 124, 155, 181, 192
Mathews, Shailer, 12
Matthiesen, F. O., 170–71
Maurin, Peter, 69, 77–82, 87, 92, 157
Mays, Benjamin, 166
McCarraher, Eugene, 89, 91, 235n171
McCarthy, Eugene, 101
McGiffert, Arthur Cushman, 24
McKanan, Dan, 218
McKinley, William, 108
Mills, C. Wright, 4
missionaries, 7, 43, 45, 59, 227n55
Mitchell, H. L., 62, 66–67
Moltmann, Jürgen, 202
Monthly Review, 217
Moody, Dwight, 43–44
Moral Majority, 209–10, 216
Moral Mondays movement, 210–11
Morgenthau, Henry, Jr., 137–38, 148
Moses, Robert, 134, 189
Mott, John, 7
Muhammad, Elijah, 204–5
Murray, Pauli: background of, 193–94, 207–8; and civil rights movement, 171–72, 193–94, 196, 199–202; and diversity, 68, 193–99, 205; religion of, 11, 172, 194–95, 199
Muste, A. J., 3, 7–8, 15–18, 48, 54, 170; background of, 23–26; and Brookwood Labor College, 11, 22–23, 30–40; criticism of Marxism, 20–22, 42, 58, 181; criticism of social gospel, 13, 28, 41; death of, 96; labor movement, 29–42, 76, 179, 192; and Reinhold Niebuhr, 123–25; and peace activism, 96–98, 100, 122–25, 130, 178, 189; and "Return to Pacifism," 20, 22–23, 41–43, 97; scholarship on, 5, 23, 31–32; and World War I, 22, 26–29; and World War II, 95, 122–25, 130–31, 149

National Association for the Advancement of Colored People (NAACP), 197, 211
National Organization for Women (NOW), 199
Native American religion, 11, 109–10
neoliberalism, 216, 252n27
neo-orthodox Christianity, 40, 123. *See also* Christian realism
New Brunswick Theological Seminary, 23
New Deal, 11, 57–58, 62–63, 76, 82, 111–20, 127, 130, 133, 137, 146, 195
New Left: early development of, 2–4, 58, 92, 135, 152, 157, 169, 181–82, 192, 246n46; fragmentation of, 191–93, 198, 202, 209, 213; ideology of, 9, 181–82, 189–90; leadership problems, 198; and religion, 13, 172, 191–92, 212
New Republic, 40, 103, 141–44, 148
New Worker's School, 195
New Yorker, 93
New York Herald-Tribune, 139
New York intellectuals, 1
New York Review of Books, 208
New York Times, 139, 173, 211
New York University, 24
Nicaragua, 192
Niebuhr, Reinhold, 10, 42, 62, 64, 66, 98, 103–6, 123–25, 160, 162, 164–65, 190
nuclear weapons, 42, 96
Nye Committee, 119

Obama, Barack, 216, 252n27
O'Gara, James, 101
Old Left: disillusionment of, 1–3, 22, 80, 92, 94, 100, 150–52, 177, 213–14; and labor, 4, 22, 58, 145, 174, 188; realignment of, 2–4, 10, 149–50, 173, 189, 199, 213
Oneida community, 159
original sin, 18, 40

258   Index

pacifism, 3–6, 20, 22–23, 26–31, 41–42, 54, 95–101, 105–6, 122–26, 178, 182, 193, 200–202. *See also* Mahatma Gandhi
Page, Kirby, 53, 104–5
Paine, Thomas, 208
Parks, Rosa, 167–68
Partisan Review, 92
Peabody, Francis, 12
Pegler, Westbrook, 113–14, 136
People Improving Communities Through Organizing (PICO), 211
Pepper, Claude, 138
personalism, 15, 88–89, 166, 194, 200
Phillips, Maxine, 212, 214–16
PM, 148
politics (magazine), 1–2, 93, 135. *See also* Macdonald, Dwight
Popular Front, 99–100, 131, 145
Populist movement, 117
Potsdam Conference, 137
Powers, J. F., 101
pragmatism: general, 6, 106, 133, 165; pragmatism, 203, 206–7, 212
Presbyterian church, 11, 108–9, 157, 194
Preston, Andrew, 107
Priestly, Joseph, 208
Progressive Citizens of America (PCA), 148
progressive movement, 13–14, 25–26, 31, 45, 57, 224n31; disillusionment of, 7–8, 20–21, 28, 47. *See also* democratic socialism
Progressive Party (1924), 109
Progressive Party (1948), 18, 132–50, 155–56, 169–70. *See also* Wallace, Henry A.
Providence Farm. *See* Delta Cooperative Farm(s)

Quakerism, 11, 26, 29, 173, 176, 182–83, 193–94

racial issues, 4, 14, 18, 56, 63, 66–68, 134, 138, 157–58, 166–69, 171, 194–207, 214–16. *See also* black radicalism; civil rights movement
Radest, Howard, 175
Randolph, A. Philip, 193, 196
Ransom, Reverdy, 56
Rauschenbusch, Walter, 12, 25, 57, 60, 105
realpolitik, 122

Red Scare, 1, 3, 11, 135–69, 182, 194, 216. *See also* Communism, and anticommunism
Reinhold, H. A., 85, 89–90
religious conservatives, 3, 10, 14, 18, 213, 216–18; and religious right, 4–5, 18, 209, 211–13
religious history, 4, 6–7, 9–14, 19, 209–19
Republican Party, 25, 109, 111, 136, 210–11, 216
Reuters, 211
revolution. *See* socialism, revolution
Robinson, Bernice, 167
Robinson, Jo Ann Ooiman, 32
Rochdale Farm. *See* Delta Cooperative Farm(s)
Rockefeller, John D., 52
Roerich, Nicholas, 135–36
Roos, Charles, 110–11
Roosevelt, Eleanor, 63, 138, 196
Roosevelt, Franklin D., 106–7, 111–14, 118, 127–28, 132–37, 141, 146, 148–49, 196
Rorty, Richard, 206
Roe v. Wade (1973), 209
Ruskin, John, 83
Rustin, Bayard, 134
Ryan, John A., 73, 82

Sanders, Bernie, 19, 212–13
Saturday Evening Post, 115–16, 127
Schuster, George, 77
Sermon on the Mount. *See* Jesus Christ, and Sermon on the Mount
Shaw, Bernard (George), 49
Silone, Ignazio, 2–3, 133, 135, 150–55, 170, 176–77, 180, 183, 191–92, 213
Sinclair, Upton, 72
Smith, Adam, 128
social democracy, 40, 43, 54, 67
social gospel, 20, 45, 105, 213; application of, 7, 13, 24–26, 42, 159, 203; eschatology of, 13, 40, 202–3; historiography on, 13–14, 229n3; proponents of, 12, 21, 25, 60, 73, 105, 177, 186; and racial issues, 57, 166, 229n3
socialism: and democracy, 2–5, 8, 19, 23, 48, 58, 61, 115, 160, 164, 170–71, 195; and orthodox doctrine, 1, 3–8, 15–16, 21, 61, 71, 85–87, 92, 135, 151–54, 160, 176, 188, 218; and revolution, 1, 8, 10, 16, 41, 115,

132, 170, 180, 208; and the state, 3, 16, 61, 81, 218; and terminology, 6, 14, 16, 19, 85–88, 91–92, 132, 186, 188, 219; and time to achieve, 5–6, 8, 10, 15, 18, 32–33, 36, 48, 60, 71, 105, 126, 164–65, 191, 208–9, 219. *See also* Communism; Marxism
Socialist Party of America, 7, 16, 26, 39–40, 58, 61–62, 71, 76, 146–50, 160, 164, 174, 194, 213
Society of Friends. *See* Quakerism
Socrates, 93
Southern Christian Leadership Conference (SCLC), 166–67
Southern Tenant Farmers' Union (STFU), 56, 62–64, 67, 146–48
Soviet Union, 1, 8, 22–23, 34–35, 49–51, 58, 81–82, 86, 92, 114, 137–39, 143, 179, 212. *See also* Communism; Red Scare
Spanish-American War (1898), 26
Spanish Civil War, 174
Spelman College, 173, 185, 187
Stalin, Joseph, 51, 144, 179; opposition to, 3, 143, 213
Stern, Frederick, 172
Stevenson, Adlai, 196
Straight, Michael, 138
Student Non-Violent Coordinating Committee (SNCC), 167, 185, 187–90, 196
Students for a Democratic Society (SDS), 172, 189–90, 196
Student Volunteer Movement (SVM), 7, 45. *See also* Young Men's Christian Association (YMCA)
Suzuki, Daisetz, 183
Swartz, David, 210–11, 251n5

Taft, William Howard, 24–25
Taylor, Alva, 163
Theoharis, Liz, 217
Theosophy, 11, 135–36
Thomas, Norman, 7–9, 39, 58, 61–62, 66, 76, 86, 146, 148–50, 154, 162, 194
Thurman, Howard, 166
Tolstoy, Leo, 70, 72–73, 93
Trine, Ralph Waldo, 109
Trotsky, Leon/Trotskyites, 20, 40, 92, 178–79
Truman, Harry S., 11, 18, 132–38, 143–49, 182
Trump, Donald, 216–17

Tuskegee Institute, 61
Tyrrell, Ian, 59

Union Theological Seminary, 24, 158–59, 162, 164
United Nations, 119, 134, 137, 142–43, 194
University of Chicago, 159–60
University of Illinois, 71
University of Michigan, 189
University of North Carolina, 194
University of Tennessee, 62
University of Wisconsin–Madison, 31
Urban League, 195
U.S. Catholic, 90
US Civil War, 174, 187, 193
US Supreme Court, 67, 166, 209
utopianism, 2, 15, 20, 32, 40, 83–84, 87–88, 148, 152, 159, 218

Vanderbilt University, 163
Victorian era, 12–13
Vietnam War, 156; and protests, 42, 96, 189, 209

Wagner, Robert F., 138
Wallace, Harry C., 108, 111
Wallace, Henry A., 8, 12, 63, 208; background of, 108–12; death of, 156; and guru letters, 135–36; and New Deal, 11, 111–20, 127–30, 137, 142, 145–46; and presidential campaign of 1948, 18, 112, 124, 132–50, 155–56, 169–70, 241n35, 242n52; socialist identity, 113–14; and World War II, 99, 106–7, 117–31, 135
Waller, Odell, 197–90
Wallis, Jim, 210, 213
Ward, Harry F., 12, 35, 158
War of 1898. *See* Spanish-American War
Washington Post, 209
Washington Star, 121
Watergate scandal, 209
Weil, Simone, 2, 170, 179–83, 192
Wells, H. G., 49
Wesley, John, 71
West, Cornel, 11, 203–8, 216–18, 252n27
West, Don, 157, 163
Wheeler, Burton, 119
Wilson, H. H., 156
Wilson, Woodrow, 26–27, 71, 118, 120–21, 141

Wisconsin School for Workers, 31
Woll, Matthew, 34–35
Workers Defense League, 197
World War I (Great War), 6–8, 10, 12–13, 20–22, 26–29, 42–48, 60, 69, 96, 149, 224n31
World War II, 10, 42, 94–99, 107, 117–32, 135, 182. *See also* Eddy, Sherwood, and World War II; Muste, A. J., and World War II; Wallace, Henry A. Wallace, and World War II

X, Malcolm, 204–5

Yale University, 44, 193
Young Men's Christian Association (YMCA), 7, 11, 21, 42–45, 49, 51–52, 57, 59, 119, 157–58, 162–63, 209
Young, Andrew, 167

Zellner, Bob, 167
Zinn, Howard, 173, 185

ACKNOWLEDGMENTS

This book would not have been possible without Robert Lockhart and the University of Pennsylvania Press. During the publication process, I also had help from the exceptional scholar Doug Rossinow, who made the book undeniably better with his insights. Doug has been a guardian angel, reading my work and bringing opportunities into my orbit. Thank you.

I would also like to thank the colleagues who accompanied me on this long journey: Guy Ketch, Mark Lynn, Leslie Abadie, Will Jones, William Reese, Tony Michels, John Kaminski, John Hall, James Danky, Isaac Lee, Jeremi Suri, Jennifer Ratner-Rosenhagen, Charles Cohen, Britt Tevis, Campbell Scribner, Robbie Gross, Debbie Sharnak, James McKay, Christine Lamberson, Dan Hummel, Alex Hinrichs, David Fields, Rivka Maizlish, Brad Baranowski, Simon Balto, Naomi Williams, Kevin Walters, Katherine Guenon, Skye Doney, Megan Stanton, Erin Kramer, Libby Tronnes, Ashley Barnes-Gilbert, Charlie Cahill, Scott Mobley, Gregory Jones-Katz, Ben Shannon, Tony Gulig, Sean Dinces, Paul Buhle, Staughton Lynd, Ron Granieri, Rosanne Currarino, James Carlson, and Zozan Pehlivan. I am lucky to be part of such a kind and thoughtful community of scholars.

Special mention goes out to Michael D. Gambone, whose professional and personal example continues to serve as a high standard.

And, saving the best for last, I extend my deepest gratitude to my husband, Dan, whose love and support have made this and all my dreams possible.

CPSIA information can be obtained
at www.ICGtesting.com
Printed in the USA
LVHW041952311019
636011LV00001B/2

9 780812 251654